The Fundamental Principles of Finance

Finance is the study of value and how it is determined. Individuals, small businesses and corporations regularly make use of value determinations for making strategic decisions that affect the future outcomes of their endeavors. The importance of accurate valuations cannot be overestimated; valuing assets too highly will lead to investing in assets whose costs are greater than their returns, while undervaluing assets will lead to missed opportunities for growth. In some situations (such as a merger or an acquisition), the outcome of the decision can make or break the investor. The need for solid financial skills has never been more pressing than in today's global economy.

The Fundamental Principles of Finance offers a new and innovative approach to financial theory. The book introduces three fundamental principles of finance that flow throughout the theoretical material covered in most corporate finance textbooks. These fundamental principles are developed in their own chapter of the book, then referred to in each chapter introducing financial theory. In this way, the theory is able to be mastered at a fundamental level. The interactions among the principles are introduced through the three precepts, which help show the impact of the three principles on financial decision-making.

This fresh and original approach to finance will be key reading for undergraduate students of introduction to finance, corporate finance, capital markets, financial management and related courses, as well as managers undertaking MBAs.

Robert Irons, PhD, is Associate Professor of Finance at Illinois Wesleyan University, USA. He has taught undergraduate and MBA students for over 20 years and is published in numerous academic journals, including the *Journal of Investing* and the *Journal of Portfolio Management*. Prior to teaching full time, Dr. Irons worked as a financial analyst for such firms as AT&T and United Airlines.

The Fundamental Principles of Finance

Robert Irons

 Routledge
Taylor & Francis Group

NEW YORK AND LONDON

First published 2020
by Routledge
52 Vanderbilt Avenue, New York, NY 10017

and by Routledge
2 Park Square, Milton Park, Abingdon, Oxon OX14 4RN

Routledge is an imprint of the Taylor & Francis Group, an informa business

© 2020 Taylor & Francis

Library of Congress Cataloging-in-Publication Data
A catalog record for this book has been requested

ISBN: 978-1-138-47751-3 (hbk)
ISBN: 978-1-138-47752-0 (pbk)
ISBN: 978-0-429-29497-6 (ebk)

Typeset in Times New Roman
by Apex CoVantage, LLC

Visit the eResources: www.routledge.com/9781138477520

Contents

Figures

Tables

1 The Fundamental Principles of Finance

Finance is the study of value and how it is determined. While different types of assets are valued using different specific methods, the underlying principles are the same for each method. It is those underlying principles, and their impact on value, that are the subject of this chapter. The material covered here will be seen in various forms throughout the next seven chapters of the book; this present chapter serves as an introduction to these principles and a guide to their comprehension. A command of these principles will aid in understanding the theory introduced in the coming chapters.

The chapters that follow this one introduce the theory of finance as applied to such things as determining the value of an asset (such as a security, or even a firm); assessing risk and ascertaining the appropriate return for the perceived level of risk; and establishing the optimal level of each source of funds to minimize the firm's costs and thereby maximize its intrinsic value. Each remaining chapter offers theory in a different specific area of finance—for example, valuing bonds, valuing stocks or valuing a potential investment in operating assets. The current chapter serves to explain in detail the fundamental principles of finance, to show that the fundamental principles flow through the remaining chapters and to promote how comprehension of these fundamental principles can aid in understanding how the theory in the remaining chapters is interrelated.

There are three fundamental principles that flow throughout the theory of finance and that interact within the theory discussed in the following chapters. These three principles are not directly related to each other—each stands on its own—but they work together in shaping financial theory. The interactions among these principles are highlighted in the three precepts that are discussed later in the chapter. These precepts show how the principles combine to affect theory, and therefore how we can better understand the theory through the use of the fundamental principles.

The Three Fundamental Principles of Finance

The First Fundamental Principle (FP1): The value of any asset is equal to the present value of the cash flows the asset is expected to produce over its economic life.

This first principle is at the heart of the valuation process and is the basis of all methods used for determining the value of virtually anything: a stock or bond being issued by the firm, an investment project the firm is considering or even the firm itself. This principle can be clarified by deconstructing it into smaller phrases that can be understood at a more basic level.

The value of any asset is equal to:

- **the present value**—present value and its calculation are discussed in Chapter 2, "The Time Value of Money." For now, it is enough to understand that a dollar today does not have the same value as a dollar one year from today. A dollar today can be invested to earn interest and will therefore be worth more than a dollar in one year's time. Thus, the ability to invest and earn interest means that a dollar today is worth more than a dollar one year from today. This basic truth indicates the need for evaluating investments in terms of dollars today—their present value.

- **of the cash flows**—the basis of value for an asset stems from the cash flows the asset will produce. Those cash flows, put into current dollar terms (their present value), are summed to determine the value of the asset. The nature of the asset will determine the nature and timing of the cash flows produced by the asset. The cash flows produced by a bond are different from the cash flows produced by a stock and are also different from the cash flows produced by an asset used in production. In any case, value will be calculated as the sum of the present values of the expected future cash flows.
- **the asset is <u>expected</u> to produce**—the word "expected" is underlined here to emphasize the fact that the cash flows to be produced by the asset are to be forecasted and therefore are a matter of judgment. It is possible that three different analysts attempting to value the same asset will produce three slightly different sets of expected cash flows, since they may each make different assumptions. There is much use of judgment in finance, and analysts who develop good judgment get paid very well. You are not expected to have good judgment in business at this time in your career, when you are just starting out. However, college is your opportunity to develop your judgment. Firms hire people with good judgment to manage their business, and those managers whose judgment proves effective climb the corporate ladder successfully. Therefore, it is in your best interests to put your own judgment to the test, in this course as well as in other courses. Even if finance is not your chosen field, if you wish to succeed in business, it is your judgment that will convince others of *your* value to the firm.
- **over its economic life**—different assets have different expected lives. For example, when a firm purchases a new machine for use in production, it assigns an economic life, based on the nature of the asset, for purposes of depreciation. Some production assets have shorter lives (5–10 years), while others have much longer lives (20–30 years). Also, while bonds have a limited expected life (they have a date at which they mature), stocks are expected to last forever. Therefore, the economic life of the asset in question will have an impact on the cash flows it is expected to produce.

Thus, when we are attempting to value an asset, we must determine:

- The discount rate (i.e., the cost) that is appropriate for the perceived level of risk for the given asset (which will be used to calculate the present value of the cash flows);
- The size and the timing of the cash flows the asset is expected to produce; and
- When the asset is expected to be sold or taken out of service (when its economic life ends).

The discount rate to be used for calculating the present value of the cash flows is determined by the level of risk associated with the asset in question, and thus will vary from asset to asset and from firm to firm. This will be discussed further in Chapter 3, "Risk and Return," as well as in the discussion of the second fundamental principle. It is enough at this point to understand that different types of assets will use different discount rates to determine the present value of their cash flows.

The cash flows associated with an asset can take on different forms. When a firm offers a new product, or improves an existing product, it does so with the expectation that the new (or improved) product will increase sales, and thus the cash flows for the product will include additional sales revenue. In a different scenario, a firm may invest in a new technology to produce an existing product because the new technology will decrease production costs, leading to higher profitability on the product. In that case, the cash flows for the project will include the reduced operating costs offered by the new technology.

The economic life of the asset will be determined by the nature of the asset as well as the intended use of the asset. Most physical assets (trucks, machines or buildings) fit into prede-termined asset classes that estimate their economic life (e.g., the MACRS asset classes used for calculating depreciation). In addition, the firm may have reasons for using a different economic life than the one suggested by the asset class. For example, if the product in ques-tion will no longer be sold after a future date, then the asset used to produce the product may have effectively reached the end of its economic life at that date. The expected economic life of the asset must be established in order to be able to determine the time span over which cash flows can be expected and, with that, its value.

The general method outlined in the first fundamental principle will be used to establish the value of a firm's bonds, their common stock, their preferred stock, any capital investments they are considering and even the firm itself. Thus, the current market value of any asset can be seen as the sum of the value of the cash flows it is expected to produce, assuming all of the cash flows were to be received today, rather than over an extended period of time.

The Second Fundamental Principle (FP2): There is a direct relationship between risk and return; as perceived risk increases, required return will also increase (and vice versa), holding other things constant.

Risk is typically understood as the chance of a bad outcome. In finance, risk is identified as the probability of not earning the return you expect from your investment over a given period of time. In statistics class, you are taught that the expected value of a variable is the mean, or the arithmetic average, of the variable. In the same way, the expected value of a data set is its mean, and the perceived risk of the data set is the likelihood of the outcome being other than its mean. That likelihood is measured using the standard deviation of the data set.

The standard deviation of a data set essentially measures the average deviation from the mean among the observations in the data set. In other words, it shows how likely the actual observations are to vary from their average. If the actual observations are very close to their mean, the standard deviation will be small, indicating that there is a small tendency for the observations to be different from their mean, or a large likelihood of achieving the expected value. If the actual observations are very different from their mean, the standard deviation will be larger, indicating a larger tendency for the observations to be different from their mean, or a smaller likelihood of achieving the expected value. This tendency reflects the behavior of the returns over the period in question—some period of time in the past. If we assume that the data will behave similarly in the future as they did in the past (a big assump-tion), then we can use the standard deviation as a measure of the likelihood of the observa-tions varying from their mean in the future. There are two issues with using the standard deviation in this way.

First, as mentioned above, assuming that past behavior will be replicated in the future is a big assumption, and there is no basis in fact for making such an assumption. However, barring any specific reason to believe otherwise, it is as good an assumption as any we can possibly make. If we have reason to believe certain things about the future, things that may or may not differ from the past, we can build that knowledge into our calculations of the mean and standard deviation of the returns in the future by using a probability distribution. We will in fact use this method in Chapter 3, "Risk and Return."

Second, there is an issue with using the standard deviation as a measure of risk, since it measures *any* deviation from the mean, lower or higher. While returns lower than the mean are disappointing, returns higher than the mean are welcome—they increase our wealth. Treating higher-than-expected returns the same as lower-than-expected returns doesn't seem right. However, until statistical theory offers a better metric, we will use the standard deviation, since it does in fact offer some insights into the behavior of the data. A simple example will help to make this point.

Table 1.1 contains the annual returns for two different stocks (Stock A and Stock B) over a five-year period. The arithmetic mean (or expected) return over the period is the same for both stocks:

$$\bar{x}_A = \frac{.048 + .058 + .055 + .059 + .05}{5} = .054 \text{ or } 5.4\%$$

$$\bar{x}_B = \frac{-.025 + .031 + .094 + .026 + .144}{5} = .054 \text{ or } 5.4\%$$

However, if you look at the raw data in the table, it is apparent that these two stocks' returns are not the same. Stock A's returns get as low as 4.8% and as high as 5.9%, while over the same period Stock B's returns get as low as −2.5% and as high as 14.4%. Clearly, Stock B's returns have a higher tendency to vary from their mean. The standard deviation of the returns for each stock quantifies this:

$$s_A = \sqrt{\frac{(.048 - .054)^2 + (.058 - .054)^2 + (.055 - .054)^2 + (.059 - .054)^2 + (.05 - .054)^2}{5 - 1}}$$

$$= .0048 \text{ or } 0.48\%$$

$$s_B = \sqrt{\frac{(-.025 - .054)^2 + (.031 - .054)^2 + (.094 - .054)^2 + (.026 - .054)^2 + (.144 - .054)^2}{5 - 1}}$$

$$= .0657 \text{ or } 6.57\%$$

Thus, while both stocks have the same expected return over the five-year period, Stock B's returns had a greater tendency to vary from their mean during the period. Stock B's higher standard deviation (more than 10 times as high!) indicates a higher likelihood for its investors not to get their expected return. The interpretation of these statistics is that, for this five-year period, Stock B's returns were riskier than Stock A's returns. This can be seen easily if we plot the returns against their mean, as in the following graphs.

Table 1.1 Returns for Two Stocks Over Five Years

	Stock A	Stock B
Year 1	.048	−.025
Year 2	.058	.031
Year 3	.055	.094
Year 4	.059	.026
Year 5	.05	.144

In the graphs in Figure 1.1, the black dots represent the returns for each year, while the dashed grey line represents the mean return during this period. Over the five-year period in question, the returns to Stock A hover around their mean without deviating very far, an indication that their standard deviation is small. The returns to Stock B, on the other hand, vary significantly from their mean, indicating that their standard deviation is much larger. For an investor looking to put their money into either Stock A or Stock B in the future, it would make sense to choose A over B, since while both have the same expected return, B has more risk. Why take on the additional risk associated with Stock B when you can get the same expected return from Stock A without the additional risk? The rules of rational investing in these cases are simple:

- If two investments have the same expected return but different levels of risk, choose the investment with less risk;
- If two investments have the same level of risk but different expected returns, choose the investment with the higher expected return.

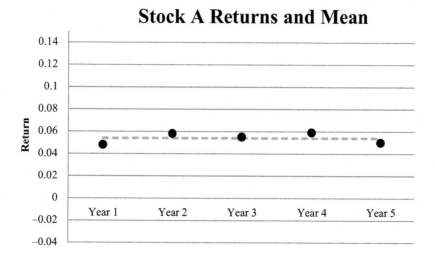

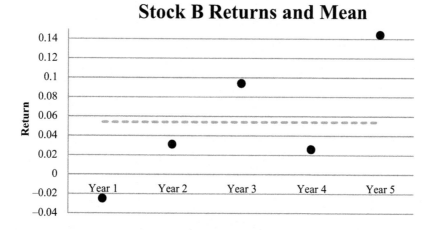

Figure 1.1 Annual and Mean Returns, Stock A vs. Stock B

Rational investors will either maximize their expected return for a given level of risk, or minimize the risk for a given level of expected return. Thus, rational investors will require a higher level of return for investments with a higher level of perceived risk, and be willing to accept lower levels of return for investments with less perceived risk. This is the essence of fundamental principle two: as perceived risk increases, required return will also increase, holding other things constant.

> **The Third Fundamental Principle (FP3): There is an inverse relationship between price and yield; if an asset's price increases, its return will decrease (and vice versa), holding other things constant.**

Yield is simply another word for return, more specifically the percentage return. This fundamental principle is based on the relationship between the terms of a fraction: as the denominator of a fraction increases, holding the numerator constant, the value of the fraction decreases. This can be shown mathematically:

$$\frac{1}{2} > \frac{1}{3} > \frac{1}{4} > \frac{1}{5}, \text{ or } 0.50 > 0.33 > 0.25 > 0.20$$

For an example of how this works, suppose you bought a $1,000 bond at the beginning of the year that pays $100 interest annually. At the end of the year, your percentage return on the bond would be 10% ($100 cash flow ÷ $1,000 investment = 0.10). Next, suppose that after the New Year starts, you want to sell the bond, and it has gone up in price to $1,080. Ignoring what the increase in price does to your returns, since the annual payment is fixed, that increase in the price will cause the yield the bond pays to decrease. The person who buys the bond from you will get the same $100 payment at the end of the year. However, since they paid more for the bond, that person will earn a lower yield (percentage return): $100 ÷ $1,080 = 0.0926 or 9.26%. Thus, the increase in the price of the bond has led to a decrease in the percentage return on the bond. Similarly, if the bond had gone down in price to $925, the new bond owner would earn a higher yield ($100 ÷ $925 = 0.1081 or 10.81%).

As will be seen in Chapter 5, "Bond Valuation," the market value of a bond already in circulation will vary in line with fundamental principle three based on changes to interest rates in the market. Bonds are issued at interest rates that equate their face value with their market value. While the face value of a bond never changes, its market value will change over time inversely with changes to market interest rates.

The Three Precepts

As stated earlier in this chapter, the three fundamental principles work independently of each other. However, they do interact, and their interactions can be better understood through the use of the three precepts. These precepts explain interactions between the fundamental principles in ways that help clarify the impact of the fundamental principles.

The Oxford Dictionary defines a precept as "a general rule intended to regulate behavior or thought." The three precepts offered here are intended to guide your thoughts through the maze of financial theory by showing how the fundamental principles interact and how theory is driven by those interactions. The precepts are specific rules designed to give insight into how the fundamental principles work in shaping financial theory.

The First Precept (PR1): The present value of a cash flow (or an asset) is inversely related to its discount rate; increasing the discount rate decreases the present value (and vice versa), holding other things constant.

The first precept reflects the interaction between fundamental principles one and three, and it is similar to the third fundamental principle in that it is mathematical in nature. The discount rate used to calculate the present value of a cash flow is determined by the nature of the cash flow (or the asset it is derived from) as well as the relative riskiness of the cash flow (or the asset it is derived from). Different types of assets will require different discount rates; PR1 tells us that the discount rate used will affect the value determined for the asset.

This first precept relates the impact of the first fundamental principle (FP1), concerning how value is determined, with the impact of the third fundamental principle (FP3), showing the relationship between the value of an asset and the return it earns. When we discount cash flows to determine their present value (or the present value of the asset that produces the cash flows), we are removing value to account for returns to investors over time. In this way, we can equate current cash flows with future cash flows by assuming they will earn a given return over a particular period of time. Understanding how cash flows in two different time periods can be economically equivalent is an important part of financial theory and will be discussed in more detail in Chapter 2.

The Second Precept (PR2): The timing of the cash flows of an asset is important; sooner is better (later cash flows are more heavily discounted, reducing their present value).

The second precept shows another interaction between fundamental principles one and three; it relates to the timing of the cash flows associated with an asset. It is similar to the first precept in that it is driven by a mathematical relationship, but it is different in that risk is not the issue here; time is. A cash flow that occurs at the end of the first time period is discounted for one period to obtain its present value, while a cash flow that occurs at the end of the second time period is discounted for two periods to obtain its present value. As will be discussed in detail in Chapter 2, "The Time Value of Money," discounting is the removal of value from the cash flows in order to pay the firm's investors. The further out the cash flows occur, the more value gets removed in the discounting process, and consequently the lower the present value. Therefore, an asset for which larger cash flows come earlier in its economic life will have a higher present value than another similar asset for which the larger cash flows come later, since the earlier large cash flows will not be discounted as much. This will be made clearer in the discussion on present value in Chapter 2.

These first two precepts show us that the present value of a cash flow is affected by the size of the cash flow, the timing of the cash flow and the discount rate used to determine its present value. The third precept shows us that the discount rate used is a reflection of the riskiness of the cash flow.

The Third Precept (PR3): The present value of a cash flow (or an asset) is inversely related to its perceived risk; the higher the risk, the higher the discount rate, and therefore the lower the present value.

The third precept shows the interaction between fundamental principles two and three. It relates the discount rate used for calculating the present value of a cash flow with the level of risk associated with the cash flow (or the asset producing the cash flow). While the first fundamental principle (FP1) shows how value is determined through the discounting process, the third fundamental principle (FP3) indicates that the value can change if the discount rate changes. This third precept tells us why the discount rate may be changed.

Fundamental principle two (FP2) indicates the positive relation between risk and return, while fundamental principle three (FP3) describes the negative relation between return and value. Since risk and return are positively correlated (as per FP2), risk must be negatively correlated with value (as per FP3). Thus, if an asset or a cash flow is determined to have above-average risk, its present value will be lower than if it were of average risk, and vice versa. This occurs because, in the discounting process, we adjust the discount rate to account for the difference in risk. In this way, if two different assets have identical cash flows but different levels of risk, the value of the lower-risk asset will be greater than the value of the higher-risk asset. This is because the higher-risk asset will be valued using a higher discount rate to account for the higher level of risk—we are increasing the denominator of the fraction, where the cash flow in question is the numerator of the fraction.

Differentiating Between the Principles and the Precepts

The three fundamental principles describe relationships among the different forces that impact value: the size, timing and nature of the cash flows produced by the asset and the relative riskiness of the asset or its cash flows. These principles apply when valuing any type of asset and can therefore be used when attempting to determine a value when confronted with some new type of asset. Regardless of the nature of the asset, its value lies in the cash flows that the asset is expected to produce. These principles flow throughout financial theory, in some form or another, whenever we are attempting to determine an asset's value, its riskiness or its expected return. Therefore, if we understand the fundamental principles, we can intuit what to expect when confronted with a financial situation with which we may be unfamiliar.

While the principles describe the forces that impact value, the precepts describe interactions between the principles that can be utilized to better understand the theory of finance. PR1 describes part of the mechanics of valuation: holding other things equal, increasing the discount rate will decrease the value of an asset or a cash flow, and vice versa. This tells us that if we have two assets that have identical cash flows, and the two assets have different discount rates (for whatever reason), then we can intuit that the asset with the lower discount rate will have the greater value. We know this without having to calculate anything, because the mathematical mechanics described in PR1 tell us so.

PR2 indicates that the timing of the cash flows will have an impact on the asset's value. This occurs because of the discounting process; the further out in time a cash flow occurs, the more value is removed during the discounting process, and therefore the lesser the present value of the cash flow.

We can take this one step further: the structure of the cash flows an asset is expected to produce has an impact on the value of that asset as well. If most of the asset's large cash flows arrive early in its economic life, those cash flows will be discounted less (i.e., will have less value removed), and therefore the present value of the cash flows will be greater. Similarly, if an asset has most of its large cash flows being produced later in its economic life, those cash flows will have more value removed during the discounting process, and therefore the present value of the cash flows will be lesser. We can intuit this without calculating anything thanks to PR2, which helps us understand the mechanics of the discounting process.

PR3 tells us that riskier cash flows will have lower present values, while less risky cash flows will have higher present values. This occurs because the discount rate can be adjusted for risk—increased for cash flows of higher-than-average risk, and decreased for cash flows of lower-than-average risk. Therefore, if we have two assets with identical cash flows, but with different levels of risk, the riskier asset will have a lower value than the less risky asset. The reason behind this is that the discounting process removes more value from the riskier asset (with the higher discount rate) than it does from the less risky asset (with the lower discount rate). We can intuit this with help from PR3, which tells us the impact of risk on the discounting process, without having to calculate anything.

This also ties in with the second fundamental principle; since both assets have the same cash flows, the riskier asset will have not only the lower value but also the higher expected return. Once again, this is the mechanics of mathematics—the higher risk asset will have a lower value in the denominator, but the same cash flow in the numerator, as the less risky asset. Therefore, the value of the fraction (the percentage return) will be higher. In fact, the higher discount rate is used for the riskier asset specifically to pay a higher return to the firm's investors, in order to compensate them for taking on the higher level of risk. Thus, PR3 gives us one possible explanation for PR1, an explanation that is grounded in financial theory, and in FP2.

Making Use of the Principles and Precepts

As was mentioned previously, the next seven chapters in this book introduce the theory of finance and how it is used for valuation. There is a chapter on how to value a firm's bonds, another on how to value their stock and another on how to value the projects the firm is considering investing in for production purposes. We will review how to value a single future cash flow as well as a series of future cash flows. We will see how the costs of the different sources of funds are incorporated into the value analysis, and how those costs may be adjusted to account for risk. Seven different chapters, covering different areas of valuation, occur later in this book. Each covers a different area of financial theory. Yet each of those chapters makes use of the three fundamental principles described in the current chapter. Therefore, each remaining chapter can be better understood by having a solid understanding of the three fundamental principles and the three precepts.

Chapter 2, "The Time Value of Money," discusses how to value different types of cash flows associated with different types of investment vehicles. For example, suppose you were to win the lottery, and you were given a choice of how to collect your winnings: a single cash flow now, or an annual cash flow for the next 20 years. How would you choose between those offers? FP1 is the basis for valuing these two choices, and PR1 tells you if the discount rate the lottery firm is using to calculate the single cash flow payment is reasonable. Similarly, it is likely that at some point in the future you will own a credit card (if you don't own one already). The credit card company offers you credit and charges you an annual percentage rate (APR) for the use of the credit. In Chapter 2, you will learn that the APR they quote you is not the rate you will actually pay. This discrepancy is explained by FP1. When compounding (or discounting) is done more frequently than annually, the future value (or present value) changes due to the change in frequency. This result is addressed by FP3.

Chapter 3 describes the relationship between risk and return, and how return is affected by risk. In this chapter, we will see that while investing in a single stock can earn you a higher expected return than investing in a number of stocks, the lower expected return you earn from the group of stocks is safer than the return you may earn from the single stock. This result, and the desirability of this result, is explained by FP2. The impact of risk on value is explained directly by PR3, and indirectly by PR1 (since risk affects the discount rate used to calculate the value).

Chapter 4, "The Term Structure of Interest Rates," shows how interest rates are determined in the market. The material in this chapter shows very clearly how FP2 works in practice. PR3 examines the inverse relationship between value and the risk, while PR1 describes the inverse relationship between value and the discount rate. These two precepts are linked by the direct relationship between risk and return, since the return to bondholders is used as the discount rate for determining the market value of bonds.

Chapter 5, "Bond Valuation," explains how a firm's bonds are valued and why their value changes over time. Suppose you were to buy a newly issued bond from Microsoft for $1,000 that had a 10-year maturity. If you decide to sell the bond after five years, there is a good chance that you will not get $1,000 for the bond when you sell it—maybe more, maybe less, but not $1,000. FP3 explains why this is so, and PR1 shows how the true market value is determined.

Chapter 6 discusses different methods for determining the value of a firm's common equity (its common stock). As will be seen, the basic model for determining the value of a common stock is based on the dividends the stock is expected to pay over time. The future dividends the stock is expected to pay are determined by making an assumption about the rate at which the dividend is expected to grow over time. There are three separate assumptions that are used for this purpose: that the dividend will not grow at all; that it will grow at a constant future rate; or that it will grow at a nonconstant rate for a period of time before eventually settling down to grow at a constant rate. The impact of these different assumptions is explained by FP1 and FP3, and the methods used for calculating the value of the stock are described by PR1 and PR2.

Chapter 7, "Capital Budgeting Decision Methods," details the various methods used to determine the value of the production projects in which the firm may choose to invest. There are several metrics given for deciding among a set of possible investments, each looking at the project from a slightly different perspective. The process for determining the cash flows of a project is given in detail, and the value metrics themselves are explained thoroughly in terms of all three fundamental principles as well as all three precepts. This is one of the most important chapters in the book, as investing in projects that earn more than they cost is the key to making a business grow.

Chapter 8 explains the theory behind determining the firm's weighted average cost of capital—the cost of the money the firm raises to invest in new production assets. Each source of funds (debt, preferred equity and common equity) is valued differently, using different assumptions, but all follow the fundamental principles outlined in this chapter. The weighted average cost of capital is the basis of the discount rate used for valuing the firm's investment projects, and all three fundamental principles impact the methods used in the calculation.

Whenever these issues arise in the coming chapters, you will be reminded of these principles and precepts, and how they impact the theory in question. Understanding the theory at a fundamental level enables you to draw conclusions and make decisions when confronted with new theoretical questions. Just as a coach in sports drills the players on fundamentals to make them better players, this book will drill you on the fundamentals of financial theory to make you a better financial analyst. This chapter serves as the basis for those fundamental understandings; refer to it whenever you confront a theoretical issue that puzzles you. It is your best bet for understanding the complicated theory to follow.

Summary

The three fundamental principles are the basis for all of the theory addressed in the following seven chapters of this text. The three precepts help to understand how the theories interact and how you can make use of the theories to solve problems. Having a solid understanding of these principles and precepts will aid in the understanding and use of the theory. The theory in each of the coming chapters is grounded in one or more of these principles, and it will aid your understanding of the theories to find the link between the theories and the underlying principles.

End of Chapter Problems

1. Describe in your own words the nature of the relationship between risk and return, how changes in one affect changes in the other and what human trait is responsible for that relationship.
2. Describe in your own words the method for determining the value of an asset.
3. Describe in your own words the nature of the relationship between the price of an asset and the percentage return it earns, how changes in one affect the other and the basic principle that determines that relationship.
4. Describe in your own words the relationship between the value of an asset and the discount rate used to calculate its value.
5. Describe in your own words the relationship between the discount rate used to value an asset and the risk of the asset, as well as the relationship between the risk of an asset and the value of the asset.
6. Describe in your own words the impact of the timing of an asset's cash flows on the value of the asset.
7. What purpose do the principles given in this chapter serve?
8. What purpose do the precepts given in this chapter serve?
9. Suppose you purchased a corporate bond for its par value of $1,000 when it was issued. The bond pays a 10% coupon ($100) annually. After two years, you sell the bond to another investor for $950. How will the change in the bond's market value affect the new owner's yield on the bond?
10. The production manager at a manufacturing plant wants to invest in a new technology for producing the firm's product. This new technology will replace one of the employees currently used to produce the item. How can you determine the value of this new technology?
11. You win a contest for which you get to pick your prize. Your options are:

    a. $1,000 in the first month, $2,000 in the second month, $3,000 in the third month, and so on for one year.
    b. $5,000 per month for one year.
    c. $12,000 in the first month, $11,000 in the second month, $10,000 in the third month and so on for one year.

    Which prize should you pick?
12. The marketing manager at your firm shows you an analysis he performed of a new production process that he believes will reduce production costs and show a slight profit after taking into account the cost of operating the new technology. While the marketing manager believes the project is of average risk, you believe the new technology is riskier than the projects the firm normally invests in. How will this affect your evaluation of the new technology?

2   Time Value of Money

The material covered in this chapter is the framework upon which the rest of the chapters in the book are built. The conception of the time value of money gets at the very heart of virtually every calculation done from this point forth. That is because the calculations used are driven by the fundamental principles, as will be seen.

This chapter covers the mathematical methods (and formulas) used to calculate the value of cash flows when either pushing them out in time (to calculate a future value) or pulling them back in time (to calculate a present value). The methods take into account the fact that corporations use other people's money (from debtors or common stock holders) to fund their operations, and those investors deserve to be paid for the use of their money.

The Cost of Money

Like everything else in life, money has a cost; that is, raising money costs money. Corporations raise money in two general forms: debt (borrowing money) and equity (selling partial ownership in the firm). The cost of debt is interest. To the borrower, the interest rate represents cost, while to the lender the interest rate represents income (known as its yield or return). Equity has two costs: dividends (quarterly payments of cash) and capital gains (increases in the stock's market price). To the firm these are costs, while to the firm's shareholders they are income. So, the total yield paid to equity holders can be broken down into the dividend yield and the capital gains yield. The cost of debt is discussed in detail in Chapter 4, "The Term Structure of Interest Rates." The costs of equity are discussed further in Chapter six, "Stock Valuation."

The Fundamental Principles in Action

FP1 equates the value of an asset with the present value of the cash flows the asset is expected to produce. This principle is clearly seen when calculating the present value of single or multiple cash flows, and is applied (but not so clearly) when calculating the present value of annuities. FP3 asserts the inverse relationship between the price of an asset and its yield, or return. This principle is seen when discounting is done more frequently than annually—this effectively increases the discount rate, causing the present value of the cash flows to decrease. The interaction between FP1 and FP3 is seen in PR1, which states that increasing the discount rate decreases the present value of cash flows.

Understanding Why Money Has Time Value—Economic Equivalency

People save their money so that it can earn interest over time. They are free to consume their income now, but choose to postpone consumption and instead invest their money in order to have more money available in the future. Thus, money has time value because investing it will lead to having additional funds available in the future. In this way, a dollar today is worth more than a dollar due one year from today, since it can be invested today to be worth more than a dollar one year from now. In other words, a dollar today and a dollar one year from today are not economically equivalent, since the dollar today has the potential to be worth more than one dollar one year from now.

For example, if today you deposit $1,000 into a savings account that pays 5.0% APR (annual percentage rate) compounded annually, at the end of one year you will have $1,000(1.05) = $1,050 in the account. For this situation, given the 5% yield, $1,000 today and $1,050 one year from today are economic equivalents; that is, $1,000 today is economically equivalent to $1,050 one year from today, given the 5% return on the account. If you knew that you had the 5.0% return available on the savings account, then you should be indifferent between receiving $1,000 today or receiving $1,050 one year from today, since they are economically equivalent.

The interest earned in the savings account is income to the account holder and expense to the bank. The account holder deposits the money in order to earn interest and thus have even more money available in the future. The bank pays the interest to the account holder so that they can use their money to invest elsewhere (like making loans for cars or houses) at a rate of return that is higher than the interest paid to the account holder. The bank can earn a higher return because they tend to make investments that have more risk than a savings account, and therefore tend to earn a higher return than the savings account pays.

FP2 states that the interest rate earned on invested money is dependent upon the amount of risk the investor is willing to bear. The least amount a rational investor should be willing to accept for postponing consumption of their income is the nominal risk-free rate (r_{rf}), or the interest rate paid on an investment that bears no risk other than the risk of inflation. In this way, the nominal risk-free rate represents the pure time value of money—the cost paid purely for postponing consumption, without taking on any risk other than inflation. Beyond that, the return the investor earns should increase with their willingness to bear more risk. The types of risks borne by debtholders and their costs, as well as the nominal risk-free rate and how it is determined, are discussed in Chapter 4, "The Term Structure of Interest Rates." The types of risks borne by shareholders and their costs are discussed in Chapter 3, "Risk and Return."

Adjusting Cash Flow Values Over Time

The time value of money is calculated moving both forwards and backwards in time. Determining the value of a current cash flow (or series of cash flows) at some point in the future is known as calculating their future value (FV), and the mathematical method for calculating future values is known as compounding. Establishing the value today of a cash flow (or series of cash flows) expected in the future is known as calculating their present value (PV), and the mathematical method for calculating present values is known as discounting.

Compounding, or calculating future values, results in the cash flows growing larger over time as they continue to earn compound interest. Thus, the multiplier used to calculate the future value of a single cash flow will be greater than one. How much greater than one it is will depend upon the interest rate used and the number of periods in the future required. This will be shown in greater detail in the section "Future Value and Compounding."

Discounting, or calculating present values, results in cash flows growing smaller the further back in time the value is calculated. For this reason, the multiplier used to calculate the present value of a single cash flow will be less than one. How much less than one it is depends upon the interest rate used and the number of periods back in time required. This will be made clear in the section "Present Value and Discounting."

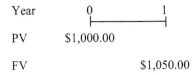

Figure 2.1 The Future Value of $1,000 Invested to Earn 5% APR Over One Year

Note that discounting involves the removal of value over time. The value removed represents the return that would be earned by the money if it were available to be invested today. In later chapters, you will see that:

- The present value of a bond is calculated by removing the required yield on the bond over the life of the bond;
- The present value of a stock is calculated by removing the required return on the stock;
- The present value of a production project is calculated by removing the cost of money to all investors (bond holders and shareholders); and
- The present value of the firm is calculated by removing the cost of money to all investors (bond holders and shareholders).

Thus, when valuing an asset, the purpose of discounting is to account for the return the firm owes to its investors for being able to use their money. In this chapter, we will be valuing future cash flows, and in this case the discount rate represents the *opportunity cost* of the investment—the yield on the next best investment available.

A tool that is helpful in time value calculations, particularly for complex time value problems, is the time line. The time line is used to list cash flows based on when they occur, whether those cash flows are being compounded to calculate a future value or discounted to calculate a present value. The time line in Figure 2.1 represents the example used in the prior section on economic equivalency.

Unless otherwise indicated, we will assume that the time periods on the number line represent years. With this assumption, period zero represents today, and the beginning of year one. Period one represents one year from today, the end of year one, and the beginning of year two. In later sections we will change the periods from years to smaller units such as months, weeks or days.

Future Value and Compounding

Compound interest is earned on both the principal (the initial cash flow) and on the accrued interest. Compound interest can be calculated using discrete time (specified intervals, such as years, months or weeks) or continuous time. This section deals with discrete compounding. Continuous compounding is treated later in the chapter.

If i percent interest is compounded annually, the principal and any accrued interest will grow by i percent each year. At the end of n years, the principal P and accrued interest will have grown at i percent per year n times, as per the following equation:

$$\text{FV}_n = P \times \left(1 + i\right)_1 \times \left(1 + i\right)_2 \times \left(1 + i\right)_3 \times \ldots \times \left(1 + i\right)_n$$

Since the principal is multiplied by the same amount each year, the equation can be written more efficiently by using an exponent, with the value of the exponent equal to the number of years included in the future value calculation:

$$FV_n = P(1+i)^n$$

The term $(1 + i)^n$ is the future value interest factor $(FVIF_{i,n})$; that is, the term $(1 + i)^n$ calculates the future value of a cash flow when interest is compounded annually at i percent for n years. The equation above can be rewritten as:

$$FV_n = P(FVIF_{i,n})$$

FV of a Single Cash Flow

If you deposit $100 into an account that pays 10.0% APR (annual percentage rate) interest compounded annually, and leave it there for five years, how much will be in the account at the end of the five-year period?

At the end of each year, the amount in the account will increase by 10.0%. At the end of one year, the account will have $100(1.1) = $110. At the end of two years, the account will have $110(1.1) = $121. At the end of three years it will have $121(1.1) = $133.10. At the end of four years, $133.10(1.1) = $146.41, and at the end of five years, $146.41(1.1) = $161.05. This process is reflected in the time line in Figure 2.2:

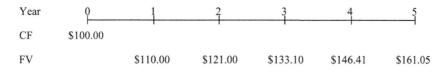

Year	0	1	2	3	4	5
CF	$100.00					
FV		$110.00	$121.00	$133.10	$146.41	$161.05

Figure 2.2 The Future Value of $100 Invested to Earn 10% APR Over Five Years

This tedious process shows the value increasing by 10.0% per year. The FV formula above allows us to do this all in one step:

$$FV_5 = \$100(FVIF_{10\%,5}) = \$100(1.1)^5 = \$100(1.61051)$$
$$= \$161.05 \text{ (rounded to the penny)}$$

Example. Your bank offers a structured-rate certificate of deposit (CD) that offers the following yields:

For deposits up to $10,000, 3.25% APR;
For deposits between $10,001 and $50,000, 3.40% APR;
For deposits between $50,001 and $100,000, 3.50% APR;
For deposits $100,001 or more, $3.65% APR.

Regardless of how much you deposit, you must leave the money in the account for five years. You intend to deposit $25,000 in the account. How much will be in the account in five years?

Solution. For a $25,000 deposit, $i = .034$ and $n = 5$; $FV = 25,000(FVIF_{3.4\%,5}) = 25,000$ $(1.034)^5 = \$29,548.99$. Assuming a 3.4% APR with annual compounding, $25,000 today and $29,548.99 five years from today are economically equivalent.

FV of Uneven Cash Flows

To determine the future value of a series of unequal cash flows, simply sum the future values of the individual cash flows. In other words, compound each cash flow out to the future period in question, then sum those future values to get the value of the series of cash flows in that future period.

For example, suppose that, as the result of a legal settlement, you received $2,500 today, and you are expecting to receive $5,000 one year from now, $7,500 two years from now, $10,000 three years from now, and $15,000 four years from now. You are putting each payment into an account that earns 6.0% APR, compounded annually. On the day you receive the last payment (four years from now), you will need to make a down payment on a home that you intend to purchase. How much money will you have available in the account to apply towards the down payment on the house once you receive the final payment?

The first payment ($2,500 received today) will earn interest for four years, the second payment ($5,000 in one year) will earn interest for three years, the third payment ($7,500 two years from now) will earn interest for two years, the fourth payment ($10,000 in three years) will earn interest for one year and the final payment ($15,000 four years from now) will earn no interest at all, since it arrives on the day in question. Each payment (except the last) will earn 6.0% interest each year. To solve this, multiply each payment by its future value interest factor, then sum the future values.

$$FV = \$2,500\left(FVIF_{6\%,4}\right) + \$5,000\left(FVIF_{6\%,3}\right) + \$7,500\left(FVIF_{6\%,2}\right) + \$10,000\left(FVIF_{6\%,1}\right) + \$15,000$$
$$= \$2,500(1.06)^4 + \$5,000(1.06)^3 + \$7,500(1.06)^2 + \$10,000(1.06)^1 + \$15,000$$
$$= \$3,156.19 + \$5,955.08 + \$8,427 + \$10,600 + \$15,000 = \$43,138.27$$

On the day you deposit the last payment, you will have $43,138.27 available in the account.

Example. Suppose your college offered to put $500 in an account that pays 5.0% APR interest at the end of each year for every A that you earn in your undergraduate studies, with the money to be used for tuition to their MBA program. Suppose further that during your freshman year you earned five As, during your sophomore year you earned six As, during your junior year you earned five As, and during your senior year you earned eight As. How much MBA tuition money would be in that account at the end of four years when you graduate?

Solution. This problem is in fact a series of simple future value problems. At the end of your first year, the school will deposit $500(5) = \$2,500$. That deposit will earn 5.0% for three years until the end of year four, at which time it will be worth $2,500(1.05)^3 = \$2,894.06$. That sum represents the future value of your freshman year as of the end of year four. This same method is used for each year of school, with the number of years compounded (n) decreasing by one each year. The sum of each year's FV calculation is the amount of MBA tuition money that will be in the account:

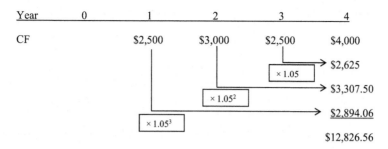

Figure 2.3 Calculating the Sum of the Future Values of the Cash Flows

$$FV_1 = \$500 \times 5 \times FVIF_{5\%,3} = \$2,500(1.05)^3 = \$2,894.06;$$

$$FV_2 = \$500 \times 6 \times FVIF_{5\%,2} = \$3,000(1.05)^2 = \$3,307.50;$$

$$FV_3 = \$500 \times 5 \times FVIF_{5\%,1} = \$2,500(1.05)^1 = \$2,625.00;$$

$$FV_4 = \$500 \times 8 \times FVIF_{5\%,0} = \$4,000(1.05)^0 = \$4,000.00;$$

$$\$2,894.06 + \$3,307.50 + \$2,625.00 + \$4,000.00 = \$12,826.56$$

You would have $12,826.56 in tuition credit for the MBA program. The time line in Figure 2.3 depicts the cash flows in the account and how their future value is calculated.

Present Value and Discounting

Discounting, the procedure for calculating the present value of a cash flow, determines the economic equivalent today of a cash flow to be received in the future, assuming a given discount rate. While compounding adds interest over time to calculate the future value of the cash flow, discounting removes interest going back in time to determine the present value of the cash flow. The discount rate in this calculation represents the opportunity cost for the cash flow—the interest rate you would earn (or pay) if the cash flow was available today to invest.

Discounting and compounding are inverse methods, in that one undoes the other. The future value interest factor ($FVIF_{i,n}$) is written as $(1 + i)^n$ and is multiplied by the cash flow to determine its future value n periods in the future when compounded at i percent per period. To determine the present value of a cash flow, we must determine the present value interest

factor ($PVIF_{i,-n}$), which is written as $(1+i)^{-n} \left[or \ \dfrac{1}{(1+i)^n} \right]$, and is multiplied by the future

cash flow to determine its economically equivalent value today.

The negative exponent in the PVIF indicates that the calculation is a present value calculation; the calculation is moving backwards in time to determine what the future cash flow is

worth in a prior period. Note that $(1 + i)^{-n}$ and $\dfrac{1}{(1+i)^n}$ are mathematically equivalent, and therefore calculate the same present value. To determine this, use a calculator or an Excel spreadsheet to calculate the value of $(1.05)^{-2}$ and $\dfrac{1}{(1.05)^2}$ and you will arrive at the same answer (0.9070294785). This proves that both multipliers provide the same solution. For your purposes, this means that you can use either of these multipliers in your calculations; if you don't like working with negative exponents, just use the fractional multiplier instead. Also note that $1.05^2 = 1.1025$, and that $1.05^2 \times 1.05^{-2} = 1.1025 \times 0.9070294785 = 1.00$. This shows that compounding and discounting are inverse operations: discounting undoes what compounding does.

PV of a Single Cash Flow

In the prior section on future value calculations, we determined that a deposit today of $100 compounded at 10% annually for five years will produce a future value of $161.05. Suppose you were expecting to receive a cash flow of that exact amount five years from today. If you had the option of either waiting five years to receive $161.05 or accepting a discounted payment today, what discounted payment would be economically equivalent? In other words, what is the present value of $161.05 five years from now at a discount rate of 10%?

$$PV = 161.05(PVIF_{10\%-5}) = 161.05(1.1)^{-5} = 161.05(0.6209213231) = \$100$$

Thus, with a discount rate of 10%, $161.05 to be received in five years is economically equivalent to $100 to be received today. We can prove the economic equivalence by compounding the $100 for five years at 10% APR, which gives us a future value of $161.05.

Example. You win a lottery prize that offers you a choice: you can accept a payment of $100,000 ten years from today, or you can accept the present value of that $100,000 payment today. If the lottery firm uses a 7.3% discount rate, what is the present value of that future $100,000 payment?

Solution. You must calculate the PVIF for a 7.3% discount rate for ten years:

$$PV = \$100,000(PVIF_{7.3\%-10}) = \$100,000(1.073)^{-10} = \$100,000(0.49431385) = \$49,431.39$$

Determining the Correct Exponent

Figure 2.4 is a tool that can be useful for determining the proper exponent to use in the FVIF or PVIF when compounding or discounting.

The tool is an equation in which the first space is the period in which the cash flow starts, and the last space is the period in which the cash flow ends. We must add the + or − symbol and the number of periods necessary to move the cash flow from the period represented by the first space number to the period represented by the last space number.

So, for example, suppose you are depositing $1,000 in the bank today, intending to leave it there for four years. During that time, you will receive 6.5% APR interest, compounded annually. How much will be in the account at the end of the four-year period? For this problem, you are given the PV ($1,000 in period 0) and you are told to calculate the FV in period 4. For this problem, the first space in the equation is 0 and the last space in the equation is 4:

$$0 + / - \_ = 4$$

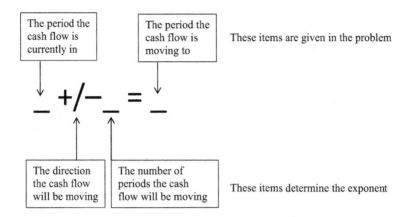

Figure 2.4 Equation for Determining the Exponent in FV or PV Calculations

The only way to get from zero to four is to add 4:

$$0 + 4 = 4$$

Therefore, the exponent needed for the FVIF is +4, or simply 4:

$$FV_4 = \$1,000\left(FVIF_{6.5\%,4}\right) = \$1,000\left(1.065\right)^4 = \$1,000\left(1.28646635\right) = \$1,286.47$$

Example. On your 21st birthday, your grandmother set up a trust for you that will pay you $50,000 on your 26th birthday. The day after your 21st birthday, your uncle offers to loan you the present value of the $50,000 trust, if you pay him 7.0% APR interest compounded annually on the funds. Using your uncle's discount rate, what is the present value of the trust?

Solution. If today is period zero, then you will receive the $50,000 in period five (at the end of five years). The cash flow is arriving in period five, but you need to determine its value if it were to arrive in period zero. So, the first space in the equation is 5 and the last space is 0:

$$5 +/-\_ = 0$$

The only way to get from five to zero is by subtracting 5, therefore the exponent is −5:

$$5 - 5 = 0$$

$$PV = \$50,000\left(PVIF_{7\%,-5}\right) = \$50,000\left(1.07\right)^{-5} = \$50,000\left(0.71298618\right) = \$35,649.31$$

Your uncle will give you $35,649.31 today and collect the $50,000 on your 26th birthday, for which he will earn 7.0% per year for the five years he spends waiting to be paid.

PV of Uneven Cash Flows

To determine the present value of a series of unequal cash flows, simply sum the present values of the individual cash flows. In other words, discount each cash flow to the present (period 0), then sum those present values to get the present value of the series of cash flows.

For example, suppose that, as the result of a lawsuit, you expect to receive cash flows of $10,000 in one year, $15,000 in two years, $20,000 in three years and $25,000 in four years. Your lawyer negotiates a counter-offer of a single cash payment today, for which you are willing to pay 8.5% interest as the discount rate (your opportunity cost of funds). If the opposing lawyers agree on your counter-offer, how much of a cash payment will you receive today?

The first payment of $10,000 will be discounted at 8.5% for one year, the second payment of $15,000 will be discounted for two years, the third payment of $20,000 will be discounted for three years, and the fourth payment of $25,000 will be discounted for four years. Sum those discounted values to get the present value of the series of cash flows, or the value of the single cash payment today.

$$\begin{aligned}
PV &= \$10,000\left(PVIF_{8.5\%,-1}\right) + \$15,000\left(PVIF_{8.5\%,-2}\right) + \$20,000\left(PVIF_{8.5\%,-3}\right) + \$25,000\left(PVIF_{8.5\%,-4}\right) \\
&= \$10,000(1.085)^{-1} + \$15,000(1.085)^{-2} + \$20,000(1.085)^{-3} + \$25,000(1.085)^{-4} \\
&= \$10,000(0.92165899) + \$15,000(0.84945529) + \$20,000(0.78290810) + \$25,000(0.72157428) \\
&= \$9,216.59 + \$12,741.83 + \$15,658.16 + \$18,039.36 \\
&= \$55,655.94
\end{aligned}$$

This shows that the value of this series of cash flows is equal to the sum of the present value of the individual cash flows, as per FP1.

Compounding/Discounting More Often Than Annually

Banks, financial firms, or businesses that extend credit generally quote an annual rate (APR) for the transaction being considered. For example, when you buy a new car, the dealer will quote you an annual interest rate for financing the purchase. Similarly, if you have a credit card that you use to make retail purchases, the credit card company will quote you an annual interest rate paid on the account. However, in both of these examples, interest is not paid annually. Since car payments and credit card payments are made monthly, the interest paid on the car loan and on the credit card debt is compounded monthly. For each loan, the result is that you pay a higher *effective* annual interest rate.

Whenever you are calculating either a future value or a present value of a cash flow for which interest is paid more often than annually, you must make two adjustments to the formula:

- You must divide the APR by the number of compounding (or discounting) periods per year to determine the **periodic interest rate**;
- You must multiply the number of years being calculated by the number of periods per year to determine the **number of periods** being calculated.

Note that when compounding or discounting is done more frequently than annually, your time line will no longer be marked in years. For example, if payments are made monthly, the periods on the time line will be in months.

For example, if you deposit $100 into an account that pays 10.0% APR, with interest compounded quarterly, and leave it there for five years, how much will be in the account at the end of the five-year period?

This problem was solved earlier in this chapter assuming annual compounding, but now we are told that compounding will be done quarterly (i.e., every three months, or four times per year). Therefore, you must change the APR into a periodic rate and the number of years into the number of periods:

- .10 ÷ 4 = .025 or 2.5% periodic rate;
- 5 × 4 = 20 periods.

Use these inputs in the future value calculation to determine the future value with quarterly compounding:

$$FV = \$100\left(FVIF_{2.5\%,20}\right) = \$100(1.025)^{20} = \$100(1.638616) = \$163.86 \text{ (rounded)}$$

Thus, with quarterly compounding, the future value increases from \$161.05 to \$163.86.

The Effective Annual Rate (EAR)

The previous problem showed that as compounding is done more frequently, the actual interest paid exceeds the quoted annual rate (APR). The result is that, when calculating a future value, more frequent compounding results in a higher future value. As will be seen, when calculating a present value, more frequent discounting results in a lower present value (the opposite result, as would be expected from an inverse mathematical operation). In either case, the result is that the party that is paying the interest is actually paying a higher rate of interest than the quoted rate. This is reflected in the EAR, or effective annual rate:

$$EAR = \left(1 + \frac{i}{m}\right)^m - 1$$

where i is the quoted annual interest rate (APR) and m is the number of compounding periods per year.

This can be verified using the previous example. If your bank pays savings account interest of 10.0% APR with compounding being done quarterly, the effective annual rate is calculated as:

$$EAR = \left(1 + \frac{.1}{4}\right)^4 - 1 = 1.025^4 - 1 = .103813 \text{ or } 10.3813\%$$

Using this as the annual rate, \$100(1.103813)^5 = \$163.86 (rounded), which matches the answer given above.

Example. Your credit card quoted you 17.99% interest annually charged on purchases, but you are expected to make payments monthly. Given this, what effective annual interest rate are you being charged?

Solution. For this problem, $i = .1799$ and $m = 12$. The EAR is calculated as indicated above:

$$EAR = \left(1 + \frac{.1799}{12}\right)^{12} - 1 = 1.0149916667^{12} - 1 = .195500 \text{ or } 19.55\%$$

So, while your credit card company quotes you an annual rate of 17.99%, you are effectively paying 19.55% annual interest.

The Impact of EAR on FV and PV Calculations of Single Cash Flows

As the previous section showed, compounding (or discounting) more often than annually increases the rate of interest paid (or earned) per year. Since compounding and discounting are inverse operations, this increase in the interest rate has the opposite effect on FV calculations of single cash flows than it does on PV calculations:

- When compounding more frequently than annually, the FVIF increases, which results in an increase in the future value calculated;
- When discounting more frequently than annually, the PVIF decreases, which results in a decrease in the present value calculated.

This second observation relates to the third fundamental principle (FP3), which discusses the inverse relationship between price and yield; discounting with a higher yield (reflected in the EAR) reduces the present value of the cash flow. The impact on future value was seen in the savings account example shown above. Another simple example will show the impact on calculating present value.

What is the present value of $161.05 five years from now at an annual discount rate of 10%, with discounting being done quarterly? Once again, we must change the APR to a periodic rate and the number of years to the number of periods:

- Periodic rate is $10\% \div 4 = 2.5\%$;
- Number of periods is $5 \times 4 = 20$.

These values are used to calculate the *PVIF*:

$$PV = 161.05\left(PVIF_{2.5\%,-20}\right) = 161.05(1.025)^{-20} = 161.05(0.6102709429) = 98.2841 \approx \$98.28$$

Changing discounting from annually to quarterly reduced the present value from $100 to $98.28.

Annuities

An annuity is a series of equal cash flows paid at regular intervals for a finite period of time. For example, some lottery winners are given the choice of a single lump sum payout or a series of equal annual payments over a 20-year period. The series of payments is an annuity. Many young parents set up annuity accounts with their bank to put funds away for their child's future college expenses.

There are two types of annuities: ordinary annuities and annuities due. In an ordinary annuity, the payment comes at the end of the period, while in an annuity due, the payment comes at the beginning of the period. Using the same inputs (i.e., payment amount, interest rate, number of payments), these two types of annuities have different present values and future values due to the difference in the timing of the payments. This is an example of PR2, which states that the timing of the cash flows has an impact on the value of the cash flows.

Future Value of an Ordinary Annuity

Similar to the way we handled the future value of a single cash flow, we can reduce the math for the future value of an ordinary annuity to an interest factor that we multiply by the value of a single payment to calculate the future value of all payments being made.

$$FVIFA_{i\%,n} = \frac{(1+i)^n - 1}{i}; \quad FVA = PMT\left(FVIFA_{i\%,n}\right)$$

Example. You want to take a trip to Europe five years from now, and the trip will cost you $24,000 in total. You decide to put away $4,200 per year for the next five years in an annuity account that pays 6.0% APR interest compounded annually, with the first payment being made one year from today. Will you have enough saved in the annuity account at the end of five years to be able to pay for the trip in full?

Solution. Since the first payment is due at the end of the first year, this is an ordinary annuity.

$$FVA = \$4,200\left(FVIFA_{6\%,5}\right) = \$4,200\left[\frac{(1.06)^5 - 1}{.06}\right] = \$23,675.79$$

Your plan to put away $4,200 at the end of each year will not fully cover the cost of the trip.

Since that plan did not work, you decide to try making monthly payments rather than annual payments. However, you can only afford to put $4,200 per year into the annuity account. Therefore, your monthly payments must be $4,200 ÷ 12 = $350. Your bank agrees to compound interest monthly at the same APR, so i = .06 ÷ 12 = .005 or 0.5% per month. The number of payments (n) will increase to 5 × 12 = 60. Plug these new figures into the formula:

$$FVA = \$350\left(FVIFA_{0.5\%,60}\right) = \$350\left[\frac{(1.005)^{60} - 1}{005}\right] = \$24,419.51$$

Making the payments monthly permits you to earn enough interest to cover the full cost of the trip without having to put away any more money.

Future Value of an Annuity Due

If the annuity payments are deposited at the beginning of the period, they will earn another period's worth of interest over the same amount of time. That will cause the future value of the annuity due to be higher than the future value of the ordinary annuity by one period's worth of interest. Therefore, the way to calculate the future value of an annuity due is to compound the value of the ordinary annuity for one more period:

$$FVIFAD_{i\%,n} = \frac{(1+i)^n - 1}{i}(1+i) = FVIFA_{i\%,n}(1+i); \quad FVAD = PMT\left(FVIFAD_{i\%,n}\right)$$

Example. You want to take a trip to Europe five years from now, and the trip will cost you $24,000 in total. You decide to put away $4,200 per year for the next five years in an annuity account that pays 6.0% APR interest compounded annually, with the first payment being made today. Will you have enough saved in the annuity account at the end of five years to be able to pay for the trip in full?

Solution. Since the first payment is being made today, this is now an annuity due.

$$FVAD = \$4,200\left(FVIFAD_{6\%,5}\right) = \$4,200\left[\frac{(1.06)^5 - 1}{.06}\right](1.06) = \$25,096.34$$

By making the payments an annuity due, you will have more than enough to cover the cost when the five-year period is over.

Present Value of an Ordinary Annuity

The present value of an ordinary annuity is also calculated as a single payment multiplied by an interest factor, just like with the future value. However, the interest factor is more complicated to calculate.

$$PVIFA_{i\%,-n} = \left[\frac{1-(1+i)^{-n}}{i}\right]; \quad PVA = PMT\left(PVIFA_{i\%,-n}\right)$$

Example. A major league baseball player's contract has a clause that states that if he is to be cut from the team, the owner must pay him the present value of all remaining annual payments specified in the contract, using a discount rate of 7.5%. At the time that the owner decides to cut the player from the team, the player has three years remaining on his contract. If the annual payments of $300,000 are paid at the end of the year, how much will the owner owe the player?

Solution. Since payments are made at the end of the year, this is an ordinary annuity.

$$PVA = 300,000\left(PVIFA_{7.5\%,-3}\right) = \$300,000\left[\frac{1-(1.075)^{-3}}{.075}\right] = \$780,157.72$$

Buying out the player's contract with three years remaining will cost the owner $780,157.72.

All that is required to see the connection between the PVA calculations and FP1 is to discount the annual payments separately, then sum their PVs. While this requires more work, it can help to make clear what the PVA formula does not:

$$PV_{CF1} = \$300,000(1.075)^{-1} = \$279,069.77;$$
$$PV_{CF2} = \$300,000(1.075)^{-2} = \$259,599.78;$$
$$PV_{CF3} = \$300,000(1.075)^{-3} = \$241,488.17;$$
$$\sum PV_{CF1-3} = \$279,069.77 + 259,599.78 + 241,488.17 = \$780,157.72$$

Thus, the PVA formula is a shortcut (i.e., a simplified formula) for calculating the PV of a series of equal cash flows that holds true to our first fundamental principle.

Present Value of an Annuity Due

If the annuity payments are made at the beginning of the period, they will be discounted for one less period during the present value calculation. This has the same effect as when calculating the future value of the annuity due: it increases the present value by one period's worth of interest. Therefore, the way to calculate the present value of an annuity due is to compound the value of the ordinary annuity for one more period:

$$PVIFAD_{i\%,-n} = \left[\frac{1-(1+i)^{-n}}{i}\right](1+i) = PVIFA_{i\%,-n}(1+i); \; PVAD = PMT\left(PVIFAD_{i\%,-n}\right)$$

Suppose the baseball contract above called for the player to be paid the first payment on the day he is cut, and one year later for each subsequent payment. How will that impact the present value of the annuity?

Since the payments will be made at the beginning of the year, this is now an annuity due.

$$PVAD = 300,000\left(PVIFAD_{7.5\%,-3}\right) = \$300,000\left[\frac{1-(1.075)^{-3}}{.075}\right](1.075) = \$838,669.55$$

Changing the payments from an ordinary annuity to an annuity due increases the present value by more than $58,000.

A Simple Understanding of the Annuity Due Value

When compounding an annuity to calculate a future value, the annuity due is compounded for one more period than the ordinary annuity, since the payments are made at the beginning of the period. This makes the future value of the annuity due equal to the value of the ordinary annuity multiplied by one plus the periodic rate.

When discounting an annuity to calculate a present value, the annuity due is discounted for one less period than the ordinary annuity, since the payments are made at the beginning of the period. This makes the present value of the annuity due equal to the value of the ordinary annuity multiplied by one plus the periodic rate.

This means that the value of an annuity due is equal to the value of the ordinary annuity multiplied by one plus the periodic rate, *regardless of whether you are calculating a future value or a present value*. This understanding makes calculating the PV or FV of an annuity due a simple step beyond calculating the value of the ordinary annuity.

Perpetuities

A perpetuity is simply an annuity that has no scheduled end date. An example would be a preferred stock's dividend; it is fixed in amount and paid on a scheduled basis with no end in sight. Since it has no end, a perpetuity has no simple formula for calculating its future value. However, the formula for calculating its present value is simple:

$$PV_{perpetuity} = \frac{PMT}{i}$$

where: PMT is the annual perpetuity payment; and
            i is the annual discount rate.

Example. Suppose you had the opportunity to purchase a preferred stock that pays a $50 dividend each year. If your required return on this preferred stock is 8.50%, how much should you be willing to pay for this stock?
    Solution. 50 ÷ .085 = 588.24. You should be willing to pay up to $588.24 for this preferred stock.

Amortized Loans

An amortized loan is a debt for which payments are calculated to be of equal value over the life of the loan, and which contribute to both the interest owed on the loan as well as the repayment of the principal. Early in the life of the loan, the principal owed is at its highest, and therefore the earlier payments contribute more to interest than to the repayment of the principal. Over time, the principal is reduced more and more, and so later in the life of the loan, the payments contribute more to repayment of the principal than to interest (i.e., as more principal is repaid, less interest is owed). Therefore, the makeup of the payments is mostly interest at first, but over time becomes less interest and more repayment of principal. So, while the amount of the payments does not change over time, the makeup of the payments (interest vs. principal) changes with each payment made.
    Since the payments are constant, made at fixed intervals (e.g., monthly or annually) and occur for a finite period of time (the life of the loan), the loan behaves like an annuity. This understanding permits us to use the PV annuity formula to determine the payment necessary to repay a given loan at a stated rate of interest for a specific period of time. Merely substitute the amount of the loan (PV_{Loan} in the formula below) for the PV of the annuity, and then divide by the *PVIFA*:

$$PVA = PMT\left(PVIFA_{i\%,-n}\right); PMT = \frac{PV_{Loan}}{PVIFA_{i\%,-n}}$$

Example. You borrow $4,500 from your uncle to buy a used car. He agrees to loan you the money for one year, during which you must make monthly payments, starting one month from the day you buy the car. Your uncle charges you 3.6% APR interest on the loan. What will your monthly payments be under this loan arrangement?
    Solution. PV_{Loan} is $4,500. Calculating the *PVIFA* requires a monthly interest rate: 0.036 ÷ 12 = 0.003 or 0.3% per month.

$$PVIFA_{0.3\%,12} = \left[\frac{1-(1.003)^{-12}}{.003}\right] = 11.7692; PMT = \frac{\$4,500}{11.7692} = \$382.35$$

Table 2.1 Amortization Schedule

	Monthly Payment	Amount of Interest	Amount of Principal	Remaining Balance
Month 0				$4,500.00
Month 1	$382.35	$13.50	$368.85	$4,131.15
Month 2	$382.35	$12.39	$369.96	$3,761.19
Month 3	$382.35	$11.28	$371.07	$3,390.12
Month 4	$382.35	$10.17	$372.18	$3,017.94
Month 5	$382.35	$9.05	$373.30	$2,644.64
Month 6	$382.35	$7.93	$374.42	$2,270.22
Month 7	$382.35	$6.81	$375.54	$1,894.68
Month 8	$382.35	$5.68	$376.67	$1,518.01
Month 9	$382.35	$4.55	$377.80	$1,140.21
Month 10	$382.35	$3.42	$378.93	$761.28
Month 11	$382.35	$2.28	$380.07	$381.21
Month 12	$382.35	$1.14	$381.21	$0.00

You will need to pay your uncle 12 monthly payments of $382.35 each.

For each payment, the amount of interest is equal to the remaining balance of the loan multiplied by the periodic rate. So, for example, when the first payment is made, you will still owe the entire $4,500. Therefore, the first payment contains $4,500(0.003) = $13.50 of interest. Since the payment is $382.35, that means that the first payment will contribute $382.35 − $13.50 = $368.85 towards the principal. This reduces the remaining principal to $4,500 − $368.85 = $4,131.15. The second payment will then be comprised of $12.39 of interest ($4,131.15 × .003) and $369.96 in repayment of principal ($382.35 − $12.39), leaving a remaining balance after the second payment of $3,761.19 ($4,131.15 − $369.96). Each successive payment will contribute less towards interest and more towards repayment of principal until the loan is repaid in full.

The amortization schedule in Table 2.1 reflects the breakdown of each payment into interest vs. principal over the life of the loan.

Solving for Other Variables in the TVM Calculations

There are questions asked of financial analysts that require different mathematical approaches than those used for calculating PV and FV. For example:

- I have $1,000 to invest today. What annual interest rate must I earn on my money to grow it to $1,500 in five years' time?
- If my money is invested to earn 6.51% APR, how long will it take to double my money?

The first question requires you to solve for the interest rate, while the second question requires you to find out how long it will take to achieve a financial goal (solving for the exponent). Both are future value questions relating to a single cash flow, so they would follow the FV formula: $FV = P(1 + i)^n$. In the first question you would be solving for i, while in the second question you would be solving for n.

The first question is answered by solving the equation $1,500 = $1,000(1 + i)^5$ for i. Note that i in this case is the geometric average growth rate over the period in question. To solve for i, manipulate the equation to get the term with i by itself, and simplify terms:

$$1,500 = 1,000(1+i)^5;$$
$$1,500/1,000 = (1+i)^5;$$
$$1.5 = (1+i)^5.$$

Now simply take the fifth root of each side of the equation to solve for $1 + i$, and then subtract the one to solve for i. Raising to the power 1/5 (or 0.2) is mathematically equivalent to taking the fifth root:

$$1.5^{0.2} - 1 = i = 0.08447$$

Therefore $i = 8.45\%$. To confirm our answer: $1,000(1.0845)^5 = 1,500.19$. The additional 19 cents are due to rounding the interest rate to 2 decimal places.

Example. In the first week of January 2007, the S&P 500 index fund was valued at $1,438.24. In the first week of January 2017, the S&P 500 index fund was valued at $2,278.87. What average annual growth rate did the index fund experience over that ten-year period?

Solution. $2,278.87/1,438.24 = 1.5844852$; $1.5844852^{0.1} - 1 = 0.047101$ or 4.71%. To confirm the answer: $1,438.24(1.0471)^{10} = 2,278.84$ (the difference of $0.03 is rounding error).

Example. You estimate you will need $100,000 for your daughter's college education, which will start in just 12 years. You currently have $25,000 available to invest. What average annual interest rate will you need to earn over the next 12 years to achieve your goal?

Solution. $100,000/25,000 = 4$; $4^{1/12} - 1 = 0.122462$ or 12.25%.

For the second question, solving for the exponent (the number of periods), we need to use the natural logarithm (ln). Logarithms are simply exponents—the power to which another number (the base) must be raised to obtain a given value.

$$10^2 = 100; \text{ 2 is the base 10 log of 100.}$$

Base 10 logs are the second most commonly used logs in finance, while the most commonly used logs are natural logs, whose base is e (approximately 2.7182818). The constant e is commonly used for valuation involving continuous compounding or discounting. The concept of e is explained more thoroughly later in the chapter.

To use logarithms successfully, it is necessary to follow the four main rules for logarithms:

1. $\ln(x \cdot y) = \ln(x) + \ln(y)$;
2. $\ln(x \div y) = \ln(x) - \ln(y)$;
3. $\ln(x^y) = y \cdot \ln(x)$;
4. $\ln(e) = 1$.

The natural log is used to get the variable out of the exponent position, for which the third rule above will help. Then to answer the question, if my money is invested to earn 6.51% APR, how long will it take to double my money?

- Set up the equation: $1(1.0651)^t = 2$;
- Isolate the variable term: $1.0651^t = 2 \div 1 = 2$;
- Take the natural log of both sides: $\ln(1.0651^t) = \ln(2)$;
- Apply rule #3 to the first term: $t \times \ln(1.0651) = \ln(2)$;
- Isolate the variable: $t = \ln(2) \div \ln(1.0651) = 0.693147 \div 0.063069 = 10.99$.

It would take almost 11 years to double your money at 6.51% per year.

Example. You deposited $2,500 in an account today that earns 8.50% APR compounded annually. How long will it take for your deposit to grow to $10,000?

Solution. $2,500(1.085)^t = 10,000$; $1.085^t = 10,000 \div 2,500 = 4$; $t \times \ln(1.085) = \ln(4)$; $t = \ln(4) \div \ln(1.085) = 1.386294 \div 0.08158 = 16.99$. It will take almost 17 years.

Example. You need $20,000 to pay for an around-the-world cruise. Today you have $14,000 in an investment that earns 7.5% APR. How long will it take for your investment to be worth $20,000?

Solution. $14,000(1.075)^t = 20,000$; $1.075^t = 20,000 \div 14,000 = 1.428571$; $t \times \ln(1.075) = \ln(1.428571)$; $t = \ln(1.428571) \div \ln(1.075) = 0.356675 \div 0.072321 = 4.93$, or just short of five years.

Discrete Time vs. Continuous Time

As discussed in the section on frequent compounding, increasing the number of compounding periods in a year increases the amount of compound interest earned in that year. While more frequent compounding leads to more interest, the increase in interest earned per year gets smaller as the number of compounding periods per year gets larger. For example, suppose you invest $1,000 for one year at an annual interest rate of 5%. The future value of the investment in one year based on different numbers of compounding periods per year is given below:

- Compounding annually: $1,000(1.05) = $1,050.00$;
- Compounding every six months: $1,000(1.025)^2 = $1,050.63$;
- Compounding every three months: $1,000(1.0125)^4 = $1,050.95$;
- Compounding every two months: $1,000(1.00833333)^6 = $1,051.05$;
- Compounding every month: $1,000(1.00416667)^{12} = $1,051.16$;
- Compounding every week: $1,000(1.00096154)^{52} = $1,051.25$.

While interest does increase with each rise in the number of compounding periods, the incremental increases become smaller. This function of increasing frequency has a limit; that is, as the number of compounding periods per year (m) increases, the future value of the investment approaches a maximum. This indicates that there is a limit as to how high the future value can go, because there is a limit as to how high the *FVIF* can go. That limit is known as e, which has a value of approximately 2.7182818 (rounded to seven decimal places). Mathematically that limit is expressed as follows:

$$\lim_{m \to \infty} \left(1 + \frac{1}{m}\right)^m = e$$

If the interest rate (*i*) and the number of years (*n*) are included, the formula changes slightly:

$$\lim_{m \to \infty} \left(1 + \frac{i}{m}\right)^{mn} = e^{in} = FVIF_{i\%cc,n}$$

For example, if you invest $1,000 for one year in an account that pays 5% APR compounded continuously, the future value in one year will be calculated as follows:

$$1000e^{0.05\times1} = \$1,051.27$$

The result of your calculation will be $1,051.27, which is only $0.02 higher than the amount earned from weekly compounding.

Note that you can get the same result by replacing *e* with 2.7182818:

$$\$1,000 \times 2.7182818^{.05\times1} = \$1,051.27$$

Example. For your 21st birthday, your grandmother puts $5,000 into an account that will earn 5.75% APR compounded continuously. The account cannot be accessed until you turn 28 years old. How much will be in the account on your 28th birthday?

Solution. $5,000e^{.0575\times7} = \$7,477.79$

Alternately, $5,000(2.7182818^{.0575\times7}) = \$7,477.79$

When discounting (calculating a PV), the time exponent *n* must be negative:

$$e^{-in} = PVIF_{i\%cc,-n}$$

For example, you win a contest that offers a choice of prizes: $10,000 today or $15,000 five years from today. You plan to put the money into an account that earns 6.5% APR compounded continuously to help pay for graduate school. Which prize should you choose?

There are two ways to solve this problem: compare the FV in five years of the $10,000 today to the $15,000 in five years, or compare the PV of the $15,000 in five years to the $10,000 today. We will do both:

$$FV = \$10,000e^{.065\times5} = \$13,840.30$$

Since the FV in five years of the $10,000 today is less than $15,000, the $15,000 in five years is the better choice. Alternatively:

$$PV = \$15,000e^{.065\times-5} = \$10,837.90$$

Since the PV of the $15,000 in five years is greater than $10,000, the $15,000 in five years is the better choice.

Example. On your 21st birthday, your grandmother set up a trust for you that will pay you $50,000 on your 26th birthday. The day after your 21st birthday, your uncle offers to loan you the present value of the $50,000 trust, if you pay him 7.0% APR interest compounded continuously on the funds. Using your uncle's discount rate, what is the present value of the trust?

Solution. $\$50,000e^{.07 \times -5} = \$35,234.40$

Alternately, $\$50,000(2.7182818^{.07 \times -5}) = \$35,234.40$

Continuous discounting reduced your payout by over $400 compared to annual discounting.

Calculating the effective annual rate with continuous compounding is as simple as raising e to the power of the APR and then subtracting one:

$$\text{EAR}_{CC} = e^i - 1$$

Example. Your bank is offering a CD that pays 7.0% APR with continuous compounding. What is the effective annual rate for the CD?

Solution. $e^{.07} - 1 = 0.0725$ or 7.25%.

Summary of the Principles and Precepts Applied in This Chapter

The First Fundamental Principle (FP1): The value of any asset is equal to the present value of the cash flows the asset is expected to produce over its economic life.

This principle is clearly seen when discounting single or multiple cash flows (although the formula for the PV of an annuity is not quite so clear!). This principle will arise repeatedly throughout most of the rest of the chapters of this text.

The Third Fundamental Principle (FP3): There is an inverse relationship between price and yield; if an asset's price increases, its return will decrease (and vice versa), holding other things constant.

This principle was seen when discounting was done more often than annually; more value is removed during the discount process due to more frequent discounting, and therefore the present value decreases (relative to annual discounting).

The first precept relates directly to the relationship between the PV and the discount rate:

The First Precept (PR1): The present value of a cash flow (or an asset) is inversely related to its discount rate; increasing the discount rate decreases the present value (and vice versa), holding other things constant.

More frequent discounting increases the effective annual discount rate, which in turn decreases the present value. This result is an interaction between the valuation method (FP1) and the relationship between value and yield (FP3).

End of Chapter Problems

1. Why is $1 today worth more than $1 next year?
2. What do the FVIF and PVIF represent?
3. What is an annuity?
4. What is the difference between an ordinary annuity and an annuity due?
5. You have $16,000 that you wish to invest for five years in an investment that is expected to pay 7.25% APR. How much will you have available when you cash out in five years if compounding is done:

   a. Annually.
   b. Semiannually (twice per year).
   c. Quarterly.
   d. Monthly.
   e. Weekly.
   f. Continuously.

6. You are expecting to receive a cash payment of $75,000 six years from today. If you had that money today, you would put it into an investment that will earn 6.55% APR. What is the present value of this cash flow, assuming discounting is done:

   a. Annually.
   b. Semiannually (twice per year).
   c. Quarterly.
   d. Monthly.
   e. Weekly.
   f. Continuously.

7. With an APR of 8.65%, what is the effective annual rate (EAR) if compounding occurs:

   a. Semiannually.
   b. Quarterly.
   c. Monthly.
   d. Weekly.
   e. Continuously.

   Round your answers to two decimal places (0.04428 = 4.43%).

8. You want to start a college fund for your little sister, so you arrange to put $250 per month into an annuity account that pays 6.0% APR, compounded monthly. Your first payment is due at the end of this month. How much will be in the account at the end of eight years?

9. You win a lottery that pays $5,000 per month for 20 years, starting today. You have the option of taking a lump sum today instead of the monthly payments. The lottery people tell you that, if you take the monthly payments, the money you won is expected to earn 7.25% APR, compounded monthly, for the entire 20 years it will be invested. Given these data, what is the lump sum you would expect to receive today?

10. You are scheduled to receive a cash payment of $100,000 eight years from now. An attorney offers to pay you a lump sum of $45,000 today if you sign over the rights to the $100,000 future payment. What annual interest rate is the attorney charging you for this transaction?

11. You purchase a car that costs $25,000 complete (title, license, etc.). Your bank loans you the $25,000, and in return you must make monthly payments of $484.00 per month for

five years (60 payments). Based on these data, what monthly interest rate is your bank charging you? What is the equivalent annual rate?

12. You put money into an investment that is expected to pay 8.0% interest annually. At this annual interest rate, how many years will it take for you to double your money?

13. You get an offer for a credit card that charges 13.99% interest APR, compounded monthly. What effective annual interest rate does this credit card charge?

14. You borrow $22,500 from your bank, to be repaid in monthly payments over four years (48 payments), starting at the end of the month. If the bank charges you 6.5% interest APR, compounded monthly, what will your monthly payment be?

15. You are expecting to receive the following cash flows: $1,000 one year from now, $1,500 two years from now, $2,500 three years from now, $4,000 four years from now and $5,000 five years from now. If your discount rate is 4.5%, what is the present value of these cash flows?

16. You intend to deposit the following cash flows into your bank: $750 one year from now, $1,000 two years from now, $1,250 three years from now, $1,500 four years from now, $1,750 five years from now and $2,000 six years from now. Assuming the bank pays you 6.25% interest APR, compounded annually, how much will be in your account at the end of six years (when the final payment is made)?

17. You plan to take a Caribbean cruise in five years. The cruise will cost you $15,000, with payment due exactly five years from today. You have a savings account that pays 5.5% APR, compounded monthly. The savings account currently has $4,500 in it, which you will leave in the account to help pay for the cruise. How much more must you deposit into the savings account today in order to have exactly $15,000 in the account five years from today?

Bibliography

Fundamentals of Corporate Finance, 12th edition. S. Ross, R. Westerfield and B. Jordan. McGraw-Hill Education, 2019.

Financial Management: Principles & Practice, 8th edition. T. Gallagher. Textbook Media Press, 2019.

Quantitative Methods for Finance and Investments. J. Teal and I. Hasan. Wiley-Blackwell, 2002.

3   Risk and Return

Businesses constantly face risks, some recurring (like the risk of a competitor designing a newer, better product), others new and different (like the risk of an economic recession) and all seemingly never-ending. Risks come in many different forms and different levels of severity. Part of being a good manager is being able to understand the nature of the risks the firm faces and determine the return necessary to make the risks worth bearing.

The last sentence above implies a relationship between risk and return, and that relationship is important for you to understand. That relationship is stated clearly in our second fundamental principle (FP2), which identifies the positive nature of the relationship between risk and return. This relationship is so important that it is usually a mistake to discuss an investment's return without also discussing its risk. In this chapter, we will discuss the different types of risk firms (and investors) face, how these risks are measured and how they compare to returns. We will also discuss how to calculate returns over a holding period, as well as how to calculate mean annual returns over an extended period of time.

The Fundamental Principles in Action

FP2 states that there is a direct (or positive) relationship between perceived risk and required return. This principle is clearly seen when calculating expected returns using the Security Market Line. PR3 examines the inverse relationship between value and the risk, while PR1 describes the inverse relationship between value and the discount rate. These two precepts are linked by the direct relationship between risk and return, since the return to shareholders is used as the discount rate for valuing the firm's common shares.

Measuring Return

The percentage return (or yield) on an investment is measured as the change in the value of the investment over the time period in question, plus any cash flows from the investment, divided by the value of the investment at the beginning of the time period. The numerator of this fraction is the dollar return on the investment, and dividing the dollar return by the beginning price makes it a percentage return (a percentage of the price). Stocks and bonds both have cash flows that occur during the year: dividends for stocks and interest payments for bonds.

Typically, when people in finance refer to returns, they are referring to percentage returns, not dollar returns. Percentage returns indicate the size of the return relative to size of the investment, and therefore can be used to compare returns for different investments, regardless of the amount invested. For example, suppose you and your best friend both invested for one year, each in a different stock. At the end of the year, you had earned $1,000 on your investment, while your friend had earned $500 on hers. Which of you did better? The correct answer is it depends on how much each of you invested. If you invested $5,000, while your friend invested $1,000, then she earned a 50% return while you only earned a 20% return. When we refer to returns in this textbook, we will usually be referring to percentage returns.

For stocks, the total return can be divided into the dividend yield (the percentage return from dividends) and the capital gains yield (the percentage change in the price of the stock). Similarly, for bonds, the total return can be divided into the current yield (the percentage return from interest payments) and the capital gains yield (the percentage change in the price of the bond). The equations for calculating the different yields are as follows:

- Total Yield = (Ending Price − Beginning Price + Cash Flows) ÷ Beginning Price;
- Dividend Yield = Total Dividends Received ÷ Beginning Price of Stock;
- Capital Gains Yield = (Ending Price − Beginning Price) ÷ Beginning Price;
- Current Yield = Total Interest Payments Received ÷ Beginning Price of Bond.

Let's assume you bought 1,000 shares of AT&T stock on January 2, 2017. The closing market price of AT&T common stock on that day was $42.16, so the total amount paid for the stocks (excluding transaction costs) was $42,160. During 2017, AT&T paid four dividends of $0.49 each per share, so you received cash flow of $1.96 for each share (or $1,960 in total). Let's also assume that you sold the shares on January 2, 2018, at the closing price of $37.45, for a total (excluding transaction costs) of $37,450. Based on these assumptions, your total dollar return per share for the year was −$2.75 (dividends of $1.96 minus a capital loss of $4.71), or −$2,750 for all of the shares. Based on these data, the total percentage return on the investment for the year was −6.52% (−2.75 ÷ 42.16 = −0.0652), which can be further divided into the dividend yield of 4.65% ($1.96 ÷ 42.16 = 0.0465) and the capital gains yield of −11.17% ({37.45 − 42.16} ÷ 42.16 = −0.1117). Note that these yield percentages are the same whether calculated on a per share basis or on the total amount invested—what happens to one share of AT&T stock happens to them all.

Annualized Return

In the financial markets, yields are reported on an annualized basis. This makes it easier to compare different investments. For example, the 10-year Treasury note yield on March 1, 2017 was 2.46%. That is the interest rate you would earn each year if you held the bond, not what you would earn over the entire ten-year period. In this way, you can compare the yield on 10-year bonds to the yields on 5-year bonds or 1-year bonds. Most interest rates are quoted as an annual percentage rate (APR) for that reason.

Suppose you purchased 100 shares of a common stock on June 1, 2018 for $35.00 per share and held it until September 1, 2018, when you sold it for $36.50 per share. Also suppose that during that period you received one dividend of $0.25 per share ($25.00 in total). Your total yield for this investment would be calculated as (36.50 − 35.00 + 0.25) ÷ 35 = 0.05 or 5.0%. However, this is what you earned over a three-month holding period. To compare this stock to other investments, you will need to annualize the yield. The method for this is simple:

- Add the holding period yield to one (1.05);
- Raise that number to the power of the number of holding periods it would require to last a full year (in this case, four three-month periods make up a year: $1.05^4 = 1.2155$);
- Subtract one from this figure (1.2155 − 1 = 0.2155 or 21.55%).

Thus, the annualized return for the stock would be 21.55%. This figure assumes that the three-month investment is reinvested three more times under the same conditions, and allows for compounding over the entire year.

Example. You bought stock in Alphabet Inc. (the parent company of Google) on July 31, 2018 for $1,218.19 per share. You got tired of holding it and decided to sell it on September 30, 2018 for $1,076.77 per share. Calculate the holding period and annualized returns.

Solution. The holding period is two months, so there are six holding periods in one year.

$$r_{HP} = \frac{1,076.77 - 1,218.19}{1,218.19} = -0.11609 \; or \; -11.61\%;$$

$$r_{annual} = 0.8839^6 - 1 = -0.52311 \; or \; -52.31\%$$

Average Returns

There are two different ways to calculate average (or mean) returns for an investment, and which one to use really depends on which question you need to answer:

1. What is the average annual rate you earned on this investment for a given year?
2. What is the average annual rate you earned on this investment over an extended period of time?

The first question can be answered by calculating the arithmetic mean return, while the second question requires you to calculate the geometric mean return.

Suppose you invested in a stock for five years, during which time your annual returns were 3.50%, 4.65%, −2.45%, 3.15% and 5.60% respectively. If you want to know on average what you would have earned in a single year during the time you were invested, simply add the annual yields and divide by the number of years in question: (.035 + .0465 − .0245 + .0315 + .056) ÷ 5 = .0289 or 2.89%. This arithmetic average is the best estimate of what you would have earned in a single random year during the five years that you held the stock.

While the arithmetic mean is good for isolating the return in a single year, it does not take compound interest into account and will therefore over-estimate the average return for an extended holding period. To include the impact of compounding, you must calculate the geometric return, which is a bit more complicated:

- Add one to each of the annual returns (1.035, 1.0465, .9755, 1.0315 and 1.056);
- Multiply all of the terms together (1.035 × 1.0465 × .9755 × 1.0315 × 1.056 = 1.1509064);
- Raise the product from the previous step to the power of one over the number of observations (n)—this is the same as taking the nth root of the product ($1.1509064^{1/5} = 1.028509$);
- Subtract one to get the geometric mean (0.028509 or 2.85%).

Raising the product to the 1/5 power is the same as taking the fifth root, so the rule is that you must take the root of however many numbers you are averaging. Note that the geometric mean is slightly smaller than the arithmetic mean (2.85% vs. 2.89%). This is expected, since the geometric rate takes into account returns compounded over a longer period of time than a single year.

The geometric mean can also be calculated directly from prices rather than from returns (as we did above). Suppose you bought the stock in the previous example on January 1, 2012 for $100, and then sold it on January 1, 2017 for $115.09. To calculate the geometric mean return, simply divide the sale price by the purchase price, then take the fifth root of that figure (because you held the stock for five years) and subtract one: $\{115.09 \div 100\}^{1/5} - 1 = .0285$ or 2.85%. This confirms our earlier calculation using the annual returns. You can check your answer by growing the purchase price of the stock at 2.85% for five years: $100 \times 1.0285^5 = 115.09$.

Expected Return and Risk

Up to this point, we have discussed measuring past returns and their risk. Financial analysts need to be able to estimate future returns and their risks in order to make decisions about potential investments. Once again, your training in statistics is useful in this endeavor.

In statistics, you studied probability distributions of variables and how they are used to calculate the mean and standard deviation of the variables. That same method will be used to estimate future mean returns and their standard deviation. Let us suppose that you are an equity analyst, and that you are charged with determining the expected future return of two particular stocks over the next ten years—we will call them Stock A and Stock B—in order to determine which one to invest in. You know from experience that all four phases of the business cycle (recession, expansion, boom and contraction) can occur within a ten-year period, so you need to see what the stocks' average returns have been during past business cycles. After having studied the stocks' returns over the prior 50 years, you make the following determinations:

- When the economy is expanding (heading out of a recession and towards a boom), Stock A has earned an average return of 6.60%, while Stock B earned an average of 9.60%;
- When the economy is booming (at the height of the business cycle), Stock A has earned an average return of 11.40%, while Stock B earned an average of 14.90%;
- When the economy is contracting (after the boom and heading towards a recession), Stock A has earned an average return of 4.40%, while Stock B earned an average of 2.00%;
- When the economy is in a recession (the trough of the business cycle), Stock A has earned an average return of −1.80%, while Stock B earned an average of −7.68%.

Next you meet with the firm's chief economist, who estimates the likelihood of each phase of the business cycle occurring during the next ten years. Her estimates are as follows (note that the probabilities associated with the four phases add up to 100%):

- The probability of an expanding economy is 30.0%;
- The probability of a booming economy is 25.0%;
- The probability of a contracting economy is 25.0%; and
- The probability of a recession is 20.0%.

You now have what you need to calculate the expected (mean) return and standard deviation of returns for each stock. The mean return is the weighted average of the expected returns during the different phases of the business cycle, with the weights being the probability associated with the different phases of the business cycle. So, calculating the mean returns is a simple task:

$$\hat{r}_A = .3(.066) + .25(.114) + .25(.044) + .2(-.018) = .0557 \text{ or } 5.57\%$$
$$\hat{r}_B = .3(.096) + .25(.149) + .25(.02) + .2(-.0768) = .05569 \text{ or } 5.569\%$$

Table 3.1 Expected Returns and Standard Deviations of Returns for Stocks A and B

State of Economy (i)		Stock A				
	P_i	r_i	$ri - \hat{r}$	$(ri - \hat{r})^2$	$(ri - \hat{r})^2 P_i$	
Expanding	0.30	0.0660	0.0103	0.00010609	0.000031827	
Boom	0.25	0.1140	0.0583	0.00339889	0.000849723	
Contracting	0.25	0.0440	−0.0117	0.00013689	3.42225E−05	
Recession	0.20	−0.0180	−0.0737	0.00543169	0.001086338	
				Variance	0.00200211	
	Mean $(\hat{r})$	0.05570		Std Dev	0.044744944	4.47%

State of Economy (i)		Stock B				
	P_i	r_i	$ri - \hat{r}$	$(ri - \hat{r})^2$	$(ri - \hat{r})^2 P_i$	
Expanding	0.30	0.0960	0.04031	0.0016248961	0.000487469	
Boom	0.25	0.1490	0.09331	0.0087067561	0.002176689	
Contracting	0.25	0.0200	−0.03569	0.0012737761	0.000318444	
Recession	0.20	−0.0768	−0.13249	0.0175536001	0.00351072	
				Variance	0.006493322	
	Mean $(\hat{r})$	0.05569		Std Dev	0.080581151	8.06%

The expected returns for the two stocks are virtually the same, making it difficult to choose based solely on returns. The next step is calculating the standard deviation of each stock's returns.

The method for calculating the standard deviation of a probability distribution is somewhat complex, but easy to do in Excel. The method requires the following steps:

1. Calculate the mean return for the stock $(\hat{r})$ —this was done in the step above;
2. Subtract the mean from each observed return $(ri - \hat{r})$ to obtain the set of deviations around the mean;
3. Square each of the deviations created in #2 above $\left[(ri - \hat{r})^2 \right]$;
4. Multiply each squared deviation by the probability associated with the given state of the economy $\left[(ri - \hat{r})^2 P_i \right]$;
5. Sum the weighted squared deviations created in #4 above—this is the variance of the distribution;
6. Take the square root of the variance to obtain the standard deviation of the distribution.

Table 3.1 shows the calculation of the standard deviations of returns using Excel and the method outlined above. Since the standard deviation for Stock B is almost twice as much as the standard deviation for Stock A, you can easily see that Stock A, with the lower total risk, is the better investment. Since both stocks have the same expected return, you choose the stock with the lower standard deviation of returns.

Risk and Risk Aversion

In finance, risk is defined as the chance (or probability) of not earning your expected return on an investment. Therefore, quantifying risk requires determining the uncertainty associated with the expected return on an investment. This uncertainty is measured one way if we are looking at an investment on its own (measuring its stand-alone risk), and another way when the asset is going to be held as part of a well-diversified portfolio (measuring its portfolio risk). Both measures are important, but not equally important, as will be discussed later in this chapter. It is good, even necessary, to understand the risks associated with an investment when held on its own, but the *relevant risk* of an investment is the risk it adds to a diversified portfolio. This will be discussed further in the section on the Capital Asset Pricing Model.

If the investment in question is a company, then the sources of uncertainty in the returns from the investment are also associated with specific strategic choices the firm's executives make, such as the decision to use technology vs. labor (business risk), or the decision to use debt vs. equity (financial risk).

It is also important to understand that, for many investments, risk is relative; that is, some investors might see an investment to be of reasonable risk, while others might see it to be of higher risk. This is because not all investors tolerate risk equally, and those who are less tolerant of risk are referred to as *risk averse.*

Risk aversion is not the fear of risk, but rather the unwillingness to accept it without adequate compensation. For example, Las Vegas is a popular resort area for people who like to gamble. Many people enjoy the thrill of the games whether they win or lose (although surely more if they win!). Others, like me, do not get pleasure from the games, and therefore see Las Vegas as a place to throw away your money. People like me do not get sufficient return from the games to be willing to risk our paychecks.

In the stock market, newer, younger stocks are considered riskier because they lack a track record of returns against which to measure the risks, unlike stocks like IBM or AT&T. Similarly, tech stocks can be riskier than average, since a new technological breakthrough can occur at any time, by the firm itself or one of its competitors. If you had invested in Enron Corporation in 1985 when it was founded, when it was selling at less than $10 per share, then by 2000 your investment would have been worth multiple times what you paid, as the price rose to over $90 per share. By December of 2001 you would have been wondering what happened, as the price of Enron stock had fallen to less than $1, and they were forced to file for bankruptcy due to fraudulent business practices.

The Relationship Between Risk and Return

Risk aversion is the reason why the relationship between risk and return is positive. Investors who see the intended investment as being of reasonable risk are going to require a reasonable return before investing, while those who see it as a high risk are going to require a high return. For example, suppose I offered you a wager on the roll of a single die; you pay $25 for one roll, and if the roll is an even number you win $100, while if the roll is odd, you lose your $25. You might find this wager appealing and be willing to pay the $25. What if instead the wager was $50 for a single roll to win the same $100? Would it still interest you? Perhaps not, as the potential return is not as high under those conditions. You might require a higher expected return to take on that amount of risk.

Suppose you owned shares in a stock that you felt was not likely to offer you the return you require in the future. Under those circumstances, you would likely want to sell the stock. In order for you to be able to sell it, there would need to exist another investor who sees the stock differently than you do in order to be willing to buy it. Suppose now that such an investor exists. Would the other investor need to see a different future for the stock than you do in order to be willing to buy it?

While it is possible that they may perceive the stock's future differently, that isn't necessary in order for them to be willing to buy the stock. If the new investor is less risk averse than you, they may see the same future for the stock that you do, but still be willing to purchase it because they don't require the same level of return that you do. Thus, while your risk aversion would prompt you to sell the stock, their risk tolerance would prompt them to buy it.

Types of Risk

Businesses face different types of risk on an ongoing basis, and it is important to be able to identify the different types (and sources) of risk in order to be able to properly measure them and determine how they are to be handled. The most common forms of risk experienced by businesses are *business risk, financial risk* and *portfolio risk*. Each type of risk comes from a different source and has different metrics by which they are measured.

Business Risk

Business risk is the uncertainty a firm faces with regard to its operating income (earnings before interest and taxes, or EBIT). Uncertainty in operating income leads to uncertainty in earnings, and therefore to the firm's stock price (FP1 tells us that a firm's value is derived from its expected future dividends, and dividends are paid from earnings). Therefore, controlling or reducing uncertainty in operating earnings should help control or reduce uncertainty in net income. Based on the structure of the income statement (see Chapter 9, "Analyzing and Forecasting Financial Statements"), the level of operating income is affected by changes in sales revenue, the cost of goods sold, operating expenses and depreciation. There are three ways to analyze business risk and to spot changes to business risk over time:

- Calculate the coefficient of variation (CV) of EBIT over a period of time;
- Calculate the CV of the operating margin over time;
- Calculate the degree of operating leverage (DOL) over time.

To calculate and compare these metrics, we will be using five years' worth of income statement data for Amazon and IBM, which are provided in Table 3.2. Amazon is a retailer, while IBM offers technology, support and services.

The Coefficient of Variation of EBIT

When applied to investments, the coefficient of variation (CV) measures the risk per unit of return for the variable being analyzed. Therefore, it is a measure of risk (rather than a measure of return), and so when comparing CVs for two different investments, smaller is better (i.e., minimizing risk).

The CV is calculated as the standard deviation of the variable divided by its mean (arithmetic average). When calculating statistics like the mean and the standard deviation, it is best to use as many observations as possible (a standard deviation based on two or three data points is misleading). Table 3.2 contains five years' worth of data, which will suffice. The statistics in the following analysis were calculated using Excel's AVERAGE and STDEV.S functions.

For Amazon, the mean level of operating income over the period 2013–2017 is $2,289.6 million. The sample standard deviation for the level of operating income for the

Table 3.2 Income Statements for Amazon and IBM 2013–2017

Amazon.com Inc (AMZN)

Income Statement (USD in millions except per share data)

	2013–12	2014–12	2015–12	2016–12	2017–12
Revenue	74,452	88,988	107,006	135,987	177,866
Cost of Revenue	62,766	73,518	85,061	105,884	137,183
Gross Profit	11,686	15,470	21,945	30,103	40,683
Operating Expenses					
Sales, General and Administrative	4,262	5,884	7,001	9,665	13,743
Other Operating Expenses	6,679	9,408	12,711	16,252	22,834
Total Operating Expenses	10,941	15,292	19,712	25,917	36,577
Operating Income	745	178	2,233	4,186	4,106
Interest Expense	141	210	459	484	848
Other Income (Expense)	(98)	(79)	(206)	190	548
Income Before Income Taxes	506	(111)	1,568	3,892	3,806
Provision for Income Taxes	161	167	950	1,425	769
Other Income	(71)	37	(22)	(96)	(4)
Net Income Available to Common Shareholders	274	(241)	596	2,371	3,033

International Business Machines Corp (IBM)

Income Statement (USD in millions except per share data)

	2013–12	2014–12	2015–12	2016–12	2017–12
Revenue	99,751	92,793	81,742	79,920	79,139
Cost of Revenue	51,246	46,386	41,057	41,625	42,913
Gross Profit	48,505	46,407	40,685	38,295	36,226
Operating Expenses					
Research and Development	6,226	5,437	5,247	5,751	5,787
Sales, General and Administrative	22,975	22,472	19,894	20,479	19,555
Other Operating Expenses	(296)	(34)	(147)	(1,041)	(915)
Total Operating Expenses	28,905	27,875	24,994	25,189	24,427
Operating Income	19,600	18,532	15,691	13,106	11,799
Interest Expense	402	484	468	630	615
Other Income (Expense)	326	1,938	722	(146)	216
Income Before Taxes	19,524	19,986	15,945	12,330	11,400
Provision for Income Taxes	3,041	4,234	2,581	449	5,642
Other Income		(1)			
Net Income From Continuing Operations	16,483	15,751	13,364	11,881	5,758
Net Income From Discontinuing Ops		(3,729)	(174)	(9)	(5)
Net Income Available to Common Shareholders	16,483	12,022	13,190	11,872	5,753

Source: www.morningstar.com

period is $1,853.6 million. Given these data, the CV for Amazon's EBIT over this particular period is calculated as 1,853.6 ÷ 2,289.6 = 0.8096, or 80.96%.

Interpreting this number on its own is tricky in this situation – 80.96% of what? The simplest, but not clearest, interpretation is that every unit of operating income contains approximately 81% risk. Fortunately, we do not need a clear interpretation to make use of the number; we simply need to have another number to compare it to. Since the CV measures risk, a lower number means less risk. So, to have a point of comparison, we will calculate the CV for IBM as well.

For IBM, the mean level of operating income over the period 2013–2017 is $15,745.6 million. The sample standard deviation for the level of operating income for the period is $3,360.3 million. With this, we can calculate IBM's CV as 3,360.3 ÷ 15,745.6 = 0.2134, or 21.34%. Based on the calculated CVs, Amazon's operating income is much riskier than IBM's operating income (81% vs. 21%—almost four times as risky!). So, this first level of analysis of operating income indicates that Amazon's EBIT is clearly riskier than IBM's EBIT for the period of time in question. When you have two results to compare, the value of the coefficient of variation is much clearer.

The Coefficient of Variation of the Operating Margin

While metrics for EBIT measure operating income on its own, metrics for the operating margin measure operating income relative to sales revenue (operating margin = EBIT / Revenue). Since operating income tends to vary with sales revenue (see the section on operating accounts in Chapter 9, "Analyzing and Forecasting Financial Statements"), changes to the margin over time reveal changes with regard to operating expenses relative to sales revenue. These changes are worth keeping track of, so that adverse changes in operating expenses can be quickly spotted and corrected.

Amazon's operating margin is 1.00% in 2013 (745 ÷ 74,452), 0.20% in 2014, 2.09% in 2015, 3.08% in 2016 and 2.31% in 2017. The mean level of operating margin over the period is 1.73%, and the sample standard deviation of the operating margin is 1.136%. This gives a CV for the operating margin of 65.66% (1.136 ÷ 1.73 = 0.6566).

IBM's operating margin for the period 2013–2017 is 19.65%, 19.97%, 19.20%, 16.40% and 14.91% respectively. The mean level of the operating margin over the period is 18.02%, while the sample standard deviation of the operating margin is 2.24%. With these statistics, we calculate a CV of 12.45% over the five-year period.

These results show that Amazon's operating margin is riskier than IBM's over the five-year period in question. While IBM's CV has a higher standard deviation, its mean level of operating margin is distinctly higher, making for a lower level of risk per unit of return. These results are consistent with those in the previous section with regard to the level of EBIT.

It should also be noted that while Amazon's operating margin climbed in 2015 and 2016 before falling in 2017, IBM's operating margin fell during all three of those years. This downward trend in IBM's operating margin should be of concern to the firm's managers, as well as its investors.

The Degree of Operating Leverage

Operating leverage measures the impact of changes in sales revenue on operating income. Operating leverage occurs because of the use of fixed costs in the production process. Fixed costs in operations typically stem from the use of technology in the production process rather than labor. For example, when a firm purchases a machine that can fill and pack boxes for a production line that normally takes five people, but only one person is required to fill and operate the machine. The machine is usually paid for over a period of years, either through the extension of credit by the manufacturer or from borrowing the funds, and so requires fixed payments at regular intervals. Therefore, firms that use technology in place of labor incur fixed costs associated with the purchase of the technology, which increases their operating leverage.

A high level of operating leverage means that a small change in sales revenue will result in a larger change in EBIT. An increase in sales will cause a larger increase in operating income, while a decrease in sales will cause a larger decrease in operating income. This adds to the firm's risk whenever there is a drop in sales revenue.

The degree of operating leverage (DOL) is measured as the percent change in operating income divided by the percent change in sales revenue. This means that the metric requires two periods of data, so our five years of data for Amazon and IBM will give us four DOL calculations.

From 2013 to 2014, Amazon's EBIT fell by 76.11% ([178 − 745] ÷ 745 = −0.7611), while their sales revenue grew by 19.52% ([88,988 − 74,452] ÷ 74,452 = 0.1952). These data result in a DOL metric of −3.90 (−76.11 ÷ 19.52 = −3.899). This means that, for the year 2014, an increase in sales revenue led to a decrease in operating income almost four times as large. In 2015, the DOL jumped to 57.02, while in 2016 it fell to 3.23, and in 2017 it fell again to −0.06. There was tremendous volatility in Amazon's DOL metric during this five-year period, but by 2017 it was very slightly below zero. This might be interpreted as an inconsistent use of operating leverage over the time period, making it appear that the use of operating leverage is not tied to a strategic plan (i.e., not a choice but rather an unintended outcome).

For IBM over the same period, their DOL metric was 0.78, 1.29, 7.39 and 10.20 respectively. While the 2017 numbers indicate that IBM currently has more operating leverage than Amazon (10.20 vs. −0.06), the consistent increase in IBM's DOL numbers are more indicative of the strategic use of operating leverage than those of Amazon. The inconsistent DOL metrics shown by Amazon, on the other hand, reflect a lack of managerial influence or oversight with regard to operating leverage, which in turn implies riskiness with regard to the use of operating leverage. Therefore, while Amazon shows high business risk throughout the five-year period, IBM shows high business risk (in the form of high operating leverage) in 2017.

Finally, it should be noted that over the five-year period in question, Amazon's sales revenue has been steadily climbing, while IBM's sales revenue has been steadily falling. This means that Amazon has been in a position to benefit from its use of operating leverage, although it has not done so (their most recent DOL of −0.06 indicates that an increase in sales will lead to a small decrease in operating income). It also means that IBM has been hurt by their use of operating leverage, and to a greater degree with each passing year; since DOL is increasing, decreases in revenue lead to even greater decreases in EBIT.

Financial Risk

Financial risk is the uncertainty a firm faces with regard to its net income (also known as earnings). As mentioned earlier, uncertainty in earnings leads to uncertainty in the stock price, and therefore to uncertainty in the market value of the firm (its market capitalization, calculated as the stock price multiplied by the number of shares outstanding). Based on the structure of the income statement, holding the operating earnings constant, the level of net income is affected by changes in interest and taxes. There are three ways to analyze financial risk, as well as changes to financial risk over time:

- Calculate the coefficient of variation (CV) of net income over a period of time;
- Calculate the CV of the net margin over time;
- Calculate the degree of financial leverage (DFL) over time.

We will once again use the Amazon and IBM data to calculate these metrics.

It is important to understand that while volatility in operating earnings is the outcome of operating decisions, volatility in net income is not. Changes in the level of interest are due to changes in the level of the firm's debt, which result from strategic decisions made by upper management (the CFO and the CEO), not by operating managers. Changes in the amount of taxes paid by the firm are similarly a function of the firm's accounting choices, which are made by the firm's controller, as well as by changes in the tax code, over which the firm has no direct influence. In the same way, changes to other non-operating expenses such as other income (expense) and net income from discontinuing ops are unrelated to the firm's operations, but rather tied to strategic choices made by the firm's top officers.

The Coefficient of Variation of Net Income

For Amazon, the mean level of net income over the period 2013–2017 is $1,206.6 million. The sample standard deviation for the level of operating income for the period is $1,416.8 million. Given these data, the CV for Amazon's net income over this time period is calculated as 1,416.8 ÷ 1,206.6 = 1.1742, or 117.42%.

For IBM, the mean level of net income over the period 2013–2017 is $11,864.0 million. The sample standard deviation for the level of net income for the period is $3,887.9 million. These statistics show IBM's CV to be 3,887.9 ÷ 11,864.0 = 0.3277 or 32.77%. Based on the calculated CVs, Amazon's net income is much riskier than IBM's net income (117% vs. 33%—more than 3 times as risky). So, this first level of analysis of net income indicates that Amazon's earnings are riskier than IBM's earnings for this time period.

The Coefficient of Variation of the Net Margin

While metrics for net income measure earnings on their own, metrics for the net margin measure net income relative to sales revenue (Net Margin = Net Income / Revenue). Since net income tends to vary with sales revenue (see the section on operating accounts in Chapter 9, "Analyzing and Forecasting Financial Statements"), changes to the margin over time reveal changes with regard to non-operating expenses (e.g., interest and taxes) relative to sales revenue. Monitoring this relationship is useful in understanding what may be driving changes to profitability.

Amazon's net margin is 0.37% in 2013 (274 ÷ 74,452), −0.27% in 2014, 0.56% in 2015, 1.74% in 2016 and 1.71% in 2017. The mean level of net margin over the period is 0.82%, and the sample standard deviation of the net margin is 0.88%. This gives a CV for the net margin of 107.28% (0.8803 ÷ 0.8206 = 1.0728).

IBM's net margin for the period 2013–2017 is 16.52%, 12.96%, 16.14%, 14.85% and 7.27% respectively. The mean level of the net margin over the period is 13.55%, while the sample standard deviation of the operating margin is 3.78%. With these statistics, we calculate a CV of 27.87% over the five-year period.

These results show that Amazon's net margin is riskier than IBM's over the five-year period in question. While IBM's CV has a higher standard deviation, its mean level of net margin is significantly higher, making for a lower level of risk per unit of return. These results are consistent with those in the previous section with regard to the level of earnings.

It should also be noted that while Amazon's net margin climbed in 2015 and 2016 and held steady in 2017, IBM's net margin fell during in 2016 and 2017. This recent downward trend in IBM's net margin should be of concern to the firm's managers, as well as its investors.

The Degree of Financial Leverage

Financial leverage measures the impact of changes in operating income (EBIT) on net income. Financial leverage occurs because of the use of fixed costs in financing. Fixed costs in financing are associated with the use of debt (i.e., borrowing money). When a firm takes out a bank loan or issues bonds to fund their operations, they take on the responsibility of making regular interest payments over the life of the debt. As a non-operating expense, interest has the beneficial property of being paid before taxes and thereby reducing the firm's taxable income (and so the amount of taxes paid). However, if the firm misses an interest payment, or if they cannot pay in full when it is due, they go in default of the terms of the debt. Being found in default means that the firm must declare bankruptcy, which would put them in the position of having to either restructure their debts (paying cents on the dollar) to stay afloat, or to sell off the firm's assets to pay their debts and close their doors. Even the possibility of bankruptcy can have a strong negative impact on the firm's stock price.

An increase in financial leverage means that a small change in operating income will result in a larger change in net income. An increase in EBIT will cause a larger increase in net income, while a decrease in EBIT will cause a larger decrease in net income. This adds to the firm's risk whenever operating income falls.

The degree of financial leverage (DFL) is measured as the percent change in net income divided by the percent change in operating income. Again, the metric requires two periods of data, so our five years of data for Amazon and IBM will give us four DFL calculations.

From 2013 to 2014, Amazon's net income fell by 187.96% ([−241 − 274] ÷ 274 = −1.8796), while their EBIT declined by 76.11%. These data combine for a DFL metric of 2.47 (−187.96 ÷ −76.11 = 2.47). This means that, for the year 2014, a decrease in operating income led to a decrease in net income more than twice as large. In 2015, the DFL dropped to −0.30, while in 2016 it jumped to 3.41, and in 2017 it fell drastically to −14.61. There was tremendous volatility in Amazon's DFL metric during this five-year period, and in 2017 it was actually negative. This result is interpreted to mean that for 2017, a 1% decrease in EBIT would result in a 14.6% increase in net income.

For IBM during this same period, their DFL metric was 4.97, −0.63, 0.61 and 5.17 respectively. While the 2017 numbers indicate that IBM currently has more financial leverage than Amazon (5.17 vs. −14.61), this metric was similarly volatile as it was for Amazon. IBM's EBIT fell consistently throughout the period, and in other years than 2015 their net income dropped as well. The increase in the DFL in 2017 is attributable to an unusually large provision for income taxes, which is not related to financial leverage (taxes are not fixed, nor are they a strategic choice for the firm). The negative DFL for Amazon in 2017 does seem to indicate that it had less financial leverage than IBM for that year; the slight decrease in EBIT for that year (−1.91%) resulted in an increase in net income (27.92%). However, this increase in net income can be attributed to a significant cut in income taxes, which again is not related to financial leverage.

So, for the financial risk analysis, two of the three metrics point at Amazon being riskier than IBM, while IBM has a higher DFL than Amazon. The impact of IBM's higher operating and financial leverage becomes clear when calculating the degree of combined leverage (DCL).

Degree of Combined Leverage

The degree of operating leverage and financial leverage together create the degree of combined leverage. The DCL is defined as the change in net income divided by the change in sales revenue. It is also the product of multiplying the DOL and the DFL. The DCL shows the impact of the use of fixed costs in operations and in financing together.

In 2014, Amazon's net income fell by 186.96%, while their sales revenue increased by 19.52%. This leads to a DCL of −9.63 (−186.96 ÷ 19.52 = −9.63). This can also be calculated by multiplying the DOL and the DFL together: −3.90 × 2.47 = −9.63. Amazon's DCL metrics for the period 2014–2017 were −9.63, −17.15, 11.00 and 0.91. Both the DOL and the DFL metrics are quite volatile over this period, leading to high volatility in the DCL as well. For the same period, IBM's DCL metrics were 3.88, −0.82, 4.48 and 52.74 respectively. IBM's DCL metrics were similarly volatile. As of 2017, IBM's DCL is significantly higher than Amazon's DCL, showing them to have higher overall fixed costs than Amazon.

Portfolio Risk

The assumption of portfolio risk is associated with financial firms rather than manufacturing or service firms. Portfolio risk is defined as the risk that an asset contributes to the risk of a diversified portfolio. A portfolio is simply a collection of assets for investment purposes. These assets may include stocks, bonds, mutual funds, real estate investment trusts, derivatives or virtually anything that can serve as an investment. A diversified portfolio is one that has been constructed specifically to minimize the portfolio's level of risk with regard to its returns. To construct a diversified portfolio, it is necessary to combine assets whose returns are less-than-perfectly positively correlated; that is, assets whose returns have a correlation coefficient that is less than one.

As you should remember from your statistics class, the correlation coefficient is a measure of the direction and strength of the relationship between two variables. Recall that the correlation coefficient can vary from +1 (perfect positive correlation) to −1 (perfect negative correlation). Perfect positive correlation means that as one variable changes in value, the other variable tends to change in value in the same direction and to the same degree. Perfect negative correlation means that as one variable changes in value, the other variable tends to change in value in the opposite direction and to the same degree. A correlation coefficient of 0.75 means that as one variable increases, the other tends to increase by about three-quarters as much, while a coefficient of −0.5 means that as one variable increases, the other tends to decrease by about half as much. A correlation coefficient close to zero means that the two variables do not have a relationship; one variable changing has virtually no impact on the other. To compare the relationship between two assets, we measure the correlation of their returns.

Measuring Portfolio Risk

Earlier in the chapter, it was mentioned that the relevant risk of an investment is the risk it adds to a diversified portfolio. The risk associated with a stock's returns can be divided into two types: market risk (also known as systematic risk or non-diversifiable risk) and firm-specific risk (also known as unsystematic risk or diversifiable risk). These two types of risk are very different in their impact on the returns of a diversified portfolio of assets.

Market risk is the risk associated with being in the economy, and it affects all assets, although not equally. Market risk includes things like changes in the political administration (i.e., the president or Congress), going to war or a recession. All investments are affected by market risk to some degree, and the only way to escape market risk is not to invest. Firm-specific risk, on the other hand, deals with the risks associated with the firm in question. This includes such things as a change in the firm's CEO or CFO, a fire or flood at a plant, the union going on strike or having a product made obsolete by a competitor's new product.

Firm-specific risks strike different firms at different times (as opposed to a recession, which hits every firm at the same time), so that while some firms experience isolated difficulties, other firms at the same time are doing well. The classic example of this is petroleum stocks vs. airline stocks. Probably the single most expensive operating cost for airlines is jet fuel; the cost of fuel can make or break an airline's profitability in any given quarter. If jet fuel prices are high, the petroleum stocks (like Exxon Mobil) do well while the airline stocks (like United Continental Holdings) do poorly, while if jet fuel prices are low, the airline stocks climb while the petroleum stocks fall. If you were to combine both of these stocks into a portfolio, you know that if one of the stocks has difficulty, the other is likely to do well, and so on average the two stocks are likely to have a reasonable return.

This is the essence of diversification: by combining stocks with returns that are less than perfectly positively correlated, you can construct a portfolio with total risk that is less than the combined risks of the assets in the portfolio. This occurs because, with sufficient diversification, the firm-specific risk in the portfolio can be eliminated, leaving only systematic risk in the portfolio. That is why the only relevant risk for a stock is the risk it adds to a diversified portfolio. While the metric for total risk is the standard deviation of returns, the metric for systematic risk is beta.

Beta

Beta measures the sensitivity of a stock's returns relative to the returns to the stock market. Researchers typically use the returns to the S&P 500 index fund as a proxy for the returns to the market; the S&P 500 includes the 500 largest stocks in the US and contains approximately 85% of the value of the stocks that make up the total stock market. Therefore, beta can be calculated by comparing the returns to a stock to the returns to the S&P 500.

Beta is a relative measure of risk—that is, relative to the risks involved in investing in the stock market. That makes it particularly useful for understanding the risks associated with a stock's returns. The beta of the market is always 1.0, making it a benchmark to which other stock's betas can be compared. This is where the relative nature of beta is apparent: a stock with a beta of 2.0 is twice as risky as the market, whereas a stock with a beta of 0.5 is half as risky as the market. Or, more to the point, its returns are half as risky as the market's returns.

One simple way to measure beta is to divide the covariance between the stock and the market by the variance of the market returns. These figures can be calculated using Excel's COVARIANCE.P and VAR.P functions. For example, for 2013, the covariance between Amazon's daily returns and the daily returns to the S&P 500 is 0.000068, and the variance of the daily returns to the market for that year is 0.000056. Therefore, Amazon's beta for 2013 is .000061 ÷ .000048 = 1.27 (rounded to two decimal places).

Another way to calculate beta is to run a simple regression model using the returns to the S&P 500 to predict the returns to the stock in question. Using Excel's Data Analysis Toolpak tool for regression analysis (or using the INTERCEPT and SLOPE functions), we are able to calculate that, for 2013, the regression model for predicting Amazon's returns is $Y = 0.000651 + 1.265466X$. The slope of the regression model (the coefficient for X) is the beta. Rounded to two decimal places, it is 1.27, as calculated above using the covariance/variance calculation.

Portfolio Risk and Return

Table 3.3 contains the annual arithmetic returns and betas for Amazon and IBM over the period 2013–2017, as well as the standard deviation of returns and the correlation matrix for those entities over the same period (there are no betas posted for the S&P 500 because

Table 3.3 Returns, Betas and Correlations for Amazon, IBM and the S&P 500 2013–2017

Returns	2013	2014	2015	2016	2017	Std Dev
Amazon	35.10%	−1.16%	65.57%	40.29%	76.19%	30.13%
IBM	−11.31%	−11.12%	−15.30%	46.57%	−2.56%	25.75%
S&P 500	18.99%	11.92%	−2.74%	17.45%	23.91%	10.24%

Betas	2013	2014	2015	2016	2017
Amazon	1.27	1.46	1.12	1.12	1.31
IBM	0.77	0.74	1.02	0.93	0.65

Correlation	Amazon	IBM	S&P 500
Amazon	1.000		
IBM	0.224	1.000	
S&P 500	0.497	0.560	1.000

Source: finance.yahoo.com

the market's beta is always 1.0). The standard deviations of the annual returns are included to show how volatile annual returns were during this period. It should be easy to see why Amazon has the highest standard deviation of the three—their returns were as high as 76% in 2017 and as low as −1% in 2014, while IBM's annual returns were as high as 46% in 2016 and as low as −15% in 2015. Note that the returns to the S&P 500 index fund were not nearly as volatile during this period; since it contains the 500 largest stocks, it is essentially a well-diversified portfolio. Amazon's beta varied between 1.12 and 1.46 during the period, while IBM's beta varied between 0.65 and 1.02 (these are annual betas based on daily returns). Finally, the correlation matrix shows that the returns for Amazon & IBM had a low positive correlation (0.224), while the correlations between each firm and the S&P 500 were moderately positive (around 0.5). Since the returns for Amazon and IBM have such a low correlation coefficient, they would appear to be good choices to combine into a portfolio. In this section, we will compare the return and risk for a 50/50 portfolio of the two stocks to each of the stocks held in isolation, as well as to the return and risk of the stock market.

We can use the data in Table 3.3 to calculate the expected return from a portfolio comprised of 50% Amazon and 50% IBM, as the calculation is simple: it is the weighted average of the expected returns to each stock, with the weights being calculated as the value invested in each stock divided by the value invested in the portfolio. In this case, it doesn't matter how much is being invested in each stock, as we have already determined that the weights will be 50% each. If instead we were intending to create a two-stock portfolio worth $100,000, then we would be investing $50,000 in each stock.

For the year 2013, the expected return for the 50/50 portfolio would be calculated as .5 × .3510 + .5 × −.1131 = .1190 or 11.90%. Note that in 2013 Amazon did quite well while IBM did quite poorly. Combining the two stocks in a 50/50 portfolio resulted in a very reasonable annual return. Using this same calculation, the returns to the portfolio for the years 2014–2017 would be −6.14%, 25.14%, 43.43% and 36.81% respectively.

While these calculations are simple, we cannot use the same method for calculating the standard deviation of the portfolio returns, because this calculation does not account for the effects of diversification. The calculation for the standard deviation of the portfolio is as follows:

$$\sigma_{portfolio} = \sqrt{W_a^2 \sigma_a^2 + W_b^2 \sigma_b^2 + 2W_a W_b r_{a,b} \sigma_a \sigma_b}$$

where: $\sigma_{portfolio}$ is the standard deviation of the portfolio of two stocks;
W_a is the weight of the first stock in the portfolio;
σ_a^2 is the variance of the first stock in the portfolio;
W_b is the weight of the second stock in the portfolio;
σ_b^2 is the variance of the second stock in the portfolio;
$r_{a,b}$ is the correlation coefficient between the two stocks in the portfolio;
σ_a is the standard deviation of the first stock in the portfolio; and
σ_b is the standard deviation of the second stock in the portfolio.

Since the variance of a variable is simply the square of the standard deviation, we have everything we need to calculate the standard deviation of the portfolio over the five-year period:

$$\sigma_{portfolio} = \sqrt{.5^2 (.3013)^2 + .5^2 (.2575)^2 + 2(.5)(.5)(.224)(.3013)(.2575)}$$
$$= .2190 \text{ or } 21.90\%$$

If we had calculated the standard deviation of the two-stock portfolio as simply the weighted average of the standard deviations of the two stocks, the figure would be distinctly larger (and incorrect!):

- $.5(.3013) + .5(.2575) = .2794$ or 27.94%

The difference between these two metrics is the effect of diversification—the total risk of the portfolio is less than the weighted average of the risks of the two stocks in the portfolio. This occurs because of the third term in the portfolio standard deviation metric—the one containing the correlation coefficient. If the two stocks are perfectly positively correlated (i.e., the correlation coefficient is 1.0), leaving all the other inputs the same, the calculated portfolio standard deviation is 27.94% (check this for yourself). It is the low correlation coefficient that reduces the standard deviation of the portfolio.

However, it has already been stated that the standard deviation of returns measures total risk, and the relevant risk for a portfolio is its systematic risk, which is measured by beta. Like the portfolio expected return, the beta of the portfolio is calculated as the weighted average of the betas of the stocks in the portfolio, with the weights again being the dollar amount invested in each stock divided by the dollar amount invested in the portfolio. Therefore, for 2013, the beta of the 50/50 portfolio is .5(1.27) + .5(0.77) = 1.02. Using this same method, we find that the portfolio betas for the years 2014–2017 are 1.10, 1.07, 1.02 and 0.98, respectively.

Relevant Risk and Required Return—The CAPM

FP2 states that the relationship between risk and return is positive; that as perceived risk increases, required return also increases. This principle is clearly reflected in the Security Market Line (SML) of the Capital Asset Pricing Model (CAPM).

The CAPM was proposed by William Sharpe in 1964.[1] The theory behind the CAPM is that investors will not be rewarded for taking on firm-specific risk; since it can be diversified away, it must be. Therefore, investors are obliged to diversify their portfolios in order to earn returns sufficient to cover the risks they bear. Since beta measures systematic risk and ignores firm-specific risk, it is useful in determining the required return for a stock that is held in a diversified portfolio. The SML uses beta to calculate the required return for any stock, given its level of systematic risk. The SML is constructed as follows:

$$r_i = r_{RF} + (r_M - r_{RF})\beta_i$$

where:　r_i is the required return for stock i;
　　　　r_{RF} is the nominal risk-free rate of return;
　　　　r_M is the return to the market; and
　　　　β_i is the beta for stock i.

The nominal risk-free rate (r_{RF}) is discussed in depth in Chapter 4, "The Term Structure of Interest Rates." It represents the minimum amount investors will accept for postponing consumption of their income in order to invest it—the term "nominal" merely means that it includes a premium to cover expected inflation. For calculation purposes, researchers use either the return on three-month T-bills or the return on 10-year T-notes as a proxy for the nominal risk-free rate. For this example, we will use the return on 10-year T-notes.

The market return (r_M) represents the return offered by the stock market for taking on the risk of investing in stocks. Since stocks are known to be riskier than bonds, investors in the stock market require a premium for taking on that risk. That premium is the term in parentheses in the SML model ($r_M - r_{RF}$): the difference between what the market is offering and the risk-free rate. That term is also known as the market risk premium (MRP). Just as the risk-free rate is what investors require to postpone consumption, the MRP is what investors require to invest in the stock market. For calculation purposes, researchers use the returns to the S&P 500 index fund as a proxy for the market return.

The MRP gets multiplied by the stock's beta to adjust the market risk premium for the level of risk associated with the stock in question. The risk-adjusted MRP [$(r_M - r_{RF})\beta_i$] is the risk premium for that particular stock. It is the MRP adjusted for the systematic risk of the returns of the given stock. Thus, an investor requires the risk-free rate at a minimum (r_{RF}) in order to postpone consumption and invest, and how much above that return the investor requires is a function of how much the stock market returns above the risk-free rate ($r_M - r_{RF}$) adjusted for the relative riskiness of the stock itself (β_i). Therefore, if you have data for the risk-free rate, the market return and the stock's beta, you can calculate how much return is required for investing in the stock.

For 2013, the yield on 10-year T-notes was 2.35%, and the return to the S&P 500 index fund was 18.99%. Based on these figures, Amazon would have had a required return of 23.48% [2.35 + (18.99 − 2.35)1.27], while IBM would have had a required return of 15.16% [2.35 + (18.99 − 2.35)0.77]. Given that Amazon had an actual return of 35.10% while IBM's return was −11.31%, it is safe to say that 2013 was a very good year for Amazon, but not a very good year for IBM!

Note that beta is only multiplied by the part of the return above the risk-free rate (the MRP, or $r_M - r_{RF}$). Since, as its name implies, it is risk-free, the risk-free rate does not get adjusted for risk. This means that, while a stock with a beta of 2.0 is twice as risky as the market, it does not earn twice as much as the market. Instead it means that the stock will earn twice as much of a risk premium as the market. For example, suppose that the risk-free rate is 3.0% and the return to the market is 8.0%. A stock with a beta of 2.0 will have a required return of 13% (3 + [8 − 3]2), which is not twice as much as the 8% market rate.

The Security Market Line of the Capital Asset Pricing Model allows us to quantify the return required on a stock based on its observed level of risk. However, it should be noted that betas are calculated after the fact and are therefore only accurate when looking back-wards in time. Using betas to forecast future returns makes the assumption that the future will be like the past, which is rarely a good assumption.

Summary of the Principles and Precepts Applied in This Chapter

The Second Fundamental Principle (FP2): There is a direct relationship between risk and return; as perceived risk increases, required return will also increase (and vice versa), holding other things constant.

The Security Market Line makes clear the direct relationship between risk and return indi-cated by FP2. Beta is the measure of systematic risk, and it is the multiplier that increases the risk premium for the stock, which thereby increases the required return for the stock.

The First Precept (PR1): The present value of a cash flow (or an asset) is inversely related to its discount rate; increasing the discount rate decreases the present value (and vice versa), holding other things constant.

In Chapter 6, we will see that the SML is used to calculate the cost of equity, which is used as the discount rate for the models used to value the firm's stock, and as part of the discount rate that makes up the weighted average cost of capital (discussed in Chapter 8).

The Third Precept (PR3): The present value of a cash flow (or an asset) is inversely related to its perceived risk; the higher the risk, the higher the discount rate, and therefore the lower the present value.

Risk affects value through its relationship with return. We know that risk and return are positively correlated due to FP2. The return to shareholders is used as the discount rate for valuing the firm's common stock and as part of the weighted average cost of capital (WACC). The WACC is used as the discount rate for the firm's capital projects, as well as for the value of the firm itself. Therefore, we can deduce that higher risk leads to a higher discount rate (and so a lower value) for the firm's equity, for the firm's intended capital investments and for the value of the firm.

End of Chapter Problems

1. A good measure of an investor's risk exposure if she only holds a single asset in her portfolio is:

   a. The expected value of the asset's returns.
   b. The standard deviation of possible returns on the asset.
   c. The correlation coefficient with the market portfolio.
   d. The normal probability distribution function.

2. In terms of risk, labor union disputes, entry of a new competitor and embezzlement by management are all examples of factors affecting:

   a.   Diversifiable risk.
   b.   Market risk.
   c.   Systematic risk.
   d.   Company-specific risk that cannot be diversified away.

3. The standard deviation is a:

   a.   Numerical indicator of how widely dispersed possible values are distributed around the coefficient of variation.
   b.   Numerical indicator of how widely dispersed possible values are distributed around the correlation coefficient.
   c.   Numerical indicator of how widely dispersed possible values are distributed around the mean.
   d.   Measure of the relative risk of one asset compared with another.

4. When we compare the risk of two investments that have the same expected return, the coefficient of variation:

   a.   Adjusts for the correlation between the two instruments.
   b.   Provides no additional information when compared with the standard deviation.
   c.   Gives conflicting results compared to the standard deviation.
   d.   Always gives us a value between 0 and 1.

5. Currently XYZ Company has a required return of 12% and a beta of 1.2. According to the CAPM, XYZ:

   a.   Can't be compared since the risk-free rate is not known.
   b.   Is less risky than the market.
   c.   Has an equal risk to the market.
   d.   Is riskier than the market.

6. Beta is best described as a measure of:

   a.   Non-diversifiable risk.
   b.   Unsystematic risk.
   c.   Total risk.
   d.   Diversifiable risk.

7. If two variables are perfectly positively correlated, it means:

   a.   Their values will change inversely to each other.
   b.   They have a correlation coefficient of -1.
   c.   They change linearly in perfect lockstep.
   d.   They have a correlation coefficient of zero.

8. You are considering investing in Digital Consolidated's common stock. Based on your perception of Digital's riskiness, you will require a return of 8.5% on their stock. Digital's most recent beta is 1.20. The risk-free rate is currently 3.25%, while the market return is currently 7.75%. Based on these data, should you invest in Digital's stock?

   a.   No, because Digital's expected return is less than your required return.
   b.   You are indifferent, because Digital's expected return is equal to your required return.

c.   Yes, because Digital's expected return is equal to your required return.

d.   Yes, because Digital's expected return exceeds your required return.

9.   You are given the following probability distribution of returns for a stock. Use the data to calculate the expected return, standard deviation of returns and coefficient of variation of returns for the stock.

Return	Probability
8.0%	0.20
10.0%	0.10
12.0%	0.40
15.0%	0.20
16.0%	0.10

10.   The beta for Beltrand Industries is 1.50. Assuming that the nominal risk-free rate is 6.0% and that the return to the market is 9.0%, what is Beltrand's required return?

11.   Farquar Manufacturing has a required return of 9.50%. If the market return is 13.0% and the nominal risk-free rate is 6.0%, what is Farquar's beta?

12.   You are a financial analyst, and you are tasked with calculating the expected return and standard deviation of returns for Kershaw Enterprises. Towards that end, you are given the following data:

- In an expanding economy, Kershaw is expected to earn 5.30%;
- In a booming economy, Kershaw is expected to earn 9.50%;
- In a contracting economy, Kershaw is expected to earn 3.50%;
- In a recession, Kershaw is expected to earn −1.20%;
- The probabilities for expansion, boom, contraction and recession are 20%, 25%, 35% and 20% respectively.

13.   You purchased 500 shares of Malfoy Manufacturing's common stock for $35.00 per share, and you sold it again one year later for $39.90 per share. During the year that you held the stock, you were paid a dividend of $2.03 per share. Calculate the dividend yield, capital gains yield and total yield for your investment.

14.   You purchased 25 corporate bonds for $985.00 each and held them for one year, at which point you sold the bonds for $965.30 each. During the year you received interest payments of $79.80 per bond. Calculate the current yield, capital gains yield and total yield on the bonds for the year during which you owned them.

15.   You purchased a stock on June 1 for $112.00 per share and promptly sold it on September 1 for $115.36 per share. Calculate the holding period return and the annualized return on the stock.

16.   You purchased a stock for $50.00 per share at the end of 2014. At the end of the years 2015–2018, the stock was worth $54.75, $59.13, $56.41 and $60.06 respectively. You sold the stock at the end of 2019 for $62.00 per share. Calculate your arithmetic and geometric mean returns for the stock during the period in which you owned it.

17.   In years 1–5 Stock A had returns of 5.6%, 7.9%, 4.2%, 1.8% and 4.5% respectively. During that same period of time the stock market had returns of 6.2%, 7.3%, 5.8%, 4.5% and 6.1% respectively. Use these data and Excel's COVARIANCE.P and VAR.P functions to calculate Stock A's beta over this five-year period.

18. Stock A's returns have a standard deviation of 7.0%, while Stock B's returns have a standard deviation of 9.0%. The correlation coefficient between Stocks A and B is 0.45. Use these data to calculate the standard deviation of a portfolio that contains 40% Stock A and 60% Stock B.

Excel Project

Table 3.4 Income Statements for Petrosian Consolidated LLC 2015–2019

	2015	2016	2017	2018	2019
Revenue	48,560	51,235	54,310	56,483	60,437
Cost of Goods Sold	22,338	23,566	24,851	25,686	26,516
Operating Expenses	10,683	11,480	11,996	11,983	12,015
Depreciation	1,457	1,486	1,493	1,521	1,535
EBIT	14,082	14,703	15,970	17,293	20,371
Interest	2,350	2,350	2,375	2,400	2,425
Taxes	4,691	4,941	5,221	5,451	5,866
Net Income	7,041	7,412	8,374	9,442	12,080

The table above contains abbreviated income statements for Petrosian Consolidated LLC for the period 2015–2019. Enter the data into an Excel spreadsheet to do a full risk analysis. Calculate the following metrics for Petrosian:

- The coefficient of variation (CV) of EBIT for the entire five-year period;
- The CV of the operating margin for the entire five-year period;
- The degree of operating leverage (DOL) for the years 2016–2019;
- The CV of net income for the entire five-year period;
- The CV of the net margin for the entire five-year period;
- The degree of financial leverage (DFL) for the years 2016–2019;
- The degree of combined leverage (DCL) for the years 2016–2019.

Use the metrics you calculate, and any other trends you may find in the data, to analyze the level of risk for Petrosian. Submit a one-page write-up of your findings (not including tables). What is happening with Petrosian's risk during this period of time?

Note

1 William Sharpe, "Capital Asset Prices: A Theory of Market Equilibrium," *Journal of Finance*, September 1964.

Bibliography

Fundamentals of Corporate Finance, 12th edition. S. Ross, R. Westerfield and B. Jordan. McGraw-Hill Education, 2019.
Financial Management: Principles & Practice, 8th edition. T. Gallagher. Textbook Media Press, 2019.
Foundations of Financial Management, 17th edition. S. Block, G. Hirt and B. Danielsen. McGraw-Hill Education, 2018.

4   The Term Structure of Interest Rates

Interest is the cost of debt. The interest rate (or yield) on a loan or a bond is a return to the lender and a cost to the borrower. Interest is charged when taking out a loan from a bank, when using a credit card and when financing a major purchase like a car. Interest is also paid by the government when issuing Treasury bonds and by firms when they use bank loans to fund operations, or when they issue bonds. In this chapter, we will discuss how interest rates are determined, the relationship between short-term and long-term interest rates and the theories that have been offered to explain that relationship.

Market interest rates are influenced by a number of different things, and the resulting changes are not always easy to understand or appreciate. For example, it is possible for inflation to be negative—for prices to fall. This is known as deflation, and at first glance it may seem to be a good thing; falling prices are good for consumers, aren't they? Yes, but they are bad for producers, and they can result in layoffs and therefore increased unemployment, which in turn can slow down the economy. In particularly bad economies, it is possible that risk-averse investors would be willing to pay for a financial institution to hold their cash, meaning that they would be willing to earn a negative interest rate. Some bonds issued by various entities in 2014 and 2015 were seen to temporarily earn negative interest rates, including some bonds issued by the US Treasury. In this chapter, we will discuss the theory of how interest rates are determined in the market, and how they can be used to compare different debt instruments.

When professionals discuss bond yields, they speak in terms of basis points. One basis point is one one-hundredth of a percentage point (0.01%, or 0.0001 in decimal format). One hundred basis points equal one percentage point.

The previous chapter examined the direct relationship between risk and return. Since interest is a return to the lender, it follows that there is a direct relationship between the perceived riskiness of the borrower and the rate of interest paid by the borrower. This relationship will be made clear in the discussion regarding the components of the nominal interest rate.

The Fundamental Principles in Action

FP2 states that there is a direct (or positive) relationship between perceived risk and required return. This principle is reflected in the numerous risk premiums that make up the nominal interest rate for various types of debt securities. The discussion of the maturity risk premium touches on the fact that changes in market interest rates have an inverse impact on bond prices, which is the basis of FP3. PR3 examines the inverse relationship between value and the risk, while PR1 describes the inverse relationship between value and the discount rate. These two precepts are linked by the direct relationship between risk and return, since the return to bondholders is used as the discount rate for determining the market value of bonds.

Real vs. Nominal Interest Rates—The Effects of Inflation

When discussing interest rates, we must specify if we are discussing real rates or nominal rates. Real rates of interest do not contain any consideration for inflation (the inflation is stripped out of them), while nominal interest rates include a premium for expectations of inflation over the life of the debt instrument. Investors concern themselves with nominal interest rates, as they expect to be compensated for inflation. Researchers tend to focus on real interest rates so that they can directly compare interest rates across different periods of time without dealing with the effects of inflation. Unless stated otherwise, this textbook will focus on nominal interest rates. We will, however, look at real rates of interest, as well as inflation. Real interest rates will be indicated as real, whereas nominal interest rates might not be designated so.

Inflation is the erosion of purchasing power; a loaf of bread may be $1.50 this year but rise to $1.65 next year. If this expectation of rising costs is not built into the interest rate earned by lenders, investors will lose purchasing power over time. For example, the change in the price of bread referred to above is a 10% increase. Assuming that prices in general are rising by 10%, if lenders are only earning 7% interest on their money, they are losing purchasing power of 3%. Since inflation is an ongoing force in the economy, prices are expected to rise on an ongoing basis. Therefore, investors will insist on receiving a premium that accounts for the future expectations of inflation over the life of the investment. A 1-year bond will include a premium for the inflation expected for next year, while a 5-year bond will include a premium to cover the expected inflation over the next five years.

The Determinants of Interest Rates

In order to be willing to postpone consumption of their income and lend their money out to others, investors must be compensated for the time during which their money is unavailable. This is the basis for the time value of money, as discussed in Chapter 2. The minimum rate of interest that lenders expect to earn is known as the nominal risk-free rate of interest, or the risk-free rate. The nominal risk-free rate (r_{RF}) is comprised of the real risk-free rate (r^*) and an inflation premium (IP)—that is, $r_{RF} = r^* + IP$. The real risk-free rate applies to interest rates of all terms (short-term or long-term) equally. It is not static, however—it can change over time.

Similarly, inflation is not constant, but can fluctuate over time. In times of rising inflation, the inflation premium will be larger for long-term rates than for short-term rates. This is because the inflation premium built into the risk-free rate will be based on the expectation of future inflation over the life of the debt instrument. Therefore, in times of rising inflation, the IP for 2-year bonds will be larger than the IP for 1-year bonds. The calculation for the IP for long-term rates will be discussed later in this chapter.

Inflation is not the only premium built into interest rates. There are a number of risks associated with bonds, and for each of those risks a premium is added to the risk-free rate to cover lenders for those various risks. The following equation indicates the nature of the risks built into interest rates for bonds:

$$i = r^* + IP + DRP + LP + MRP$$

where: i is the market interest rate;
   r* is the real risk-free rate;
   IP is an inflation premium;
   DRP is a default risk premium;
   LP is a liquidity premium; and
   MRP is a maturity risk premium.

Each of these additional premiums will be discussed in turn. Earlier in the chapter, we determined that the risk-free rate includes both the real risk-free rate and an inflation premium. Based on this understanding, the equation above can be rewritten as follows:

$$i = r_{RF} + DRP + LP + MRP$$

Note that these risk premiums cannot always be easily precisely measured, as they are theoretical constructs that are used to explain differences in interest rates on different securities. Those that can be accurately measured are clearly indicated.

The Default Risk Premium

Default is when a borrower is unable to pay either a scheduled interest payment or the repayment of the principal (the amount of the loan) in full and on time. If a borrower goes into default, they can be required to declare bankruptcy, which means that they must either reorganize and pay a portion of the debt they owe while being allowed to remain in business, or they must sell off their assets to repay the debt, which will force them out of business. The higher the perception that a firm may default (whether because they are new and have little credit history, or because they have a bad credit history), the higher the premium they will have to pay for default risk. A large, established firm like Microsoft or Exxon Mobil will pay a very small default premium, while a newer firm or a firm that has had financial difficulties in the past will pay a significantly higher default risk premium. Treasury bonds have no default risk premium because the United States government has not, to date, ever defaulted on their debt. They have come close a few times due to partisan politics in Congress, but so far it has not happened. Therefore, Treasury securities of all maturities have a zero default risk premium.

Default risk (also known as credit risk) is monitored and reported on by the rating agencies Standard & Poor's (S&P), Moody's and Fitch Group. The ratings are structured so that the highest rating reflects the lowest default risk, and therefore the lowest default risk premium.

Table 4.1 shows the credit rating system used by Standard & Poor's for rating the likelihood of default for corporate bonds. Bonds rated AAA are seen as the least likely to default and therefore will have the lowest possible default risk premium. As you go down the list, the risk of default increases, as does the default risk premium. Bonds rated BB+ or lower are non-investment grade bonds (also known as high-yield or junk bonds) and have very high default risk premiums. Many pension funds, banks, insurance companies and other institutional investors are prohibited from investing in these bonds due to their high level of default risk.

As of June 2018, there were only two US companies holding S&P's AAA rating: Microsoft and Johnson & Johnson. On February 6, 2017, Microsoft issued $4 billion worth of bonds with 10-year terms. The coupon rate for the bonds at issuance was 3.30%. On that

Table 4.1 Standard & Poor's Credit Rating System for Corporate Bonds

Long-term	Short-term	Description of Rating	
AAA	A–1+	Prime	Investment grade
AA+		High grade	
AA			
AA–			
A+	A–1	Upper medium grade	
A			
A–	A–2		
BBB+		Lower medium grade	
BBB	A–3		
BBB-			
BB+	B	Non-investment grade	Non-investment grade
BB		speculative	(junk bonds)
BB–			
B+		Highly speculative	
B			
B–			
CCC+	C	Substantial risks	
CCC		Extremely speculative	
CCC–			
CC		Default imminent	
C			
D	–	In default	

Source: www.standardandpoors.com

same day, the yield on 10-year T-notes was 2.42%. The differences between the Micro-soft bonds and the Treasury notes consist of the default risk premium and the liquidity premium; Microsoft's bonds carry default and liquidity risk while the Treasury notes do not. The difference between the coupon rate on Microsoft's bonds and the T-note yield (88 basis points) can therefore be attributed to premiums for those two risks. Given the popularity of Microsoft's bonds (they issued another $2 billion in 40-year term bonds that same day), it is likely that the bulk of that difference is related to default risk rather than liquidity risk.

The Liquidity Risk Premium

In finance, liquidity refers to the ability to turn an asset into cash quickly at a fair market value. How easy or difficult it is to sell a particular bond is a function of the size of the market in which the bond trades. The market for US Treasury bonds is huge—they are sold all over the world in incredibly large quantities—and selling them requires no more than a phone call. Their high level of liquidity means that Treasury securities do not pay a liquidity premium; just as with the DRP, the LP is zero for Treasury bonds. Bonds for large, estab-lished firms like Starbucks or Cisco have very small liquidity premiums, as there are many investors out there willing to buy the bonds of such firms. Lesser known firms whose bonds are not traded often will have higher liquidity premiums built into their interest rates, as the current owners may be forced to hold them until they mature. Of all the risk premiums listed here, the liquidity risk premium is the most difficult one to measure.

The Maturity Risk Premium

When a bond is issued for the first time, the coupon rate (the interest rate the bond pays to the bond holder) is set so that the market value of the bond is equal to the par value (or face value). This is done by setting the coupon rate at issuance equal to the rate paid by other current bonds of similar risk and maturity. However, over time market interest rates change. Often this is due to actions taken by the Federal Reserve Bank; the Fed changes short-term interest rates to manage inflation, unemployment and economic growth. When short-term interest rates change, long-term interest rates change as well, because long-term rates are an average of current and expected future short-term rates. The mechanics of this will be discussed later in the chapter. For now, you merely need to note that, as indicated in FP3, there is an inverse relationship between value and yield. When market interest rates increase, the market values of outstanding bonds decrease, and vice versa. While this has no impact if you intend to hold the bonds to maturity, it will affect the price you are able to get when attempting to sell a bond in the market. If interest rates have increased since you bought it, the market price will be below the par value. Chapter 5 on bond valuation will show the method for determining exactly how much the price is affected by a given change in market interest rates.

The risk associated with changes in market interest rates grows with the remaining time to maturity for the bond; a 5-year bond has more opportunity for interest rate changes to occur before maturity than a 2-year bond. Therefore, bonds with longer times to maturity must compensate the bond holder for the risk of future changes in market interest rates. This compensation added to the interest rate is the maturity risk premium. Thus, if Amazon issues both 10-year and 5-year bonds at the same time, the 10-year bonds will have a higher interest rate due to the longer time to maturity (as well as five additional years of inflation). Short-term bonds (bonds with one year or less to maturity) typically do not pay an MRP. All bonds of longer maturity, including Treasury securities, require an MRP in their interest rate.

On May 11, 2009, Microsoft issued both 10-year term bonds and 30-year term bonds. The 10-year bonds offered a coupon rate of 4.20%, while the 30-year bonds offered a coupon rate of 5.20%. Since the only difference in these bonds is their time to maturity, the difference in the coupon rates can only be attributed to expected changes in future inflation (the IP) and the time to maturity (the MRP). It is very difficult to determine how much of that difference is explained by either premium.

The risk associated with rising market interest rates is known as interest rate risk: the risk that increases in market interest rates will cause long-term bond values to fall. While this risk can be avoided by investing in short-term bonds, those bonds face another form of risk, known as reinvestment rate risk. Reinvestment rate risk is this risk that when you go to reinvest your money when the security reaches maturity, you will be facing lower market interest rates.

For example, suppose you choose to invest in a 1-year bond that pays 5% coupon interest rather than investing long-term, because you believe interest rates are going to climb to 6% next year. Your plan is to earn 5% this year, cash out the bond at maturity, then invest in another 1-year bond that pays 6% interest. You have the option of investing in a 3-year bond that pays 5.5%, but you don't want to get locked in for three years at 5.5% when you believe you can get 6% next year, so you buy the 1-year bond paying 5% today. Now suppose that next year, when the bond matures, market interest rates fall to 4%. When you reinvest next year, you will be earning a lower yield than if you had purchased the 3-year bond paying 5.5%. The lesson here is that you can avoid interest rate risk or reinvestment rate risk, but not both.

Determining Interest Rates

Assume the following premiums reflect current market conditions:

r* = 2.75%;
IP (1-year bonds) = 2.20%;
IP (3-year bonds) = 2.45%;
IP (5-year bonds) = 2.60%;
DRP (AAA corporate bonds) = 0.50%;
DRP (AA+ corporate bonds) = 0.65%;
LP (Microsoft) = 0.15%;
LP (Apple) = 0.25%;
MRP = 0.1% × (t − 1) where t is the number of years to maturity.

NOTE: Microsoft bonds are rated AAA, and Apple bonds are rated AA+.

Now use these data to determine the appropriate interest rates for the following newly issued bonds:

- 1-year, 3-year and 5-year bonds for Microsoft;
- 1-year, 3-year and 5-year bonds for Apple; and
- 1-year, 3-year and 5-year Treasury securities.

The following rules, mentioned earlier in the chapter, must be kept in mind:

1. All securities must have the real risk-free rate and the appropriate inflation premium;
2. Treasury securities do not have default risk or liquidity risk premiums;
3. All bonds with maturities greater than one year must have maturity risk premiums.

Using the data given above, and these three rules, we get the following interest rates:

- Microsoft 1-year bonds: i = 2.75 + 2.20 + 0.50 + 0.15 = 5.60%;
- Microsoft 3-year bonds: i = 2.75 + 2.45 + 0.50 + 0.15 + 0.1 × 2 = 6.05%;
- Microsoft 5-year bonds: i = 2.75 + 2.60 + 0.50 + 0.15 + 0.1 × 4 = 6.40%;
- Apple 1-year bonds: i = 2.75 + 2.20 + 0.65 + 0.25 = 5.85%;
- Apple 3-year bonds: i = 2.75 + 2.45 + 0.65 + 0.25 + 0.1 × 2 = 6.30%;
- Apple 5-year bonds: i = 2.75 + 2.60 + 0.65 + 0.25 + 0.1 × 4 = 6.65%;
- 1-year Treasury bonds: i = 2.75 + 2.20 = 4.95%;
- 3-year Treasury bonds: i = 2.75 + 2.45 + 0.1 × 2 = 5.40%;
- 5-year Treasury bonds: i = 2.75 + 2.60 + 0.1 × 4 = 5.75%.

Note that Apple, with the lower credit rating, has the highest interest rates for all three bond maturities, and that the Treasury bonds, with the least amount of risk, have the lowest interest rates.

The Yield Curve

A yield curve is simply a graph that shows the relationship between short-term and long-term interest rates for a particular type of security at a particular point in time. The relationship between short-term and long-term interest rates is known as the *term structure of interest rates*; that is, the structure of interest rates with regard to the term to maturity. The relationship between short-term and long-term interest rates is clearly reflected in the yield curve. The graph plots the interest rate on the vertical axis and the time to maturity on the horizontal axis. The most common yield curve represents the rates on Treasury securities, as it is easy to hold other factors constant (other than the time to maturity). Since all Treasury securities are highly liquid and have no default risk, the differences in the observed interest rates can be attributed to differences in either maturity (the MRP) or in expected future inflation (the IP).

The graphs in Figure 4.1 show the Treasury yield curve for June 1, 2018 and for March 20, 1980. In the first graph (2018), it is readily apparent that the interest rate increases as time

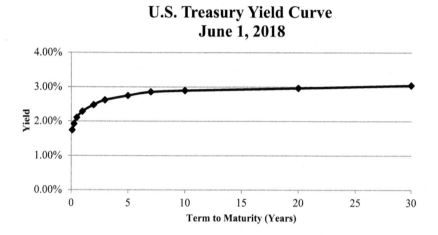

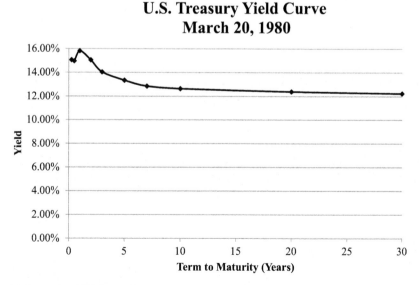

Figure 4.1 Treasury Yield Curve for June 1, 2018 and March 20, 1980

Source: www.treasury.gov, Federal Reserve Economic Database

to maturity increases; that is, long-term rates are higher than short-term rates. This is what economists refer to as a normal curve. It is considered normal because, under normal conditions, we would expect long-term rates to be higher than short-term rates due to the maturity risk premium, as well as the fact that inflation is normally expected to increase over time.

The second graph (1980) is known as an inverted curve, because short-term interest rates are higher than long-term interest rates. While the inverted shape of the yield curve stands out, another obvious difference is the overall level of interest rates—they were much higher in 1980. Inflation at that time was approximately 14.0%, whereas in June 2018 inflation was approximately 1.9%. The yield curve was inverted—that is, long-term rates were falling—due to anticipation that Ronald Reagan, who was running for president in 1980, would be able to get inflation under control. Therefore, the inflation premiums for future years were shrinking.

There are three main theories that attempt to explain the shape of the yield curve:

- The Liquidity Preference Theory states that investors prefer the liquidity of short-term debt, while borrowers prefer the security of long-term debt. In order to entice lenders to lend long-term, a premium must be paid, and the longer the term to maturity, the higher the premium. This would cause the yield curve to be normal under most conditions.
- The Market Segmentation Theory states that certain investors prefer investing for particular terms, and therefore the shape of the yield reflects current investment preferences. Under this theory, the yield curve could have any shape at any time.
- The Expectations Theory states that long-term interest rates are an average of current and expected future short-term rates. Therefore, when short-term rates are expected to rise in the future, the yield curve will be normal, whereas when future short-term rates are expected to fall, the yield curve may flatten out or even invert. So, the yield curve will be driven by expected future economic conditions, such as changes in inflation. This theory does not support the idea of a maturity risk premium, which some researchers believe does exist.

Of the three theories offered by research, the Expectations Theory can be used to analyze data in order to better understand what is happening with the changes in interest rates over time. For example, in June 2018 the 1-year Treasury rate was 2.28%, the 2-year rate was 2.47% and the 3-year rate was 2.61%. Since the 1-year Treasury rate contains no DRP, no LP and no MRP, the 2.28% rate consists of a 0.38% real risk-free rate (r*) and the 1.9% inflation premium mentioned above. If we assume that the r* is constant for years 2 and 3, then the IP for year 2 is 2.09% (2.47 − 0.38 = 2.09), and the IP for year 3 is 2.23%. We can now deconstruct the inflation premiums to see what future expectations of inflation were in June of 2018.

The 2-year IP is a geometric average of the 1-year IP in year 1 and the 1-year IP in year 2. Since the 2-year IP is higher than the 1-year IP in year 1, it is apparent that the 1-year IP has increased for year 2. We can determine the 1-year IP for year 2 by using the geometric mean approach:

$$\sqrt{\left(1 + IP_{1,1}\right) \times \left(1 + IP_{1,2}\right)} = 1 + IP_2$$

where: $IP_{1,1}$ is the 1-year inflation premium in year 1;
$IP_{1,2}$ is the 1-year inflation premium in year 2; and
IP_2 is the 2-year inflation premium.

This equation can be rewritten to solve for the 1-year inflation premium in year 2:

$$\left(1+IP_2\right)^2 \div \left(1+IP_{1,1}\right) = 1+IP_{1,2}$$

Now we can solve for $IP_{1,2}$:

1. $(1.0209)^2 = 1.04224$;
2. $1.04224 \div 1.019 = 1.02280$.

Therefore the 1-year IP for year 2 is 2.28%. This can be confirmed by plugging the figures into the geometric mean equation above:

$$\sqrt{1.019 \times 1.0228} = 1.0209$$

We can use the same method for calculating the 1-year IP for year 3:

$$\sqrt[3]{\left(1+IP_{1,1}\right) \times \left(1+IP_{1,2}\right) \times \left(1+IP_{1,3}\right)} = 1+IP_3;$$
$$\left(1+IP_3\right)^3 \div \left[\left(1+IP_{1,1}\right) \times \left(1+IP_{1,2}\right)\right] = 1+IP_{1,3}.$$

1. $(1.0223)^3 = 1.0684$;
2. $1.0684 \div (1.019 \times 1.0228) = 1.0251$.

Therefore, the 1-year IP for year 3 is 2.51%. This can again be confirmed by plugging these numbers into the 3-year equation above:

$$\sqrt[3]{1.019 \times 1.0228 \times 1.0251} = 1.0223$$

Based on this analysis, in 2018 inflation was expected to rise from 1.9% to 2.28% in 2019 and to 2.51% in 2020. This expected increase in inflation is one possible answer for why the yield curve for June 2018 is normal (upward sloping).

Bond Yields vs. Stock Returns—The Fed Model

Wall Street has a long and storied history. The New York Stock Exchange was founded in 1792, and trading in the market has grown more active over time. Data relating to the yields on bonds and the returns on stocks are available as far back as 1871. Thanks to this, there is a tremendous amount of research that has been done with regard to bond yields and stock returns. However, until relatively recently, there has not been as much research published that compares the two. The markets for bonds and stocks are separate and different, but in recent years investors have begun to move their money from one market to the other based on changes in the returns from both types of securities. The motivation for this can be explained in terms of what we learned in Chapter 3 with regard to the Security Market Line.

The SML indicates that investors insist on earning the risk-free rate (r_{RF}) at a minimum in order to postpone consuming their income to invest it. Beyond that minimum, investors require compensation related to the risks associated with investing in stocks (r_M) as well as for the risks associated with the specific stock under consideration (β). If we speak about the market in general rather than any specific stock, we can remove beta from the equation (since the market beta is 1.0) and focus on the risk-free rate and the market risk premium $(r_M - r_{RF})$.

In order to study these markets, researchers use proxies (representative substitutes) for these variables. The nominal risk-free rate is represented by the yield on Treasury securities (typically either the 3-month T-bill rate or the 10-year T-note rate), while the market return is represented by the return to the S&P 500 index fund. By comparing the yields on 10-year Treasury notes to the returns to the S&P 500 index fund over an extended period of time, we can see that while the two returns behaved differently for a very long time, at some point in the not-too-distant past the yields on bonds started behaving very much like the returns to stocks.

The graph in Figure 4.2 shows the annual returns to the S&P 500 index fund (E1/P) and the annual yields on 10-year Treasury notes (Y) going back to 1881. While it is clear that the returns to the different types of securities behaved independently for quite a while, starting in 1950[1] the two series began to track each other very closely. Researchers have posited that the change in the behavior of these variables came about because investors began to equate the returns to stocks with the yields on bonds,[2] moving their money between the two markets based on the size of the market risk premium $(r_M - r_{RF})$. This tendency for investors to benchmark the market earnings yield to the yield on 10-year T-notes is referred to as the Fed model,[3] apparently in response to a 1997 Federal Reserve Monetary Policy Report to Congress. When the market risk premium is large, investors earn enough of a return to make it worth the risk of being in the stock market, and so they move their money into stocks. When the risk premium is small, the return to stocks is no longer seen as being worth the risk, and so investors move their money into bonds. This reactionary behavior on the part of investors seems to have caused the returns on both types of securities to compete, and therefore to move very close together. This is evidence that investor behavior can affect the bond and stock markets in much the same way as economic factors can.

The field of behavioral finance is young and growing, but even at this early stage it is clear that human behavior can impact financial markets in unexpected ways that we are just

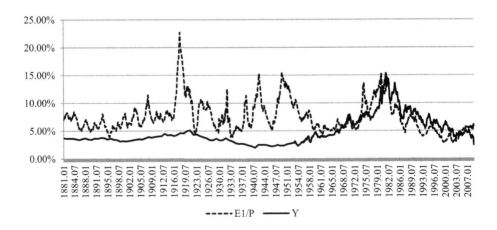

Figure 4.2 Stock Market Returns vs. 10-Year Treasury Note Yields 1881–2007

Source: Irons, R. and T. Wu, "Will the Market P/E Ratio Revert to its Mean?," *Investment Management and Financial Innovations*, 2013.

beginning to appreciate. It is inevitable that further research in this area will make the current theories on interest rates problematic, if not obsolete.

Summary of the Principles and Precepts Applied in This Chapter

The Second Fundamental Principle (FP2): There is a direct relationship between risk and return; as perceived risk increases, required return will also increase (and vice versa), holding other things constant.

The accuracy of FP2 is reflected in the numerous risk premiums that make up the nominal interest rate for debt securities. As additional risk is taken on, the required yield climbs.

The Third Fundamental Principle (FP3): There is an inverse relationship between price and yield; if an asset's price increases, its return will decrease (and vice versa), holding other things constant.

The discussion of interest rate risk, as reflected in the MRP, shows that changes in market interest rates have an inverse impact on bond prices.

The First Precept (PR1): The present value of a cash flow (or an asset) is inversely related to its discount rate; increasing the discount rate decreases the present value (and vice versa), holding other things constant.
The Third Precept (PR3): The present value of a cash flow (or an asset) is inversely related to its perceived risk; the higher the risk, the higher the discount rate, and therefore the lower the present value.

PR3 describes the inverse relationship between value and the risk. PR1 shows the inverse relationship between value and the discount rate. These two precepts are linked by the direct relationship between risk and return, since the return to bondholders is used as the discount rate for determining the market value of bonds. This will be seen again in the following chapter on bond valuation.

End of Chapter Problems

1. A normal yield curve has what general shape?

   a. Downward sloping.
   b. Concave.
   c. Inverted.
   d. Upward sloping.
   e. Convex.

2. If the real risk-free rate is 112 basis points, the maturity risk premium is 177 basis points and the 1-year inflation premium is 263 basis points, what is the nominal risk-free rate?

   a. 2.63%.
   b. 2.89%.
   c. 3.75%.
   d. 4.40%.
   e. 5.52%.

3. Which of the following items reflects the size of the market for the security in question?

   a. Real risk-free rate.
   b. Inflation premium.
   c. Default risk premium.
   d. Liquidity premium.
   e. Maturity risk premium.

4. Which of the following items reflects the time value of money?

   a. Real risk-free rate.
   b. Inflation premium.
   c. Default risk premium.
   d. Liquidity premium.
   e. Maturity risk premium.

5. Which of the following items reflects the active trading life of the security in question?

   a. Real risk-free rate.
   b. Inflation premium.
   c. Default risk premium.
   d. Liquidity premium.
   e. Maturity risk premium.

6. Which of the following items reflects the financial stability of the company that issued the security in question?

   a. Real risk-free rate.
   b. Inflation premium.
   c. Default risk premium.
   d. Liquidity premium.
   e. Maturity risk premium.

7. Which of the following items reflects the expected changes in purchasing power over the life of the security in question?

   a. Real risk-free rate.
   b. Inflation premium.
   c. Default risk premium.
   d. Liquidity premium.
   e. Maturity risk premium.

8. Which of the following rules regarding interest rate premiums are true?

   a. All bonds with maturities longer than one year must have maturity risk premiums.
   b. All securities must have the real risk-free rate and an appropriate inflation premium.
   c. US government securities do not have default risk or liquidity risk premiums.
   d. All of the above are true.
   e. None of the above is true.

9. The yield curve represents:

   a. The relationship between bond yields and stock returns.
   b. The relationship between default risk and time to maturity.

c.   The relationship between short-term and long-term interest rates.
d.   The relationship between risk and return.
e.   The relationship between yield and price.

Use the following data to answer questions 10–18.
Assume the following premiums reflect current market conditions:

r* = 3.15%;
IP (1-year bonds) = 2.35%;
IP (3-year bonds) = 2.65%;
IP (5-year bonds) = 2.90%;
DRP (AAA corporate bonds) = 0.60%;
DRP (AA+ corporate bonds) = 0.85%;
LP (AAA corporate bonds) = 0.22%;
LP (AA+ corporate bonds) = 0.30%;
MRP = 0.1% × (t − 1) where t is the number of years to maturity.

10. Calculate the interest rate for a 1-year AA+ corporate bond.
11. Calculate the interest rate for a 3-year AA+ corporate bond.
12. Calculate the interest rate for a 5-year AA+ corporate bond.
13. Calculate the interest rate for a 1-year AAA corporate bond.
14. Calculate the interest rate for a 3-year AAA corporate bond.
15. Calculate the interest rate for a 5-year AAA corporate bond.
16. Calculate the interest rate for a 1-year Treasury security.
17. Calculate the interest rate for a 3-year Treasury security.
18. Calculate the interest rate for a 5-year Treasury security.
19. The current 1-year interest rate is 6.40%, while the current 2-year interest rate is 5.80%. Given these rates, what is the expected 1-year interest rate one year from now?
20. The current 1-year interest rate is 4.74% and the expected 1-year interest rate one year from now is 5.12%. If the current 3-year interest rate is 5.22%, what is the expected 1-year rate two years from now?

Notes

1 Irons, R. and T. Wu. "Will the Market P/E Ratio Revert to Its Mean?" *Investment Management and Financial Innovations*, 2013.
2 Weigand, R. and R. Irons. "Compression and Expansion of the Market P/E Ratio: The Fed Model Explained," *Journal of Investing*, 2008.
3 Asness, C. "Fight the Fed Model," *Journal of Portfolio Management*, 2003.

Bibliography

Fundamentals of Corporate Finance, 12th edition. S. Ross, R. Westerfield and B. Jordan. McGraw-Hill Education, 2019.
Financial Management: Principles & Practice, 8th edition. T. Gallagher. Textbook Media Press, 2019.
Foundations of Financial Management, 17th edition. S. Block, G. Hirt and B. Danielsen. McGraw-Hill Education, 2018.

5 Bonds and Bond Valuation

In Chapter 4, we discussed the structure of interest rates and how they are determined, as well as the relationship between short-term and long-term interest rates. In this chapter, we will see how debt is used to fund a firm's operations or its investments, and how changes in market interest rates affect the market value of the firm's debt.

The material in this chapter shows clearly the impact of the fundamental principles and precepts in determining the value of bonds in the market. A solid understanding of these connections will help you intuit the expected changes to a bond's value in the face of changes to its cash flows, its level of risk or its discount rate.

The Fundamental Principles in Action

FP1 states that an asset derives its value from the cash flows it will produce. Bonds have very specific cash flows—interest payments and the return of the principal—and those cash flows are the basis of the model used to value bonds. FP3 indicates the inverse relationship between an asset's yield and its market value. This is clearly reflected in the mechanics of bond valuation—increases in market interest rates negatively impact bonds' market values. FP2 asserts that risk and return are directly related, and so riskier assets require higher returns. This applies to bonds as well, and it can be seen in PR1 (relating value inversely to the discount rate). Since the market interest rate is used as the discount rate in valuing bonds, bonds of higher risk will pay a higher discount rate, which will reduce the market value of the bonds.

The Basics of Bonds

A bond is a debt instrument; a loan reinforced by a detailed contract. The issuer of the bond agrees to repay the debt in full on a certain date and to make regular interest payments until that date (assuming the life of the debt is more than one year). A debtor issues a bond (a firm or a government), and a creditor buys a bond (an investor, either an individual or an institution, such as a hedge fund, or an insurance company, or a mutual fund). All bonds have most or all of the following features:

- An issue date (the date on which the bond was issued), a maturity date (the date on which the contract ends, and the loan amount is repaid) and an original maturity (the time between the issue date and the maturity date). Thus, a bond that is issued on March 1, 2018 and is due to mature on March 1, 2028 has an original maturity of ten years. On

March 1, 2019, the bond will have nine years remaining to maturity, but its original maturity will always be ten years.

- A par value, or face value, which is usually $1,000 or some multiple thereof. It is clearly marked on the face of the bond.
- A coupon interest rate (or coupon rate), which is the percentage of the par value that the holder of the bond will earn annually. Thus, a $1,000 par value bond with a 4.50% coupon rate will pay $45.00 in interest per year. Interest payments are typically made semiannually (twice a year), and so the investor in this case would receive $22.50 interest per bond every six months.

  Most bonds have fixed interest payments, but there are some variable interest rate bonds. Variable rate bonds tend to have their interest payments tied to some other rate, such as the LIBOR (London Interbank Offer Rate), or the rate of inflation. For this chapter, we will assume that the bonds in question have a fixed coupon rate.

  Note that there are bonds without coupons, known as zero coupon bonds, or zeros. These are bonds whose time to maturity is less than one year. With limited time to maturity, paying interest payments is inefficient, so instead the bond's price is discounted to account for the interest to be earned (these are also known as original discount bonds). For example, a 6-month, $1,000 par Treasury bill with an APR of 3.50% will sell for $982.95 at issue: $1,000(1.035)^{-0.5} = 982.95.

- A schedule of interest payment dates as well as the date for the return of the principal (the face value). On the maturity date, the investor will receive both the return of the par value and the final interest payment.
- The bond indenture, which specifies features intended to protect either the debtor or the creditor. Such features may include collateral offered in case of default, provisions for early payoff or warrants or conversions. A warrant is a feature that permits the creditor to purchase the debtor's common stock at a specified price during the life of the bond. Once the firm's stock goes above that price, exercising the warrants leads to a quick profit. This feature is an option that has intrinsic value, and therefore bonds with warrants usually offer a lower interest rate than comparable bonds without them.

  Convertible bonds are bonds that can be traded in for the firm's common stock at a specific ratio. For example, a $1,000 par value convertible bond may be issued with a 20:1 conversion ratio, meaning that a single bond can be traded in for 20 shares of the firm's common stock. Since the bond is worth $1,000, it will pay for the creditor to convert the bond if the firm's common stock goes above $50 per share ($50 × 20 = $1,000). The difference between a warrant and a convertible bond is that with the warrant the creditor gets to keep the bond, but the convertible bond must be traded for the common stock.

- A call provision permits the debtor to recall the bonds (buy them back) before the bond's maturity date, but after some period of time has passed from the issue date. This period of time during which the bonds cannot be called is known as the call protection period. If a 10-year maturity bond has three years of call protection, then once three years has passed, the firm has the option to recall the bonds early, but must pay a call premium to the bondholders (an amount above the par value). This premium may be a dollar amount or a percentage. A debtor will be motivated to call bonds early when market interest rates have fallen, which will permit the firm to issue new bonds at a much lower interest rate and thus save money on future interest payments.

Bonds can be secured by specific assets (such as mortgage bonds), or they can be unsecured; unsecured bonds are known as debentures. In the case of a default, debentures are not collateralized, so the bondholders have a general claim against the issuer rather than a specific claim against their assets.

Calculating the Value of a Bond

As per FP1, the value of a bond is the present value of its expected future cash flows. Those cash flows are the scheduled interest payments and the return of the principal at maturity. The single most important detail to remember about valuing bonds is that the discount rate to use is the bond's yield to maturity (YTM)—this is the current market interest rate for bonds of similar risk and of similar maturity. At issue, the YTM for the bond is its coupon rate—i.e., the bond's coupon rate is set so that the bond sells at par. Over time, market interest rates change, and those changes in market interest rates cause changes in the market values of outstanding bonds. FP3 tells us that there is an inverse relationship between yield and value, which means that if market interest rates increase, bond prices will decrease. Note that if you hold the bond from its issue until it matures, you will earn the coupon rate for the entire time and will be repaid the par value at maturity. The YTM only becomes an issue when the bond is being sold before it matures, and that is because the YTM is used as the discount rate for valuing the bond.

As stated above, the cash flows for a bond are the periodic interest payments and the return of the principal. Since the interest payments are fixed and come at regular intervals for the life of the bond, they are an annuity, and their present value is calculated using the present value annuity interest factor. The return of the principal is a single cash flow to be received in the future, so its present value is simply the present value of a single cash flow. The sum of these two calculations is the market value for the bond. For a bond that makes interest payments annually, the equation to use to value the bond is as follows:

$$
\begin{aligned}
V_{Bond} &= PMT\left(PVIFA_{YTM,-n}\right) + Par\left(PVIF_{YTM,-n}\right) \\
&= PMT\left[\frac{1-(1+YTM)^{-n}}{YTM}\right] + Par(1+YTM)^{-n} \\
&= \frac{PMT}{YTM}\left[1-(1+YTM)^{-n}\right] + Par(1+YTM)^{-n}
\end{aligned}
$$

where: *PMT* is the annual coupon payment (coupon rate × par value);
YTM is the bond's yield to maturity (the market rate for bonds of similar risk and maturity);
Par is the bond's face value; and
n is the number of years to maturity.

If the bond pays interest semiannually (twice per year, as most bonds do), then three things happen to the formula:

1. The PMT is cut in half (since the annual interest amount is divided over two payments);
2. The YTM is cut in half to make it a periodic rate; and
3. The number of years is doubled to derive the number of semiannual periods.

The formula for the value of a bond with semiannual payments is modified to account for this:

$$V_{Bond} = \frac{PMT}{2}\left(PVIFA_{YTM \div 2,-2n}\right) + Par\left(PVIF_{YTM \div 2,-2n}\right)$$

$$= \frac{PMT}{2}\left[\frac{1-(1+YTM \div 2)^{-2n}}{YTM \div 2}\right] + Par(1+YTM \div 2)^{-2n}$$

$$= \frac{PMT/2}{YTM/2}\left[1-\left(1+\frac{YTM}{2}\right)^{-2n}\right] + Par\left(1+\frac{YTM}{2}\right)^{-2n}$$

$$= \frac{PMT}{YTM}\left[1-\left(1+\frac{YTM}{2}\right)^{-2n}\right] + Par\left(1+\frac{YTM}{2}\right)^{-2n}$$

As we discussed in Chapter 2, when cash flows are discounted more frequently than annually, the present value of the cash flows decreases. This can be seen when valuing a bond with both annual and semiannual interest payments. For example, suppose you are interested in purchasing a $1,000 par value bond with six years remaining until maturity. The coupon rate for the bond is 5.0%, but interest rates have gone up since the bond was issued, and the current YTM for the bond is 5.80%. How much should you be willing to pay for this bond? Calculate the value of the bond assuming both annual and semiannual interest payments.

Before you begin to calculate, you can get some insight regarding the bond's market value by comparing the coupon rate and the yield to maturity. In this case, the YTM is greater than the coupon rate, because interest rates have risen since the bond was issued. According to FP3, this means that the value of the bond has decreased, so the bond should be selling at a slight discount. If you calculate the value of this bond as being $1,000 or higher, you will have made a mistake, and you will need to check your work. In this way, FP3 helps us intuit the answer to the problem.

With annual interest payments:

$$V_{Bond} = \frac{\$50}{.058}\left[1-(1.058)^{-6}\right] + \$1,000(1.058)^{-6} = \$247.42 + \$712.99 = \$960.41$$

With semiannual interest payments:

$$V_{Bond} = \frac{\$50}{.058}\left[1-(1.029)^{-12}\right] + \$1,000(1.029)^{-12} = \$250.34 + \$709.60 = \$959.94$$

The bond with annual interest payments is selling at a slight discount ($39.59), and making semiannual interest payments lowers the market value of the bond by another $0.47.

Bond Values Over Time

Let's assume that you choose to purchase the semiannual bond and hold it for one year. Presuming market interest rates don't change during the year, what will happen to the price of the bond? Under these conditions, we would expect the price of the bond to increase slightly. If market interest rates hold steady, the value of the bond will slowly head towards par over time until the maturity date, at which point its value *will* be par. So discounted bonds will increase in price (holding other things constant), and bonds selling at a premium will decrease in price. Figure 5.1 shows what happens to bond prices over time, holding market interest rates constant.

In Figure 5.1, the premium bond (with values above par) represents a 20-year bond with a 5% coupon rate and a 4% YTM. Since the coupon rate is higher than the discount rate, the bond sells for more than par at all times except at maturity, when it sells for par. The discount bond (with values below par) represents the same 20-year bond with the same 5% coupon rate but with a 6% YTM. Since the current market interest rate is above the coupon rate, the bond sells at a discount at all times except at maturity, when it sells for par. Holding the market interest rates constant, bonds selling at either a discount or a premium will head towards par over time. Thus, for premium bonds we expect the price to fall over time, which will increase the current yield and decrease the capital gains yield. For discount bonds, we expect the price to rise over time, which will decrease the current yield and increase the capital gains yield. In both cases, assuming market interest rates do not change, these component yield changes will offset each other, and the total yield will remain the same.

As the graph indicates, over time the bond will slowly change more and more in value, at an increasing rate, until the maturity date, at which point the bond's value will be par. Bonds selling at a premium will fall in price, while those selling at a discount will rise in price. For

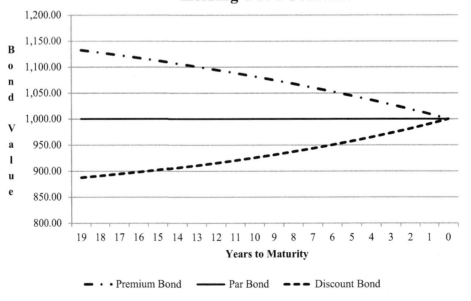

Figure 5.1 Changes in Bond Values Over Time Holding Market Interest Rates Constant

the bond considered above, assuming semiannual interest payments, the increase in price over one year is small:

$$V_{Bond} = \frac{\$50}{.058}\left[1-(1.029)^{-10}\right]+\$1,000(1.029)^{-10} = \$214.34+\$751.36 = \$965.70$$

The bond will have increased in price by $5.76 by the end of the first year. Referring to the return calculations from Chapter 3, we can now calculate the current yield, capital gains yield and total yield for the bond over the year:

* Current Yield = 50 ÷ 959.94 = 0.0520 or 5.20%;
* Capital Gains Yield = 5.76 ÷ 959.94 = .0060 or 0.6%;
* Total Yield = .052 + .006 = .058 or 5.8%.

Notice that the total yield is equal to the YTM; this is not a coincidence. Since other bonds of similar risk and maturity earn 5.8% annually, the market priced this bond to earn the same yield. If we follow this bond for one more year, holding market interest rates constant, we will see the same general results:

$$V_{Bond} = \frac{\$50}{.058}\left[1-(1.029)^{-8}\right]+\$1,000(1.029)^{-8} = \$176.23+\$795.57 = \$971.80$$

* Current Yield = 50 ÷ 965.70 = 0.0517 or 5.17%;
* Capital Gains Yield = (971.80 − 965.70) ÷ 965.70 = .0063 or 0.63%;
* Total Yield = .0517 + .0063 = .058 or 5.8%.

Once again, the bond rose slightly in price, and once again the total yield on the bond was 5.80%. Since the price rose during the year, the capital gains yield increased, but the current yield decreased.

Using Excel to Calculate Bond Prices

Bond prices can be calculated using Excel's PRICE function, which requires the following inputs:

* The settlement date (the beginning of the time period of interest—the date on which the bond is purchased)—must be entered as a date;
* The maturity date—must be entered as a date;
* The coupon rate;
* The yield to maturity;
* The redemption (assumes face value is 100); and
* The frequency of interest payments—1 is annual, 2 is semiannual.

The settlement and maturity dates can be entered as any two dates that are the correct number of years apart. As you can see in Table 5.1, I used January 1, 2000 and January 1, 2006 for the 6-year bond in the previous example. Finally, since the function thinks this is a $100 par bond, we must multiply the output by 10 to make the par value $1,000 (if it were a $5,000 par bond, we would need to multiply the output by 50).

Table 5.1 Determining a Bond's Value Using Excel's PRICE Function

Settlement	1/1/2000	
Maturity	1/1/2006	
Rate	0.05	
Yield	0.058	
Redemption	100	
Frequency	2	
Price function	95.9945	<-- =PRICE(B1,B2,B3,B4,B5,B6)
Market price	959.945	<-- =B7 * 10

Table 5.2 Using Excel's RATE Function to Calculate a Bond's Yield to Maturity

nper	12	
pmt	25	
pv	−959.94	
fv	1000	
type	0	
rate	2.90%	<-- =RATE(B1,B2,B3,B4,B5)
YTM	5.80%	<-- =B6 * 2

The PRICE function determines that the bond is selling at 95.9945% of its face value. Therefore, the market value of the bond is $1,000 × .959945 = $959.94. If this were a $5,000 bond, its market price would be $5,000 × .959945 = $4,799.72.

Calculating a Bond's Yield to Maturity

Solving for a bond's yield to maturity requires us to solve for the discount rate, which means we must use either a financial calculator or an Excel function—the RATE function. The RATE function can be used for this purpose because the interest payments are an annuity and are used as the payments needed for the function. The current market value of the bond is its present value, and the bond's par value is its future value. One important issue is that since coupon payments are made semiannually, we must use the semiannual payment amount and the number of semiannual payments in the calculation. This means that the RATE function will leave us with a semiannual YTM, which must be doubled in order to obtain the annual YTM.

Table 5.2 shows the Excel inputs needed to calculate the bond's YTM. There are 12 semiannual periods in six years, and a 5% coupon rate means a $25 semiannual coupon payment for a $1,000 par bond. The present value is given as a negative number because Excel needs either the PV or the FV to be negative in order for the function to work. The future value of the bond is par ($1,000), and the type is 0 since it is an ordinary annuity (coupon payments come at the end of the period). The RATE function gives us the semiannual rate of 2.90%, which is then doubled to get the annual rate of 5.80%.

Since this bond is selling at a discount, we would expect the YTM to be higher than the coupon rate, which is the case here. FP3 tells us that the bond is selling at a discount because market interest rates have risen since the bond was issued. Intuiting these types of details can be quite helpful while doing homework or during an exam and will be of great use in a career in finance.

Calculating a Bond's Yield to Call

If a bond that you own is callable, there is the possibility that you will not be permitted to hold it to maturity. If the bond *is* called before it matures, that will affect the yield on your investment. For this reason, it is necessary to calculate the bond's yield to call (YTC). The YTC is defined as the yield you will earn if you hold the bond until the first day it can be called (the end of its call protection).

While we can still use the RATE function to calculate the YTC, there are two changes we must make to the inputs:

- You must reduce the number of periods to extend only through the bond's period of call protection; and
- You must increase the future value of the bond to include the call premium that must be paid for the bonds to be called.

We will use the same bond we have been using to show how calling a bond affects the yield on the bond. Suppose the 6-year bond you just bought was issued as a 10-year bond four years ago, and that the bond was callable but has five years of call protection. That means that after the fifth year is over (i.e., your first year owning the bond), the bonds are able to be called by the issuer. If market interest rates fall between the time you purchase the bond and the time the bond is called, the firm may be motivated to call the bonds and issue new bonds with a lower interest rate. Let us suppose that is the case here, and that the firm contacts you that your bond is being called after you will have owned it for just one year. In return, you will be paid a call premium of one interest payment ($25). To calculate the YTC, we simply assume that the bond will be called once the call protection is over. Therefore, we change the inputs to the RATE function by reducing the number of interest payments to two (nper = 2) and increasing the future value to $1,025 (to include the $25 call premium).

The top of Table 5.3 compares the YTM and YTC calculations for the same bond. Notice that for the YTC calculations the number of payments was reduced to two and the future value was increased by the call premium. The YTC is far higher than the YTM because,

Table 5.3 Calculating Yield to Call Using the RATE and IRR Functions

nper	12	nper	2	
pmt	25	pmt	25	
pv	−959.94	pv	−959.94	
fv	1000	fv	1025	
type	0	type	0	
rate	2.90%	rate	5.90%	<-- =RATE(E1,E2,E3,E4,E5)
YTM	5.80%	YTC	11.79%	<-- =E6 * 2

Using the IRR Function

	0	1	2
Cash flows	−959.94	25	1050

IRR	5.90%	<-- =IRR(B10:D10)
YTC	11.79%	<-- =B13 * 2

thanks to the call premium, you are receiving three interest payments in the amount of time in which you would normally only receive two. In addition, the price, which is currently below par, is expected to rise to par within one year. All of this works together to drive the YTC to over twice as much as the YTM.

The bottom of Table 5.3 illustrates how you can use Excel's IRR function to calculate the bond's YTC. The theory of the IRR will be discussed in Chapter 7, "Capital Budgeting Decision Methods." For now, we will discuss only how to use the IRR function.

To calculate the IRR, we need to show the cash flows on a time line, as indicated in Table 5.3. The time line covers two semiannual periods for owning the bond. The purchase of the bond is a negative cash flow in time period zero. At the end of six months, you will receive one interest payment of $25, and at the end of another six months you will receive one more $25 interest payment, the $25 call premium, and the $1,000 par value, totaling $1,050. The investment's internal rate of return (IRR) per semiannual period is shown to be 5.90%, which is then doubled to obtain the annual rate. Note that the semiannual rate is really 5.896%, which doubles to 11.792%. Formatting to two decimal places causes the rounding error to show.

Duration and Its Use

Interest rate risk, which we discussed in the previous chapter, is the risk that market interest rates will rise while you are holding long-term bonds, causing the market value of those bonds to fall. This relationship is described in FP3, and it is the justification for the maturity risk premium added to long-term interest rates. Generally speaking, the longer the time to maturity remaining for a bond, the larger its maturity risk premium. That is because the longer the time remaining in the life of the bond, the more opportunity there is for market interest rates to change. This relationship between time and interest rate risk causes long-term bonds to be more sensitive to interest rate changes than short-term bonds.

Figure 5.2 shows the prices for three different $1,000 par value, 5% coupon bonds. The only difference between the bonds is their time to maturity; they are a 1-year bond, a 10-year bond and a 20-year bond. The graph shows what happens to the bond prices when market interest rates fall to 4% and 3%, as well as what happens when market interest rates climb to 6% and 7%. The first thing that you should notice is that all of the graph lines have a negative slope—they go from upper left to lower right, meaning that as the YTM increases the bond price decreases. This is what we would expect based on FP3. The second thing that should strike you is that at a 5% YTM they all have the same value—par ($1,000). When the YTM and the coupon rate are the same, the bond's value is par, regardless of maturity.

A closer look should make it plain that the 10-year bond has much larger changes to its price than the 1-year bond, and that the 20-year bond has even larger price changes than the 10-year bond. This analysis permits us to draw the conclusion that *the longer time to maturity for a bond, the more its price changes in response to a given change in market interest rates*. A similar analysis offers insights as to how the bond's coupon rate affects its price.

Table 5.4 shows what happens to the price of a 20-year maturity bond for different levels of coupon rate when market interest rates change. The top section shows the model for valuing a bond using Excel's PRICE function. All three models have the same YTM (5%), but the coupon rates are different: 8%, 5% and 2%, from left to right. This part of the analysis sets the base case. The second section shows what happens to these bond values when the yield to maturity changes. For all three bonds, the price increases as the YTM falls. This is what we would expect to see due to our understanding of FP3 and PR1.

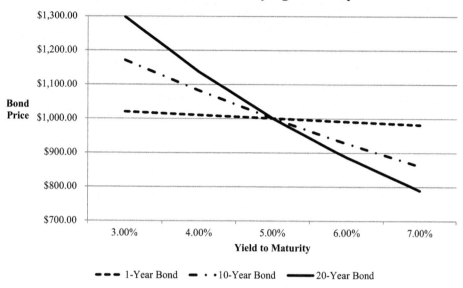

Figure 5.2 Price Changes for 5% Coupon Bonds of Varying Maturity

Table 5.4 Comparing Bond Price Changes at Varying Coupon Rates

Settlement	1/1/2000	1/1/2000	1/1/2000	
Maturity	1/1/2020	1/1/2020	1/1/2020	
Rate	**0.08**	**0.05**	**0.02**	
Yield	0.05	**0.05**	0.05	
Redemption	100	100	100	
Frequency	2	2	2	
Price function	137.65	100.00	62.35	
Market price	1,376.54	1,000.00	623.46	

	Coupon Rate			
YTM	8%	5%	2%	
10%	828.41	571.02	313.64	<-- =PRICE(D$1,D$2,D$3,$A12,
7%	1,106.78	786.45	466.12	D$5,D$6) * 10
4%	1,547.11	1,136.78	726.45	
1%	2,266.03	1,723.44	1,180.86	

% Price Change				
10%	−39.82%	−42.90%	−49.69%	<-- =(D12 / D$8) − 1
7%	−19.60%	−21.36%	−25.24%	
4%	12.39%	13.68%	16.52%	
1%	64.62%	72.34%	89.40%	

The third section shows the second section's percent price change from the original price (in the top section). Thus, when we vary the YTM from 10% down to 1%, the value of the 8% coupon bond varies from a 40% fall in price to a 65% rise in price. At the same time, the 5% coupon bond's value varies from a 43% fall in price to a 72% rise in price, while the 2% coupon bond's value varies from a 50% fall in price to an 89% rise in price. This analysis permits us to draw the conclusion that *the lower the coupon rate for a bond, the more its price changes in response to a given change in market interest rates.*

Given these understandings about bond sensitivities, it would be helpful to investors if there were a metric that measures the sensitivity of a bond's value to changes in market rates. In fact, there are two: the duration and the modified duration.

The Macaulay duration for a bond is calculated as:

$$D_{Macaulay} = \frac{\sum_{t=1}^{n} \frac{Pmt_t}{(1+YTM)^t}(t)}{V_{Bond}}$$

where: Pmt_t is the cash flow in period t;
YTM is the periodic yield to maturity (usually semiannual periods); and
V_{Bond} is the bond's market price.

The fraction in the numerator is the present value of each cash flow, which is multiplied by the number of periods until the cash flow is received (which acts as a weight for each cash flow), and then the sum of those weighted present values is divided by the bond's current value. This metric is interpreted as the average number of periods that the bond's present value of cash flows remains outstanding. Note that for semiannual bonds, the duration is the number of semiannual periods and therefore should be divided by two to obtain the number of years.

Macaulay's duration measures a bond's sensitivity to interest rates by way of the following calculation:

% Change in V_{Bond} = (% Change in YTM)(−Duration)

Thus, the percent change in a bond's price is proportional to its duration. A zero coupon bond, which has no payments until it matures, has a duration equal to its maturity. Coupon bonds have a duration that is shorter than their current maturity. Duration also decreases as the coupon rate increases.

The modified duration simply discounts the duration for one more period:

$$D_{Modified} = \frac{D_{Macaulay}}{\left(1+\dfrac{YTM}{m}\right)}$$

where: m is the number of periods per year (two for semiannual bonds).

The modified duration is known to offer slightly more accurate estimates of the expected change in a bond's price for a small change in the YTM. The modified duration is used in place of the Macaulay duration in the equation above to estimate the percent change in the value of the bond. Note that both the duration and the modified duration assume a linear relationship between the change in YTM and the change in the bond's price. In fact, the relationship between YTM and price is nonlinear, so duration and modified duration only work well for small changes in yields.

Imagine having to calculate the Macaulay duration or the modified duration for a 20-year bond by hand. With 40 cash flows, it would take up an entire sheet of paper. Fortunately, Excel has both a DURATION function and an MDURATION function that make life easier for us. They also make life easier because you can tell the functions that the bond is semiannual, and for output they will give you the number of years rather than the number of periods.

Table 5.5 uses the same three bonds from Table 5.4 to show how the duration and modified duration work. The first section is simply the data used for pricing the bond. The second section calculates the duration and modified duration for each bond to two decimal places. Note that the duration and modified duration both increase as the coupon rate for the bond falls. The third section calculates the expected change in the bond's price using the equation above for both the duration and the modified duration, assuming a 10 basis point fall in the YTM (i.e., YTM drops from 5.00% to 4.90%). The fourth section calculates the actual percent change in the bond's price, again based on a 10 basis point fall in the YTM. As you can see, the results in the fourth section are very close to the modified duration results in the third section, and also not very far from the duration results as well.

It should be noted that, as discussed above, the duration and modified duration of a bond also change with regard to changes in a bond's time to maturity. Using a simple 5% coupon rate bond that has a 5% YTM and semiannual payments, with a 5-year maturity its duration is 4.49 years (modified duration 4.38 years), while with a 10-year maturity the same bond's

Table 5.5 Using Duration and Modified Duration to Estimate Changes to Bond Prices

Settlement	1/1/2000	1/1/2000	1/1/2000	
Maturity	1/1/2020	1/1/2020	1/1/2020	
Rate	**0.08**	**0.05**	**0.02**	
Yield	0.05	**0.05**	0.05	
Redemption	100	100	100	
Frequency	2	2	2	
Price function	137.65	100.00	62.35	
Market price	1,376.54	1,000.00	623.46	

Duration	11.71	12.87	15.42	<-- =DURATION(D1,D2,D3,D4,D6)
Modified D	11.42	12.55	15.05	<-- =MDURATION(D1,D2,D3,D4,D6)

Based on a 10 basis point fall in the YTM

% change—Duration	1.17%	1.29%	1.54%	<-- =−0.001 * −D10
% change—Mod. D	1.14%	1.26%	1.50%	<-- =−0.001 * −D11

Price @ 5.00% YTM	1,376.54	1,000.00	623.46	<-- =PRICE(D1,D2,D3,D4,D5,D6) * 10
Price @ 4.90% YTM	1,392.39	1,012.66	632.93	<-- =PRICE(D1,D2,D3,0.049,D5,D6) * 10
Change in price	15.85	12.66	9.47	<-- =D18 − D17
% change in price	1.15%	1.27%	1.52%	

duration is 7.99 years (modified duration 7.79 years) and with a 20-year maturity the dura-tion is 12.87 years (modified duration 12.55 years). For bond traders, knowing the sensitivi-ties of the bonds in their portfolios will allow them to protect the value of their bonds from expected changes in market interest rates.

Summary of the Principles and Precepts Applied in This Chapter

> **The First Fundamental Principle (FP1): The value of any asset is equal to the pre-sent value of the cash flows the asset is expected to produce over its economic life.**

The valuation model used in the chapter shows how a bond's cash flows (interest payments and the return of principal) are used as the basis of the bond's value.

> **The Third Fundamental Principle (FP3): There is an inverse relationship between price and yield; if an asset's price increases, its return will decrease (and vice versa), holding other things constant.**

This relationship is clearly shown in this chapter, as the bond's value moves inversely with the changes in market interest rates. This relationship is also implied through PR1:

> **The First Precept (PR1): The present value of a cash flow (or an asset) is inversely related to its discount rate; increasing the discount rate decreases the present value (and vice versa), holding other things constant.**

Bond prices rise because market interest rates fall. This is because the market interest rate is used as the discount rate for calculating the present value. If market interest rates suddenly fall, bonds that were previously seen as adequate are likely to suddenly appear more attrac-tive, since their coupon rates are higher than those for newly issued bonds of the same risk and maturity.

End of Chapter Problems

1. If the yield to maturity on a bond increases, what will happen to the bond's current yield?

    a. It will increase.
    b. It will decrease.
    c. It will remain the same.
    d. There is not sufficient information to answer this question.

2. If the yield to maturity on a bond increases, what will happen to the bond's capital gains yield?

    a. It will increase.
    b. It will decrease.
    c. It will remain the same.
    d. There is not sufficient information to answer this question.

3. Which of the following items is not a feature of a bond?

    a. Par value.
    b. Call premium.

    c.   Coupon rate.
    d.   Dividend yield.
    e.   Original maturity.

4. Which of the following items is not used in calculating the value of a bond?

    a.   Coupon payment.
    b.   Duration.
    c.   Yield to maturity.
    d.   Par value.
    e.   Years to maturity.

5. Suppose a 10-year, 6% coupon bond is issued, and one year later similar bonds are issued paying 5.85% coupons. What will happen to the market value of the first bond?

    a.   Since it is a 10-year bond, its maturity is not long enough for the value to change.
    b.   The first bond's value will fall slightly.
    c.   The first bond's value will fall very much.
    d.   The first bond's value will rise slightly.
    e.   The first bond's value will rise very much.

6. You are concerned about your bond portfolio because market interest rates are expected to fall. Which of these items is also expected to fall?

    a.   The bond's market price.
    b.   The bond's call premium.
    c.   The bond's time to maturity.
    d.   The bond's duration.
    e.   The bond's current yield.

7. You are torn between investing in a 20-year US Treasury bond or the new 20-year bond that Google just issued. Which of the two should pay the higher coupon rate?

8. On June 1, 2018, the US Treasury issued new 20-year, $1,000 par value bonds paying a 4.40% coupon semiannually. On June 1, 2019, similar T-bonds were paying 4.65% coupons. What was the market value of the 2018 bonds as of June 1, 2019?

    Use the following data to answer questions 9–13.

    You bought a newly issued 10-year, 5.50% coupon bond (with semiannual coupon payments) on May 1, 2018. You decided to check the value and yields on the bond annually, so that you can keep track of your wealth. Your first check was to be done on May 1, 2019. On April 15, 2019, the yield to maturity for the bond changed to 5.20%. Assume this new YTM remains the same throughout this set of problems.

9. For your one-year anniversary of owning the bond, calculate the market price, the current yield, the capital gains yield and the total yield for the bond for the past year. What has changed? To what do you attribute the change (specifically, not "the change in the YTM")?

10. For your two-year anniversary of owning the bond, calculate the market price, the current yield, the capital gains yield and the total yield for the bond for the past year. What has changed? To what do you attribute the change (specifically, not "the change in the YTM")?

11. For your three-year anniversary of owning the bond, calculate the market price, the current yield, the capital gains yield and the total yield for the bond for the past year. What has changed? To what do you attribute the change (specifically, not "the change in the YTM")?

12. For your four-year anniversary of owning the bond, calculate the market price, the current yield, the capital gains yield and the total yield for the bond for the past year. What has changed? To what do you attribute the change (specifically, not "the change in the YTM")?

13. For your five-year anniversary of owning the bond, calculate the market price, the current yield, the capital gains yield and the total yield for the bond for the past year. What has changed? To what do you attribute the change (specifically, not "the change in the YTM")?

14. You bought a 10-year, 6.20% semiannual coupon bond three years ago for its face value of $1,000. When you attempted to sell the bond today, you were told that the market price being offered today is $985.00. What is the current yield to maturity for this bond?

15. You are interested in purchasing a newly issued $1,000 par, 20-year, 4.80% semiannual coupon bond. While reading the indenture you see that the bond has five years of call protection, and that the call premium is one interest payment. What is the yield to call for this bond?

16. You are interested in purchasing a newly issued $1,000 par, 20-year, 4.80% semiannual coupon bond. Calculate the duration and the modified duration for the bond.

17. You are interested in purchasing a newly issued $1,000 par, 20-year, 4.80% semiannual coupon bond. You believe that the yield to maturity on the bond will increase to 4.90% during the first year that you own the bond. Use the duration and modified duration that you calculated in problem 16 to estimate the percent change in the price if your belief in the YTM proves accurate.

Bibliography

Fundamentals of Corporate Finance, 12th edition. S. Ross, R. Westerfield and B. Jordan. McGraw-Hill Education, 2019.

Financial Management: Principles & Practice, 8th edition. T. Gallagher. Textbook Media Press, 2019.

6   Stocks and Stock Valuation

There are two main types of stocks issued by corporations: common stock and preferred stock. Common stock represents ownership in the firm, and therefore some influence over the firm's strategic choices, but only to the degree to which you own shares. For example, owning 500,000 shares of Microsoft common stock may seem impressive, but in 2018 Microsoft had 7.68 billion shares outstanding. Those 500,000 shares represent a 0.0065% share of ownership—not enough to sway a vote. In addition, for some firms, ownership of common stock comes with quarterly cash dividends. For 2017, Apple shareholders received quarterly dividends, one of $0.57 per share, and three of $0.63 per share each. So, your 10,000 shares would have earned more than $5,700 in dividends for the year: the gift that keeps on giving.

Preferred stock is more of a hybrid security, in that it has features similar to both common stock and bonds. For example, preferred stock pays a dividend, but it is a fixed dividend, whereas common dividends are expected to grow (more about that later). Since it is fixed, the preferred dividend is more like an interest payment. In the case of bankruptcy, preferred shareholders are higher on the list than the common shareholders. Also, if the firm suspends both preferred and common dividends for a period of time, before they can pay any new common dividends, they must pay all of the preferred dividends that went unpaid during the period of dividend suspension.

In Chapter 4, we learned that the cost of debt is interest. There are two costs to stock: dividends and capital gains. So, the total yield on a stock is comprised of dividend yield and capital gains yield. Since stock returns are more volatile than interest rates, most stocks typically have required returns that are higher than the YTM on investment grade bonds. In this chapter, we learn the very basics of how to value a stock.

The Fundamental Principles in Action

FP1 states that an asset derives its value from the cash flows it will produce. For many stocks, the cash flows are the dividends paid to common shareholders. For stocks that do not pay dividends, the cash flow from assets (CFFA) valuation model will be discussed. FP3 indicates the inverse relationship between an asset's yield and its market value. This is clearly reflected in the mechanics of the dividend discount model used to value a stock. FP2 asserts that risk and return are directly related, and so riskier assets require higher returns. This applies to stocks as well, and it can be seen in PR1 (relating value inversely to the discount rate). Since the required return on the firm's stock is used as the discount rate in valuing the stock, stocks of higher risk will pay a higher discount rate, which will reduce the market value of the stocks.

The Basics of Stocks

As mentioned above, common stock represents ownership in the firm as well as a claim to the common dividends paid by the firm. Preferred shareholders do not have ownership claims, but they do have claims to the preferred dividends paid by the firm, and in the case of bankruptcy they get in line ahead of the common shareholders for claims against the firm's assets. So common shareholders purchase stocks in order to obtain dividends and/or to obtain capital gains (i.e., see the stock price rise over time), while preferred shareholders purchase stocks for the security of the income (the preferred dividend is more reliable than the common dividend) and to protect their investment (by being ahead of the common share-holders in the bankruptcy line). The difference between common and preferred shareholders is the risk–return tradeoff; common shareholders want growth, both in the share price and in the annual dividend, while preferred shareholders want mainly to protect their investment. Common shareholders know that growth stocks are risky because there are a number of things, both inside and outside of the firm's influence, that can affect the firm's profitability (and therefore the stock's return). The common shareholders are less risk averse and are willing to take on the risks associated with the stock's returns in the belief that the long-run returns will be high enough to justify the risks. The preferred shareholders are (relatively) more risk averse and are willing to accept lower returns on their investment in order to avoid the risks associated with the common equity market.

There is no maturity date for a stock. Without any prior knowledge, the only reasonable expectation for the life of the firm is eternity. Theoretically, this is possible; since ownership can be transferred by simply selling the shares, the firm has the potential to be in business forever. As we must make some assumptions in order to estimate the value of the stock, the assumption of eternal life is as good as any.

The major cash flows produced by stocks are the dividends. That is why the main model used to value common stocks, the dividend discount model (DDM), uses dividends as the basis of value. For firms that do not pay dividends, we will discuss the cash flow from assets model later in the chapter. The DDM is flexible enough to be useful under three different scenarios with regard to the expectation of future dividend growth:

- Zero growth—the dividend does not change over time;
- Constant growth—the dividend grows at a (relatively) constant rate for the foreseeable future; and
- Non-constant growth—the dividends grow at one or more distinctly different rates for a period of time, after which dividend growth is expected to be constant.

Each of these scenarios is sound and reasonable. The zero-growth scenario is the preferred dividend valuation model, as preferred dividends are fixed. The constant growth scenario is the normal or expected scenario: not that the dividend will grow at exactly the same rate forever, but that it will grow at roughly the same rate over the long term. The non-constant growth scenario will work during periods of dynamic change, like when a firm introduces a new product that makes the competition's products obsolete, or when a firm is struggling to overcome the loss of a lawsuit.

When valuing bonds, we used the yield to maturity (YTM) as the discount rate, as this is the required return to the firm's bondholders. When calculating the present value of divi-dends, we will use the cost of common equity (r_e) as the discount rate. As will be discussed in Chapter 8, "Capital Structure and the WACC," the cost of common equity is the percentage return the firm is required to pay its common shareholders.

The Dividend Discount Model

The dividend discount model requires the last dividend paid (D_0), the expected future dividend growth rate (g) and the required return on the firm's common equity (r_e) in order to estimate the firm's intrinsic common stock price. It is an intrinsic price because it is assumed that all relevant information about the firm and its stock are known. That assumption includes any relevant non-public information, good or bad. For example, if the firm were about to release a new product that will make its competitors' products obsolete, that information would have a positive impact on both the expected future growth rate of dividends and the required rate of return on the firm's equity. Likewise, if the firm were guilty of some form of malfeasance, that would have a negative impact on the expected growth rate of dividends and the required return on equity. This was the situation for Enron in 2001, when their common stock went from being in high demand to being virtually worthless in less than a year. Their stock price in early 2001 was not an intrinsic price, as the market was unaware of their illegal and unethical accounting practices.

The DDM is also known as the Gordon model, since the paper in which it was published won Myron Gordon the Nobel Prize in Economics.[1] The DDM values a firm's common stock as the present value of all expected future dividends (in line with FP1):

$$P_0 = \frac{D_1}{1+r_e} + \frac{D_2}{\left(1+r_e\right)^2} + \frac{D_3}{\left(1+r_e\right)^3} + \ldots + \frac{D_\infty}{\left(1+r_e\right)^\infty} = \frac{D_1}{r_e - g} = \frac{D_0\left(1+g\right)}{r_e - g}$$

where: D_0 is the most recent annual common dividend already paid (time period zero is the present);

g is the expected annual percentage growth rate in dividends for the foreseeable future; and

r_e is the required annual percentage return on the firm's common equity, and $r_e > g$.

The dividends indicated in the model are annual dividends, or the sum of all four quarterly dividends in a given year. Note that, when moving to the right from the equals sign, each successive term is simply the prior term multiplied by $\frac{1+g}{1+r_e}$. So, the numerator is increasing at the dividend growth rate, and the denominator is increasing at the required rate of return on the firm's common equity. Since $r_e > g$, this means the denominator is growing faster than the numerator. This in turn means that, as both r_e and g get larger, the successive terms on the right side of the model get smaller. Since both r_e and g go to infinity, at some point in the future, the terms to the right of the equals sign go to zero. This means that at some point in the future, the present value of the future dividends goes to zero.

The model has several assumptions, all of which invite questions, but which in no way detract from the power of the model:

* g, the expected growth rate in the firm's dividends, is assumed to be constant over time (not absolutely constant but reasonably constant);
* r_e, the required cost of equity, is also assumed to be constant over time; and
* $r_e > g$.

Note that since g is constant, $D_1 = D_0(1 + g)$, and $D_2 = D_0(1 + g)^2$, and so on. The first two assumptions listed above are simplifying assumptions that make the math easier—they are not held to be absolutely true, but in order to be able to calculate a value, such assumptions are necessary. The third assumption is important, but again for mathematical reasons. If

$r_e = g$, then the fraction will be undefined. Also, if $r_e < g$, then the model will give a negative stock price, which is nonsensical.

Preferred Stock Valuation

This is the scenario with zero growth. As indicated earlier, the preferred dividend is fixed. Therefore, to use the DDM to value preferred stock, we rework the model assuming $g = 0$. This requires two changes to the model:

- Since $g = 0$, $D_1 = D_2 = D_3$, so the preferred dividend is simply referred to as D_p;
- The denominator reduces to r_p, the cost of preferred equity.

Making these changes results in the following version of the model:

$$P_p = \frac{D_p}{r_p}$$

where: P_p is the market price of the preferred stock;
D_p is the preferred dividend (which is fixed); and
r_p is the required return on the firm's preferred stock.

Note the strong resemblance to the model given for the PV of a perpetuity in Chapter 2. Since no growth is expected, the model is simplified.

Example. Nussbaum Manufacturing's annual preferred dividend is $8.00. Your assessment of the stock's risk convinces you that you would require a 12.5% return in order to purchase the stock. How much should you be willing to pay for Nussbaum's preferred equity?

Solution. $8 \div .125 = 64$. You should be willing to pay up to $64.00 for Nussbaum's preferred equity.

Example. Farquar Industries' preferred stock is currently selling for $150. If their annual preferred dividend is $12.00, what is the required return on Farquar's preferred stock?

Solution. $150 = 12 \div r_p$; $r = 12 / 150 = .08$. The required return is 8.00%.

Common Stock Valuation With Dividends—Constant Growth

Under normal competitive conditions, all firms realize a time at which the number of good investment opportunities levels off, and sales growth, as well as growth in the stock price, also levels off. From time to time the firm may have an exceptional episode, such as when it introduces a new product, which may offer temporary increases in the sales growth rate. During those times, value can be determined using the non-constant growth approach, discussed later in this chapter. Beyond those times, the firm will likely grow its sales, its stock price and its dividend at a relatively constant rate.

This is the DDM scenario with constant growth, which uses the model in its original form. The model requires the next future annual dividend, which it estimates using the most recent past annual dividend and the expected future growth rate for the dividend. Thus, if the firm recently paid an annual dividend (D_0) of $0.80 per share, and the dividend is expected to grow at a rate of 5.0% per year (g), then $D_1 = 0.80(1.05) = 0.84. When attempting to solve DDM-based problems, make sure of which dividend you are given. If it is D_1, you may plug it into the model as is. If it is D_0, you must grow it by one year to transform it into D_1.

Example. Milford Consolidated just paid an annual dividend of $1.20, and the dividend is expected to grow at a rate of 5.0% per year for the foreseeable future. If the required return on Milford's common stock is 9.0%, what is the intrinsic value of their shares?

$$\text{Solution. } P_0 = \frac{1.20(1.05)}{.09-.05} = \$31.50.$$

Example. Wyatt Systems Inc.'s common stock currently sells for $22.00 per share. Their most recent annual dividend was $1.10, and it is expected to increase by 10.0% per year. What is the required return on Wyatt's common stock?

$$\text{Solution. } P_0 = 22 = \frac{1.10(1.10)}{r_e-.10}; \ 22(r_e-.10)=1.21; \ r_e-.10 = \frac{1.21}{22} = .055;$$
$$r_e = .055+.10 = .155 \ or \ 15.5\%$$

Example. Garland Metals expects their annual common dividend to grow at a rate of 5.0% per year, and the required return on their common stock is 8.0%. If their common stock is currently selling for $21.00 per share, what was Garland's last dividend (D_0)?

$$\text{Solution. } P_0 = 21 = \frac{D_0(1.05)}{.08-.05}; \ 21(.08-.05)=.63 = D_0(1.05); \ D_0 = \frac{.63}{1.05} = \$0.60$$

Common Stock Valuation With Dividends—Non-Constant Growth

This is the scenario with non-constant growth. Periods of expected non-constant growth are not common, but neither are they rare. For example, when a firm introduces a product that is new to the market (i.e., there are no competitive products), the firm can charge whatever they think the market will bear for the new product. During this period, the firm earns abnormal profits, which attracts other firms to the product. It will take the other firms a little while, but eventually they will be in a position to produce a similar product, and they will sell it for a lower price than the original in order to gain market share. As time passes, more competitors will introduce their own similar products, each one driving the price lower. Eventually the higher-cost producers will be unable to compete on price, and the market for the product will stabilize, leaving a reasonable number of competitors, each earning normal profits. At that point, normal growth is expected for all competitors moving forward, unless and until another new product is developed.

In this scenario, the firm's analysts will estimate the expected growth in revenue associated with the new product. They will estimate not only the rate of growth but also the period of time during which non-constant growth is expected. So, for the scenario above, the firm's analysts may estimate that it will take two full years for the first competitor to introduce their product, with additional new competitors' products arriving every six months for the following three years, after which the market would be expected to stabilize. Once this is determined, the analysts would estimate the increase in sales revenue for each year before the market is expected to stabilize. Suppose they determine that for the first two years revenue will increase by 20%, then revenue growth will fall to 15% in year 3, 12% in year four and 9% in year five, after which revenue is expected to grow at the normal (constant) rate of 6%.

With revenue growth rates determined, it becomes a simple matter to estimate the intrinsic common stock price at the beginning of the product's introduction.

The method simply follows FP1; we assume that the common dividend will grow at the non-constant rates of revenue growth during the non-constant growth period. Once the firm returns to constant growth, the DDM can be used to calculate the value of the remaining constant growth dividends. Then we simply discount the non-constant growth dividends, as well as the DDM value calculated after the non-constant growth period, and then sum those present values to obtain the intrinsic price. So, the steps to be used are as follows:

1. Draw a time line that extends for one year longer than the expected non-constant growth period (you will need one constant growth dividend for the DDM);
2. Populate the time line with dividends by growing the last dividend (D_0) at the non-constant growth rates for the entire non-constant growth period (however many years non-constant growth is expected);
3. At the end of the non-constant growth period, use the first constant growth dividend in the DDM to value the remaining future dividends. Note that the value the DDM gives belongs in the time period prior to the first constant growth dividend (the DDM uses D_1 to determine P_0, therefore if the first constant growth dividend is D_5, the value the DDM gives will be P_4);
4. Discount the non-constant dividends as well as the DDM value to period zero (the present) using the firm's required cost of common equity to determine the present value of the future dividends; and
5. Sum the present values of all the dividends to obtain the intrinsic value of the stock.

For example, let's suppose that a firm introduces a new product today, and that the product is expected to grow the firm's revenues as indicated above (20% in years 1 and 2, 15% in year 3, 12% in year 4, 9% in year 5, and 6% from year 6 on). Let's also assume that the firm's last dividend (D_0) was $1.00, and that their required cost of common equity (r_e) is 11%. Using the growth rates given, and rounding the dividends to no more than four decimal places, the cash flows for the time line are as follows:

- $D_1 = \$1.00 \times 1.2 = \$1.20;$
- $D_2 = \$1.20 \times 1.2 = \$1.44;$
- $D_3 = \$1.44 \times 1.15 = \$1.656;$
- $D_4 = \$1.656 \times 1.12 = \$1.8547;$
- $D_5 = \$1.8547 \times 1.09 = \$2.0216;$
- $D_6 = \$2.0216 \times 1.06 = \$2.1429.$

The firm's analysts are expecting five years of decreasing non-constant growth, followed by constant growth beginning in year 6. Therefore, our time line is six years long, to include all five years of non-constant growth as well as the first year of constant growth. Next we use the first constant growth dividend in the DDM to value all remaining future dividends. Since the first constant dividend is D_6, the DDM will give us P_5:

$$P_5 = \frac{D_6}{r_e - g} = \frac{2.1429}{.11 - .06} = \$42.8589$$

Notice that for the DDM we used the constant growth rate, because at that point in time the dividend is expected to grow at the normal constant rate.

Our next step in the process is to discount the cash flows back to period zero at the firm's cost of common equity (again, rounding to at most four decimal places):

- $PV(D_1) = 1.20 \times 1.11^{-1} = \$1.0811$;
- $PV(D_2) = 1.44 \times 1.11^{-2} = \$1.1687$;
- $PV(D_3) = 1.656 \times 1.11^{-3} = \$1.2109$;
- $PV(D_4) = 1.8547 \times 1.11^{-4} = \$1.2217$;
- $PV(D_5) = 2.0216 \times 1.11^{-5} = \$1.1997$;
- $PV(P_5) = 42.8589 \times 1.11^{-5} = \$25.4347$.

Now these present values are summed to arrive at the intrinsic value of the stock:

$$P_0 = 1.0811 + 1.1687 + 1.2109 + 1.2217 + 1.1997 + 25.4347 = 31.3168 = \$31.32$$

Figure 6.1 shows the time line for the problem as well as the discounting of the cash flows and the summing of the present values to arrive at the solution. D_6 is crossed out on the time line because it was used to calculate P_5, and so it should not be discounted or summed since it is already included in P_5. In the figure the cash flows in year 5 were summed before discounting. This does not change the valuation in any way.

The method described here is perfectly in line with FP1: we determine the cash flows expected over the life of the stock, discount them to the present and then sum their present values. This method merely permits us some flexibility with the expected growth rates during the non-constant growth period.

Example. Putnam Electronics is introducing a new laser measuring device that is accurate at measuring areas to within a square inch. Since the device has no current competition, the firm expects sales revenues to increase by 24% in the first year. They expect at least one competitor in year 2, so they expect revenue growth in year 2 of only 18%. More competition is expected in year 3, reducing the revenue growth to 14% for that year. In year 4, they expect revenue growth to return to its normal 9% annual rate and remain there from that point forward. Their most recent dividend was $1.50, and their required return on equity is 13.50%. Considering the introduction of the new product, what is the intrinsic price of their stock?

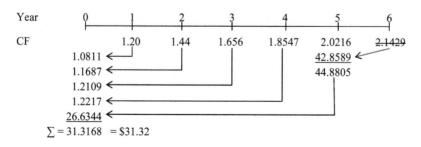

Figure 6.1 Calculating the Intrinsic Value of a Non-Constant Growth Stock

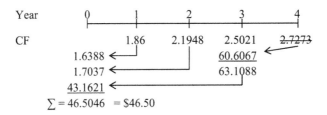

Figure 6.2 Solving a Non-Constant Growth Stock Problem

Solution. Putnam's analysts are expecting three years of non-constant growth, followed by normal growth starting in year 4. Thus, the time line should be four years long, and should contain the following cash flows:

- $D_1 = \$1.50 \times 1.24 = \$1.86$;
- $D_2 = \$1.86 \times 1.18 = \$2.1948$;
- $D_3 = \$2.1948 \times 1.14 = \$2.5021$;
- $D_4 = \$2.5021 \times 1.09 = \$2.7273$.

Next, we use D_4 in the DDM in order to calculate P_3:

$$P_3 = \frac{2.7273}{.135 - .09} = \$60.6067$$

Now we must discount dividends 1–3 and P_3 back to the present:

- $PV(D_1) = \$1.86 \times 1.135^{-1} = \$1.6388$;
- $PV(D_2) = \$2.1948 \times 1.135^{-2} = \$1.7037$;
- $PV(D_3) = \$2.5021 \times 1.135^{-3} = \$1.7113$;
- $PV(P_3) = \$60.6067 \times 1.135^{-3} = \$41.4508$.

And, finally, we sum the present values to obtain the intrinsic value of the stock:

$$P_0 = 1.6388 + 1.7037 + 1.7113 + 41.4508 = 46.5046 = \$46.50$$

Figure 6.2 shows the time line for the problem with the cash flows, as well as the discounting of the cash flows and the summing of the discounted cash flows. While somewhat complex, the method is rather straightforward, and it follows FP1 to the letter.

Common Stock Valuation Without Dividends—The Cash Flow From Assets Model

For stocks that do not pay dividends, the cash flow from assets (CFFA) model provides a method for valuation that is similar in construction to the non-constant growth method, but for which the cash flows used are the firm's cash flow from assets (also known as free cash flow). Cash flow from assets is defined as operating cash flow less the amounts needed to invest in operating assets:

CFFA = Operating cash flow − Net capital spending − Changes in
Net Working Capital

It is the cash that is available to be distributed to the firm's investors—its bondholders and share-holders—after investment is made to support operations. This is reflected in the CFFA identity:

CFFA = Cash Flow to Creditors + Cash Flow to Stockholders

This identity provides a check for the work done to calculate CFFA, as will be seen.

The CFFA model values the firm using the Gordon model, substituting the firm's cash flow from assets for dividends and the firm's weighted average cost of capital (WACC) as the discount rate. The process is simple in conception, but can be complex in implementation:

-
$$V_{Operations(t)} = \frac{CFFA_{t+1}}{WACC - g_{CFFA}} = \frac{CFFA_t\left(1 + g_{CFFA}\right)}{WACC - g_{CFFA}}$$

This adapted Gordon model calculateds the value of the firm's operations, based on the cash flows from operations;

- Adding the value of non-operating assets determines the value of the firm (non-operating assets typically include marketable securities and any non-operating long-term assets);
- Subtracting the value of debt and preferred stock from the value of the firm gives the value of the firm's common equity; and
- Dividing the value of common equity by the number of shares outstanding offers an estimate of the firm's intrinsic common stock price.

That is the method in a nutshell; there are many details involved in the process.

Understanding Operating Accounts

The model above calculates the value of operations. The metric is identified in this way because it is based on cash flow from assets, and cash flow from assets is calculated from operating cash flows. To more fully understand cash flow from assets and the FCF valuation model, it is essential to understand the concept of operating accounts.

Operating accounts are accounts on the income statement and the balance sheet that are directly impacted by changes in the amount of sales revenue. These accounts are known to change along with sales revenue, and these relationships will be used as the basis for fore-casting financial statements in Chapter 9, "Analyzing and Forecasting Financial Statements." For now, we simply need to be able to identify the operating accounts.

There are two operating accounts in the income statement:

- Cost of goods sold (COGS);
- Operating expenses (also known as sales, general and administrative expenses; or SG&A).

The COGS account is the accounting value of the items sold during the period covered by the financial statement. By definition, this account should vary directly with sales. The SG&A account includes such things as salaries, commissions and wages. As sales increase, we would expect sales commissions to increase, and possibly for higher wages due to overtime or adding workers or an additional shift to production. It also includes expenses for maintenance of the firm and its machinery, which would also increase when production ramps up to fill the increase in sales.

For this chapter, we will be dealing with the operating accounts in the balance sheet, of which there are six:

- Cash (or cash and cash equivalents)—a current asset account;
- Accounts receivable—a current asset account;
- Inventory—a current asset account;
- Fixed assets net of depreciation—a long-term asset account;
- Accounts payable—a current liability account;
- Accrued expenses (or accruals)—a current liability account.

Some firms also use a prepaid expenses account (as a current asset account) to prepay ongoing operating expenses, in which case the prepaid expenses account should also be considered an operating account.

Firms hold cash "just in case"—if a truck or a machine breaks down, or if a supplier offers a great deal on an item for buying a large quantity. Many firms recognize the relationship between cash and sales by holding cash as a percentage of sales (2% of sales is a common policy). Any cash beyond that required by the level of sales is then invested in money market instruments such as commercial paper or Treasury bills, which are recognized in an account titled marketable securities (or something similar). Marketable securities is not an operating account, but cash is. Accounts receivable is the amount of sales owed by customers using store credit accounts (rather than paying with cash or a credit card). Assuming the firm's credit policy is not changed, an increase in sales would be expected to lead to an increase in accounts receivable. Inventory has a similar relationship with sales, since inventory consists of items produced (or in production) to fulfill sales orders.

The final operating asset account on the balance sheet is fixed assets net of depreciation, or net property, plant and equipment. Fixed assets are the machines used to produce the product or service, so there should be some relationship between the quantity of fixed assets on hand and the amount of sales orders that can be filled on a timely basis. It is not a direct relationship, as it is with cash or accounts receivable, since fixed assets have issues related to capacity (how many units can be produced in a given period of time). However, any increases in fixed assets are recognized as an investment in operations.

Calculating Cash Flow From Assets

Calculating a firm's cash flow from assets for a given year is a four-step process that requires two years of financial statement data for the firm in question:

1. Calculate OCF (operating cash flow) for the given years.

   a. OCF = EBIT + Depreciation – Taxes

2. Calculate NCS (net capital spending) for the given years.

   a. NCS = Net Fixed Assets (given year) − Net Fixed Assets (prior year) + Depreciation

3. Calculate CNWC (changes in net working capital) for the given years.

    a. CNWC = NWC (given year) − NWC (prior year)

4. CFFA = OCF − NCS − CNWC

Since two years of data are required for the metric, with five years' worth of financial statements you can calculate four years' worth of cash flow from assets.

Using the Cash Flow From Assets Model to Value a Firm's Common Equity

Table 6.1 contains five years of income statements and balance sheets for Exemplar Manufacturing, a medium-sized firm that manufactures capital equipment. These financial statements are to be used to estimate Exemplar's common stock price using the cash flow from assets model. Note that all figures in the financial statements are in millions of dollars.

For this example, you are a financial analyst working for a mutual fund brokerage house. Exemplar has issued new debt and common equity in each year from 2014 to 2018, and they are preparing to issue new securities again in 2019. Your supervisor has asked you to determine if Exemplar's new common stock should be added to one or more of the firm's mutual funds. Your initial research on the firm uncovered the following facts which will be useful in the analysis:

- Exemplar's common stock currently sells for $10.44 per share;
- The firm's weighted average cost of capital (WACC) is 12.75%; and
- The firm currently has 300 million common shares outstanding.

You must start this analysis by calculating OCF, NCS, NCWC and the firm's CFFA for 2015–2018.

OCF starts with EBIT (earnings before interest and taxes), also known as operating income, which is on the income statement. For 2015, this figure is $972 million. In 2015, the firm had $6 million in depreciation and they paid $184 million in taxes, both of which are also on the income statement. Therefore, for 2015, Exemplar's OCF is 972 − 6 − 184 = $794 million. Using this same approach, OCF for 2016–2018 is $841 million, $1.04 billion and $1.113 billion respectively.

Net capital spending (NCS) is calculated as ending net fixed assets (NFA) minus beginning net fixed assets plus depreciation. NFA is found on the balance sheet, and depreciation is on the income statement. For 2015, ending NFA is $2.393 billion, beginning NFA is $2.302 billion and depreciation is $6 million. So, for 2015, NCS = 2.393 − 2,302 + 6 = $97 million. NCS for 2016–2018 is $555 million, $701 million and $750 million respectively.

Change in net working capital (CNWC) is calculated as ending NWC minus beginning NWC. Net working capital (NWC) is defined as current assets minus current liabilities. For 2015, Exemplar had $2.049 billion in current assets and $544 million in current liabilities, so NWC for 2015 is 2,049 − 544 = $1.505 billion. For 2014, NWC was 1,557 − 599 = $958 million. So, for 2015, CNWC is 1,505 − 958 = $547 million. CNWC for 2016–2018 is $92 million, $128 million and $120 million respectively.

Finally, to calculate CFFA, you subtract NCS and NCWC from OCF. So, for 2015, CFFA = 794 − 97 − 547 = $150 million. CFFA for 2016–2018 is $194 million, $211 million and $243 million respectively.

Table 6.1 Financial Statements for Exemplar Manufacturing, Inc. 2014–2018

Balance Sheet ($Millions)

	2014	2015	2016	2017	2018
Cash	25	42	45	52	55
Marketable Securities	121	267	283	302	324
Accounts Receivable	637	963	1,021	1,103	1,180
Inventory	774	777	824	890	952
Total Current Assets	1,557	2,049	2,173	2,347	2,511
Net Fixed Assets	2,302	2,393	2,944	3,640	4,386
Total Assets	3,859	4,442	5,117	5,987	6,897
Accounts Payable	325	372	394	426	456
Notes Payable	100	50	53	57	61
Accrued Expenses	174	122	129	139	149
Total Current Liabilities	599	544	576	622	666
Long-Term Debt	571	636	674	728	779
Total Liabilities	1,170	1,180	1,250	1,350	1,445
Common Stock	840	896	950	1,026	1,098
Retained Earnings	1,849	2,366	2,917	3,611	4,354
Total Common Equity	2,689	3,262	3,867	4,637	5,452
Total Liabilities and Equity	3,859	4,442	5,117	5,987	6,897

Income Statement ($Millions)

	2014	2015	2016	2017	2018
Net Sales	1,268	2,113	2,240	2,585	2,766
Cost of Goods Sold	630	1,050	1,113	1,202	1,286
Gross Income	638	1,063	1,127	1,383	1,480
Operating Expenses	50	85	90	97	104
Depreciation	5	6	4	5	4
Operating Income (EBIT)	583	972	1,033	1,281	1,372
Interest	59	98	102	110	118
Earnings Before Taxes	524	874	931	1,171	1,254
Taxes (21%)	110	184	196	246	263
Net Income	414	690	735	925	991
Dividends	104	173	184	231	248
Addition to Retained Earnings	310	517	551	694	743
EOY Price of Common Stock	33.42	38.16	44.21	49.39	55.36
# Shares Outstanding (millions)	100	107	113	122	130

The CFFA identity was given earlier in the chapter as a way to check your work on calculating cash flow from assets. Once again, the identity is as follows:

CFFA = Cash Flow to Creditors + Cash Flow to Stockholders

Cash flow to creditors is defined as interest paid minus net new borrowing. For this calculation, we define net new borrowing as the change in long-term debt. For 2015, interest paid was $98 million, while net new borrowing is the difference between long-term debt for 2015 ($636 million) and 2014 ($571 million), or $65 million. Thus, for 2015, cash flow to creditors is 98 − 65 = $33 million. Cash flow to creditors for 2016–2018 is $64 million, $56 million and $67 million respectively.

Cash flow to stockholders is defined as dividends paid minus net new equity raised. Net new equity raised is simply the ending amount of common stock minus the beginning amount of common stock (not including retained earnings). For 2015, dividends paid were $173 million. Common stock was $896 million in 2015 and $840 million in 2014, indicating that the firm increased common stock by 896 − 840 = $56 million in 2015. So, for 2015, cash flow to stockholders is 173 − 56 = $117 million. Cash flow to stockholders for 2016–2018 is $130 million, $155 million and $176 million respectively.

Given the figures derived above, CFFA for 2015 is calculated as 33 + 117 = $150 million, which matches the figure we calculated using operating cash flows. Likewise, the CFFA figures for 2016–2018 using the CFFA identity are $194 million, $211 million and $243 million respectively.

At this point, you can determine the growth rates for cash flow from assets over each of the past three years, and use these as a basis for g_{CFFA} in the model. The growth rate is calculated as the most recent value divided by the prior value, minus one. Therefore g_{2016} = (194 ÷ 150) − 1 = 0.2933, or 29.33%; g_{2017} = (211 ÷ 194) − 1 = 0.0876, or 8.76%; and g_{2018} = (243 ÷ 211) − 1 = 0.1517, or 15.17%. These numbers are all positive but inconsistent, indicating that Exemplar's cash flow from assets has been growing, but not at a steady rate, over the past few years. This creates conflict for the analysis.

If the growth in CFFA were reasonably steady, we could use the average growth rate over the period for the model. The average growth rate for CFFA 2016–2018 is 17.75%, which will not work due to an assumption of the CFFA model, which is that the growth rate in CFFA must be less than the discount rate (WACC) of 12.75%. Only one of the three years had a growth rate in CFFA that was less than 12.75% (2015 = 8.76%). Since you must make the g_{CFFA} < WACC, you can use the 8.76% growth rate for 2015, or a figure close to that. To be conservative in your growth estimate, you decide to round it down to 8.00%.

You now have everything you need to calculate the firm's intrinsic stock value using the CFFA model. Recall from the previous description of the process that non-operating assets include marketable securities and other long-term assets, as this will be needed for the second step of the process. Note that all calculations use the most recent year's data. Following the steps listed earlier in the chapter:

- Calculate the value of operations:

$$V_{operations(2018)} = \frac{CFFA_t \left(1 + g_{CFFA}\right)}{WACC - g_{CFFA}} = \frac{\$243(1.08)}{.1275 - .08} = \$5,525.05 \; million;$$

- Calculate the value of the firm: V_{firm} = $V_{operations}$ + Marketable Securities = 5,525.05 + 324 = $5,849.05 million;
- Subtract the values of debt and preferred equity to obtain the value of common equity (since Exemplar doesn't use preferred equity, we only need to subtract the debt accounts from the balance sheet): V_{equity} = V_{firm} − (Notes Payable + Long Term Debt) = 5,849.05— (61 + 779) = $5,009.05 million;
- Divide the value of common equity by the number of shares outstanding to obtain an estimate of the intrinsic common stock price: 5,009.05 ÷ 300 = 16.69684 or $16.70.

Table 6.2 Cash Flow From Assets Model Inputs and Calculations

Model Inputs		
$CFFA_{2018}$	243.00	
g_{CFFA}	8.00%	
WACC	12.75%	
$V_{MktblSec}$	324	
V_{Debt}	840	<-- = 61 + 779
# shares	300	

Model Calculations		
$V_{operations}$	5,525.05	<-- = (B2 * (1 + B3)) / (B4 − B3)
V_{firm}	5,849.05	<-- = B10 + B5
V_{equity}	5,009.05	<-- = B11 − B6
Intrinsic P_0	16.70	<-- = ROUND(B12 / B7,2)

So, by using an 8% growth rate assumption for Exemplar's cash flow from assets, you estimate the firm's common shares are worth more than $16. Given that Exemplar's common stock currently sells for $10.44, your analysis indicates that the stock price is likely to increase sharply in the near future ($16.70 represents a 60% increase over the current stock price). If you are confident in your analysis, you should recommend to your supervisor that Exemplar stock be included in one or more of the firm's mutual funds. See Table 6.2 for the inputs and the calculations for the CFFA valuation model.

Summary of the Principles and Precepts Applied in This Chapter

The First Fundamental Principle (FP1): The value of any asset is equal to the present value of the cash flows the asset is expected to produce over its economic life.

The valuation model used in the chapter shows how a stock's cash flows (dividends or cash flow from assets) are used as the basis of the stock's value.

The Third Fundamental Principle (FP3): There is an inverse relationship between price and yield; if an asset's price increases, its return will decrease (and vice versa), holding other things constant.

This relationship can be seen when looking at the structure of the DDM:

$$P_0 = \frac{D_1}{r_e - g}$$

If the required return to equity (r_e) increases, the denominator of the model will increase. This will cause the value of the fraction to decrease, and therefore the stock price to fall. For example, if $D_1 = \$2.00$, $g = .05$ and $r_e = .09$, then $P_0 = 2 \div (.09 - .05) = \$50$. However, if the required return is increased to 10%, holding everything else constant, then $P_0 = 2 \div (.1 - .05) = \$40$.

The Second Fundamental Principle (FP2): There is a direct relationship between risk and return; as perceived risk increases, required return will also increase (and vice versa), holding other things constant.

A risk-averse investor will require a higher return for a stock than an average investor. FP3 indicates that the risk-averse investor will only purchase the stock at lower prices than the average investor, which will increase the return earned by the risk-averse investor.

> **The First Precept (PR1): The present value of a cash flow (or an asset) is inversely related to its discount rate; increasing the discount rate decreases the present value (and vice versa), holding other things constant.**

Since the required return on equity is used as the discount rate, increasing the required return will decrease the present value of the stock's dividends, and therefore its intrinsic value.

End of Chapter Problems

1. Based on the DDM, if the required return on a stock increases, what will happen to the stock's price?

    a. It will increase.
    b. It will decrease.
    c. It will remain the same.
    d. There is not sufficient information to answer this question.

2. Based on the DDM, if the dividend growth rate increases, what will happen to the stock's price?

    a. It will increase.
    b. It will decrease.
    c. It will remain the same.
    d. There is not sufficient information to answer this question.

3. Which of the following items is not a characteristic of a common stock?

    a. It represents ownership in the firm.
    b. It offers the chance for the firm to remain in business forever.
    c. It gives the owner priority if the firm files for bankruptcy.
    d. It represents a claim against future common dividends.
    e. Its market value is constantly changing.

4. Which of the following items is not used in calculating the value of a stock?

    a. Cost of common equity.
    b. Interest rate.
    c. Dividend.
    d. Dividend growth rate.
    e. Cash flow from assets.

5. Under which of the following circumstances can you not use the DDM to value a stock?

    a. When interest rates are higher than stock returns.
    b. When the dividend is not expected to grow.
    c. During an economic contraction.
    d. When the dividend growth rate is higher than the required return to the stock.
    e. When the firm is expected to file for bankruptcy.

6. Which of the following items is a characteristic of preferred stock?

   a. It represents ownership in the firm.
   b. Preferred stock owners are taxed at a lower rate.
   c. It can be used to purchase the firm's bonds.
   d. It represents a claim against future common dividends.
   e. It gives the owner priority if the firm files for bankruptcy.

7. Garner Electronics pays a preferred dividend of $7.50. If the required return on Garner's preferred stock is 6.00%, what is the price of Garner's preferred stock?

8. Edwards International's preferred stock sells for $70 per share. If the required return on Edwards' preferred stock is 7.50%, how much is Edwards' preferred dividend?

9. Burkhead Sales just paid an annual dividend of $0.70, and the dividend is expected to grow at a constant rate of 7.00% in the future. If the required return on Burkhead's stock is 10.50%, what is the intrinsic price of the shares?

10. Anthony Inc.'s common stock is currently selling for $20.00 per share. Their most recent annual dividend was $0.60, and the dividend is expected to grow at the rate of 10% annually in the future. What is the required return on Anthony's common equity?

11. Fester Industries' common stock is currently selling for $30.00 per share. Next year's dividend (D_1) is expected to be $1.26. If the required return on Fester's common stock is 9.20%, what was the most recent dividend that Fester paid (D_0)?

12. Gerard Consolidated's last annual dividend was $1.40. The dividend is expected to grow by 20% this year, 16% next year, 12% the year after next and 8% from the following year forward. If the required return on Gerard's common stock is 13.50%, what is the intrinsic value of Gerard's common stock?

13. Allyson Enterprises just lost a big lawsuit. Their most recent dividend was $0.88, and that dividend is expected to grow by 2% in year 1, 4% in year 2, 5% in year 3 and 6% in year 4 and beyond. If the required return on Allyson's common stock is 10.50%, what is the intrinsic value of the stock?

14. One year ago today, you bought 600 shares of Mullen Manufacturing's common stock for $42.50 per share. During the past year you received two quarterly dividends of $0.35 each and two quarterly dividends of $0.38 each. Today the stock's market price is $44.20. Calculate the dividend yield, capital gains yield and total yield on the stock for the past year.

    Use the following data to answer questions 15–19.

    Gaspar International does not pay a common dividend. Gaspar's CFFA for 2015 was $20.0 million, for 2016 it was $21.0 million, for 2017 it was $22.05 million and for 2018 it was $23.1525 million. Gaspar's WACC is known to be 9.50%. Gaspar's balance sheet includes $26.4 million in marketable securities and $130.0 million in non-operating long-term assets. The firm currently carries $44.0 million in short-term debt, $160.0 million in long-term debt and $22.0 million in preferred equity. There are currently 10 million shares of Gaspar's common stock outstanding.

15. Use the CFFA data above to estimate the growth rate for Gaspar's cash flow from assets.

16. Use the data above and the g_{CFFA} you estimated to calculate the value of Gaspar's operations as of the end of 2018.

17. Use the data above and your calculations from questions 15 and 16 to estimate the value of the firm as of the end of 2018.

18. Use the data above and your calculations from questions 15, 16 and 17 to estimate the value of the firm's common equity as of the end of 2018.

19. Use the data above and your calculations from questions 15 through 18 to estimate the intrinsic value per share of the firm's common stock as of the end of 2018.

Note

1 Myron J. Gordon, "Dividends, Earnings, and Stock Prices," *The Review of Economics and Statistics*, 1959.

Bibliography

Fundamentals of Corporate Finance, 12th edition. S. Ross, R. Westerfield and B. Jordan. McGraw-Hill Education, 2019.
Financial Management: Principles & Practice, 8th edition. T. Gallagher. Textbook Media Press, 2019.

7 Capital Budgeting Decision Methods

Capital, in a business sense, refers to money, while a budget is basically a plan. So capital budgeting decision methods are the tools firms use to plan how they are going to invest money to grow their business. Each year firms construct a new budget for the following year—it is a long, involved process that rarely goes smoothly. The firm's managers look for new ways for the firm to expand, whether it is new products and services, new production methods, new distribution venues or the like. They champion specific projects based on their analysis of the project's potential impact on the firm's profitability, and their annual bonuses are tied to the performance of their pet projects. Thus, the annual capital budget is the largest recurring project most firms experience. Skill in budgeting is a good way to climb the corporate ladder.

The secret to growing a business is simple: invest in projects that earn more than they cost. If a project covers its own costs and the costs the firm pays its investors, any money left over can be used to invest in more projects and thereby fuel more growth. This chapter discusses the major methods used by firms to value potential investment projects, and a solid understanding of these methods is necessary to becoming a good financial analyst. We will discuss five major methods used for valuing investment projects: the payback period (PB) and discounted payback period (DPB), the net present value (NPV), the internal rate of return (IRR) and the modified internal rate of return (MIRR). Each of these methods will be shown using an Excel spreadsheet for the calculations. We will also review the method for determining the net operating cash flows for the projects based on the incremental cash flows associated with the project. Finally, we will review the method for determining the firm's optimal capital budget.

The Fundamental Principles in Action

FP1 states that an asset derives its value from the cash flows it will produce. In this chapter, we value production projects as the present value of the net operating cash flows the project is expected to produce. FP2 declares that risk and return are directly related, and so riskier assets require higher returns. In the capital budgeting process, one way to adjust the analysis for projects that have different levels of risk is to adjust the discount rate; increase the rate for projects of higher than average risk, and decrease it for projects deemed to be of lower risk. This is consistent with both PR1 and PR3. In addition, this chapter makes the truth of PR2 clear by comparing projects with distinct differences in their cash flows. Finally, we will see the impact of FP3 when we review the NPV profile.

The Capital Budgeting Decision Methods

Analysts tend to have favorite methods they use for recurring tasks, and that is also true when it comes to capital budgeting tools. However, it is best to use all of these methods for a thorough analysis of a project. The five methods discussed here have some similarities as well as some clear differences, and it is the differences that can be useful when interpreting the results.

To compare these methods, we will be using the cash flows from two different projects: Project E, which has the larger cash flows occurring early in the project's life, and Project L, which has the larger cash flows occurring late in the project's life. Each project has an initial cost (year 0 cash flow) of $1,000, which is negative (because it is a cash outflow). Each project has an economic life of four years, and each project has a discount rate of 6.0%. The only difference between the projects is the size of the cash inflows during years 1–4 (see Table 7.1 for the time lines for these projects):

- Project E has cash flows of $530, $430, $187 and $150 in years 1–4 respectively (the larger cash flows occur in years 1 and 2);
- Project L has cash flows of $190, $270, $235 and $780 in years 1–4 respectively (the largest cash flow occurs in year 4).

The Payback Period

The payback period (PB) is defined as the amount of time (in years) required to recover the initial cost of the project. It is found by calculating the cumulative cash flows for the project, starting with the initial cash outflow, then adding each cash inflow until the sum turns nonnegative (zero or higher). In the year the that the sum turns nonnegative, if the cumulative cash flow is greater than zero, that means that the payback occurred during the year, and that the full final year was not required to recover the initial cost. Therefore, you would count all of the years prior to that year and include only the part of the current year needed for full recovery of the cost. That amount is calculated as the unrecovered cost at the start of the year divided by the cash inflow during the year:

$$PB = \#\text{ of Years Prior to Full Recovery} + \frac{\text{Unrecovered Cost at Start of Year}}{\text{Cash Inflow During Full Recovery Year}}$$

Table 7.1 Cash Flows and Discount Rates for Projects E and L

	Project E				
Year	0	1	2	3	4
Cash Flow	−1,000	530	430	187	150
WACC	6.0%				
	Project L				
Year	0	1	2	3	4
Cash Flow	−1,000	190	270	235	780
WACC	6.0%				

To calculate the PB, we simply sum the project's expected cash flows at the end of each year to see when the sum reaches zero or higher. We start with Project E:

- At the end of year 1, Project E has total cash flows of −1,000 + 530 = −470;
- At the end of year 2, Project E has total cash flows of −470 + 430 = −40;
- At the end of year 3, Project E has total cash flows of −40 + 187 = 147.

Project E turns positive some time during year 3, so the PB is calculated as two full years plus the fraction of year 3 represented by the cash flow needed to break even divided by the cash flow due in year 3, or 2 + (40 ÷ 187) = 2.21 years. Next is Project L:

- At the end of year 1, Project L has total cash flows of −1,000 + 190 = −810;
- At the end of year 2, Project L has total cash flows of −810 + 270 = −540;
- At the end of year 3, Project L has total cash flows of −540 + 235 = −305;
- At the end of year 4, Project L has total cash flows of −305 + 780 = 475.

Project L turns positive some time during year 4, so the PB is calculated as three full years plus the fraction of year 4 represented by the cash flow needed to break even divided by the cash flow due in year 4, or 3 + (305 ÷ 780) = 3.39 years.

The decision rule for the payback period is simple: as long as the firm gets its money back before the project ends, the project is worth considering. Both Project E and L have payback periods of less than four years, so both are acceptable based on the PB. When comparing two or more projects using the payback period, quicker is better, because it means that the firm gets its money back sooner, and so can get it reinvested again sooner to earn more money. Therefore, if the projects are mutually exclusive (meaning that the firm can choose one or the other but not both), the firm should choose Project E, since it pays back sooner. If a project's cash flows do not turn positive within the project's economic life, then the project fails to pay back, meaning that the firm will not recover its costs and therefore should reject the project.

The payback period method has three basic flaws:

1. It does not account for the time value of money (the fact that the firm's investors require a return on their investment);
2. Cash flows beyond the payback period are ignored (it doesn't matter if it has one more or one hundred more cash flows after the initial cost is recovered);
3. The PB tells us nothing about the value of the project, unlike the NPV (which tells us how much value the project adds to the shareholders) or the IRR (which indicates the rate of return the project earns).

To address the first of these flaws, we use the discounted payback period (DPB).

The Discounted Payback Period

The discounted payback period (DPB) is defined as the amount of time (in years) required to recover the initial cost of the project after paying the firm's investors their required return. It is found by calculating the cumulative discounted cash flows for the project, starting with the initial cash outflow, then adding the present value of each cash inflow until the sum turns nonnegative. In the year the that the sum turns nonnegative, if the cumulative discounted cash flow is greater than zero, that means that the payback occurred during the year, and that the full final year was not required to recover the initial cost. Therefore, you would count all of the years prior to that year and include only the part of the discounted cash flow for the current year needed for full recovery of the cost. That amount is calculated as the unrecovered discounted cost at the start of the year divided by the present value of the cash inflow during the year, and is therefore mathematically the same as the calculation for the payback period used in the prior section. In fact, the method is the same; you are merely required to calculate the present value of the cash inflows prior to summing. For Project E:

- $PV_{CF1} = 530 \times 1.06^{-1} = \$500.00$;
- $PV_{CF2} = 430 \times 1.06^{-2} = \$382.70$;
- $PV_{CF3} = 187 \times 1.06^{-3} = \$157.01$;
- $PV_{CF4} = 150 \times 1.06^{-4} = \$118.81$.

Now we sum the discounted cash flows year by year until the sum reaches 0 or higher:

- At the end of year 1, Project E has total cash flows of $-1,000 + 500 = -500$;
- At the end of year 2, Project E has total cash flows of $-500 + 382.70 = -117.30$;
- At the end of year 3, Project E has total cash flows of $-117.30 + 157.01 = 39.71$.

Project E turns positive some time during year 3, so the DPB is calculated as two full years plus the fraction of year 3 represented by the discounted cash flow needed to break even divided by the discounted cash flow due in year 3, or $2 + (117.30 \div 157.01) = 2.75$ years. Note that the DPB is longer than the PB; discounting the cash flows to pay the firm's investors extends the time it takes for the company to break even on the project. Next is Project L:

- $PV_{CF1} = 190 \times 1.06^{-1} = \$179.25$;
- $PV_{CF2} = 270 \times 1.06^{-2} = \$240.30$;
- $PV_{CF3} = 235 \times 1.06^{-3} = \$197.31$;
- $PV_{CF4} = 780 \times 1.06^{-4} = \$617.83$.

Again, we sum the discounted cash flows year by year until the sum reaches 0 or higher:

- At the end of year 1, Project L has total cash flows of $-1,000 + 179.25 = -820.75$;
- At the end of year 2, Project L has total cash flows of $-820.75 + 240.30 = -580.45$;
- At the end of year 3, Project L has total cash flows of $-580.45 + 197.31 = -383.14$;
- At the end of year 4, Project L has total cash flows of $-383.14 + 617.83 = 234.69$.

Project L turns positive some time during year 4, so the DPB is calculated as three full years plus the fraction of year 4 represented by the discounted cash flow needed to break even divided by the discounted cash flow due in year 4, or $3 + (383.14 \div 617.83) = 3.62$ years.

It is possible for a project to have a positive PB but a negative DPB due to the discounting process. If that occurs then we say that the project has no discounted payback—it does not cover its own costs once the investors are paid. In that case, based on the DPB, the project should be rejected. That is not the case with these projects—both have positive PB and DPB. As they are mutually exclusive, the firm should choose Project E since it pays back sooner, with or without discounting the cash flows.

The discounted payback period takes care of flaw #1 above, but flaws #2 and #3 are still an issue. The next method takes care of all the flaws and is the favorite of both academics and practitioners.

The Net Present Value

The NPV method is based upon the discounted cash flow (DCF) technique learned in the chapter on the time value of money. The steps required to calculate the NPV are as follows:

1. Calculate the present value of the stream of cash flows the project is expected to produce over its economic life, discounted at the project's cost of capital;
2. Sum the present values of the stream of cash flows, including the initial cost of the project (the negative cash flow in period zero)—this sum is defined as the NPV.

The mathematical equation for the NPV is:

$$NPV = CF_0 + CF_1(1+WACC)^{-1} + CF_2(1+WACC)^{-2} + \cdots + CF_n(1+WACC)^{-n}$$
$$= \sum_{t=0}^{n} CF_t(1+WACC)^{-t}$$

where: CF_t is the expected net cash flow at the end of year t;
WACC is the project's cost of capital; and
n is the expected economic life of the project in years.

Again, cash outflows (such as the initial cost of purchasing the equipment, CF_0) are represented as negative cash flows.

The decision rule for the NPV method is simple: if the project's NPV is positive, then the project is returning more than its cost of capital and is therefore a good investment and should be accepted. If the NPV is negative, the project is returning less than its cost of capital and is therefore a bad investment and should be rejected (investing in it would destroy value, not create it). If the NPV is equal to zero, the firm is indifferent about the investment, as it returns exactly what it costs but adds no residual value to the firm. If the firm is considering mutually exclusive projects, the one with the higher NPV is to be preferred.

The NPV for Project E is calculated as follows:

$$NPV_E = -1{,}000 + 530 \times 1.06^{-1} + 430 \times 1.06^{-2} + 187 \times 1.06^{-3} + 150 \times 1.06^{-4}$$
$$= -1{,}000 + 500 + 382.70 + 157.01 + 118.81 = \$158.52$$

Since Project E has a positive NPV, it is a good investment and therefore should be accepted.
The NPV for Project L is:

$$NPV_L = -1{,}000 + 190 \times 1.06^{-1} + 270 \times 1.06^{-2} + 235 \times 1.06^{-3} + 780 \times 1.06^{-4}$$
$$= -1{,}000 + 179.25 + 240.30 + 197.31 + 617.83 = \$234.69$$

Since Project L has a positive NPV, it is a good investment and therefore should be accepted. As these are mutually exclusive projects, Project L should be chosen since it has the higher NPV.

Note that the decision methods used thus far are giving conflicting recommendations: the PB and DPB prefer Project E, while the NPV prefers Project L. Such conflicts are justification for calculating all of the capital budgeting metrics, to have as much relevant information as possible before making the decision. It should also be noted, however, that while the PB and DPB methods have the flaws mentioned earlier, the NPV method has no such flaw, and is therefore the method preferred by both academics and professionals. Therefore, the NPV results should be given more weight in the decision process than the PB or DPB results.

The Internal Rate of Return

The internal rate of return (IRR) is defined as the discount rate that forces the NPV of the cash flows to equal zero. It can also be understood as the yield to maturity of the cash flow stream. Mathematically it is:

$$NPV = CF_0 + CF_1(1+IRR)^{-1} + CF_2(1+IRR)^{-2} + \ldots + CF_n(1+IRR)^{-n} = 0;$$
$$= \sum_{t=0}^{n} CF_t(1+IRR)^{-t}$$

To calculate the IRR, you must solve for the discount rate that forces the NPV to zero. This cannot be done using math but instead requires either a financial calculator or an Excel spreadsheet. To calculate the IRR in Excel, you must use the IRR function, which only requires you to highlight the cash flows. The IRRs for Projects E and L were calculated in Excel, and the output is shown in Table 7.2.

When valuing a capital project with the IRR method, the rule is if the IRR is greater than the project's cost of capital, the project returns more than it costs and therefore should be accepted. If the IRR is less than the project's cost of capital, it returns less than it costs and should be rejected. If the IRR is equal to the cost of capital, the project returns exactly what it costs, and the firm will be indifferent to the project. In this comparison, the cost of capital is used as a "hurdle" rate; if the project's IRR clears the hurdle rate, it is acceptable.

The IRR for Project E is 14.67%, which is greater than the 6.0% WACC, so based on the IRR, Project E should be accepted. The IRR for Project L is 13.80%, which is also greater than the 6.0% WACC, so Project L should also be accepted based on the IRR analysis.

The NPV and the IRR methods essentially give the same decision; if a project has a positive NPV, its IRR will be greater than the hurdle rate. The issue between them comes about when you are analyzing mutually exclusive projects. Independent projects will receive the same accept/reject decision from both the NPV and IRR methods, but mutually exclusive projects can get conflicting results. Since the projects in question are mutually exclusive, the firm should choose the one with the higher IRR. The analysis shows that Project E has the higher IRR and so should be chosen, which is in conflict with the NPV analysis. The nature of the conflict can be seen by creating NPV profiles for the two projects.

The top panel of Figure 7.1 shows the cash flows for the two mutually exclusive projects, as well as their WACC, NPV and IRR. Both have the same discount rate, but while Project E has the higher IRR, Project L has the higher NPV. The bottom panel of Figure 7.1 is a graph known as an NPV Profile. The vertical (Y) axis for the graph is the projects' NPV, and the horizontal (X) axis is the discount rate (WACC). The lines trace the NPVs for each project at different discount rates, from 0% to 19% in 1% increments. Note that the slope for the NPV

NPV Profile - Project E vs. Project L

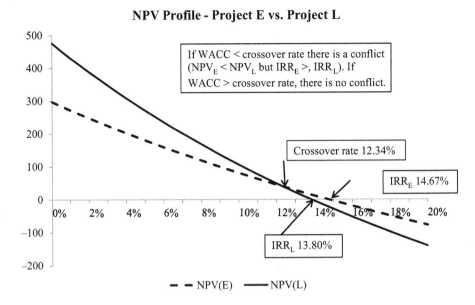

Figure 7.1 NPV Profile of Mutually Exclusive Projects

profiles is negative; as the discount rate increases, the projects' NPVs decrease. This graph shows FP3 and PR1 in action.

Notice that the NPV profile for Project E crosses the horizontal axis (NPV = 0) at just under 14% (13.8%). The point where the NPV profile crosses the X-axis is the project's IRR (NPV = 0). Notice also that the two NPV profiles are not parallel, but cross at the discount rate of 12.34%. This discount rate is known as the crossover rate, and it is the discount rate at which the NPVs for the two projects are equal.

The fact that the NPV profiles cross means that the project with the higher NPV is determined by which discount rate is used. If the crossover rate is lower than the projects' WACC, then the NPV and IRR decision rules will not have a conflict. For Projects E and L, since the crossover rate is higher than the WACC of 6%, there is a conflict between the NPV and IRR results.

Comparing the NPV and IRR Methods

The NPV and IRR methods are different perspectives on the same problem: the NPV solves for the present value of a series of cash flows given a stated discount rate, while the IRR solves for the discount rate of the cash flows given a stated present value (zero). The mathematical issue with the IRR is that there is no closed-form solution—it cannot be solved mathematically. Calculating the IRR requires either a financial calculator or a computer. Fortunately, Excel has an IRR function that makes it easy to calculate.

The discussion on the NPV profile and the crossover rate points out just one issue with the IRR method. Another significant problem with the IRR method is that projects with non-normal cash flows can have more than one IRR. A non-normal cash flow could be a large cash outflow in the middle or at the end of the project's life. For example, suppose there is a nuclear reactor in the state of Ohio that is being considered for shut down because the state utility is unwilling to put the money into the repairs necessary to keep the reactor going for the last ten years of its expected life. A private contractor estimates that they can get the reactor into working order for $15 million, and offers the state $5 million for the right to run the reactor for the next ten years. The contractor's financial analysts estimate that the reactor will produce cash flows of $50 million for each of the next ten years. However, the contractor's engineers determine that at the end of the ten-year period, the reactor will be so unstable that they will need to bury and seal off the property completely, which they estimate will cost $550 million. The contractor has a WACC of 8.0%, but they believe this project is riskier than their typical project, so they use a 9% cost of capital for the project. The project's NPV at 9.0% is $68.6 million, so it appears to be a good investment. When they calculate the project's IRR, however, they find two of them: 3.15% and 249.97%. The large cash outflow at the end of the project is creating multiple IRRs. Further, if the engineers had been using Excel for their IRR calculations, they would not have known that the project has two IRRs; the IRR function would report the low result (IRR = 3.15%), and they would be none the wiser. An NPV profile of the project would show that the graph crosses the X-axis at two points: X = 3.15% and X = 249.97%.

The biggest concern about the IRR method, however, comes from one of its assumptions: the method assumes that the project's cash flows will be reinvested at the project's internal rate of return. Since the IRR is specific to that project, however, it is unlikely that the cash flows will be reinvested at that rate (since they will be invested in a different project). The NPV method, on the other hand, assumes that the project's cash flows will be reinvested at the cost of capital, which is a reasonable assumption. Because of this concern, and because many managers prefer to evaluate investments in percentage terms (IRR) rather than in dollar terms (NPV), the modified internal rate of return (MIRR) was developed.

The Modified Internal Rate of Return

The modified internal rate of return (MIRR) came about because of a false assumption made by the IRR model: the IRR assumes that the cash flows from the project will be reinvested at the project's IRR. Theoretically, the MIRR is the same as the IRR with the exception of the change in the reinvestment rate assumption; it still represents the yield to maturity of the cash flow stream. Mathematically, however, the calculations are very different: all of the cash inflows are compounded out to the end of the project's economic life at the cost of capital (taking care of the reinvestment rate assumption). Those compounded cash flows are then summed to determine the project's terminal value, or the value of the cash flows at the end of the project's economic life. The MIRR then is the discount rate that equates the project's terminal value with the absolute value of the project's initial cash outflow (cost), so that the NPV of the project is zero. The following equation shows the mathematics of the MIRR method:

$$CF_0 + \frac{CF_1\left(1+WACC\right)^{n-1} + CF_2\left(1+WACC\right)^{n-2} + \cdots + CF_n\left(1+WACC\right)^{n-(n-1)}}{\left(1+MIRR\right)^n} = 0$$

Figure 7.2 depicts the time line for calculating a project's MIRR and shows how the method is applied. The MIRR suffers from the same mathematical drawback as the IRR—no closed-form solution—but Excel also has an MIRR function. The MIRR for Project E is

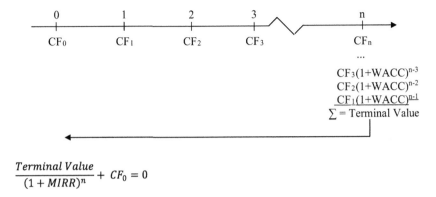

$$\frac{Terminal\ Value}{(1+MIRR)^n} + CF_0 = 0$$

Figure 7.2 Time Line for Calculating a Project's MIRR

9.97%, which is lower than the IRR but higher than the WACC. Because it assumes the firm is reinvesting the cash flows at the lower WACC, the MIRR falls below the IRR. The MIRR for Project L is 11.74%, which also falls between the WACC and the IRR, but is higher than the MIRR for Project E. Both projects are good investments because the MIRR is higher than the WACC. Since they are mutually exclusive projects, the firm would choose Project L. So, the MIRR result is consistent with the NPV result but conflicts with the IRR result.

Table 7.2 shows all the calculations necessary to perform a complete capital budgeting analysis of the projects. The calculations are simple, but the details are important:

- To use the NPV function, after you highlight the WACC as the discount rate, you only highlight the project's cash inflows inside the function; the initial cash outflow is added after the function (<u>added</u> because it is entered as a negative number). This particular detail only applies to the NPV function.
- The IRR function is the simplest, as you only need to highlight the cash flows—all of them, including the initial cash outflow, unlike with the NPV function.
- The MIRR function requires two rates to be entered, a "finance rate" and a reinvestment rate, in addition to the cash flows. Highlight the WACC for both rates. Highlight all cash flows, including the initial cash outflow.
- For the PB, cumulate the cash flows as indicated. For the calculation, highlight the number of the year for the last negative cumulative cash flow, then, using the ABS function (for absolute value—it turns negative numbers positive), add the ratio of the last negative cumulative cash flow to the value of the next cash inflow. Format the number to two decimal places.
- For the DPB, calculate the discounted cash flows using the WACC, then cumulate the discounted cash flows as indicated. For the calculation, highlight the number of the year for the last negative cumulative discounted cash flow, then using the ABS function, add the ratio of the last negative cumulative discounted cash flow to the value of the next discounted cash inflow. Format the number to two decimal places.

The next part of this chapter shows the logic and the accounting method used to determine the project's net cash flows—the numbers used in the capital budgeting analysis.

Table 7.2 Capital Budgeting Decision Tools Using Excel

	Project E				
Year	*0*	*1*	*2*	*3*	*4*
Cash Flow	−1,000	530	430	187	150
WACC	6.0%				
NPV	158.52	<-- =NPV(B4,C3:F3) + B3			
IRR	14.67%	<-- =IRR(B3:F3)			
MIRR	9.97%	<-- =MIRR(B3:F3,B4,B4)			
PB	2.21	<-- =D2 + ABS(D11 / E3)			
DPB	2.75	<-- =D2 + ABS(D13 / E12)			
Cum CF	−1,000	−470	−40	147	297
Disc CF	−1,000.00	500.00	382.70	157.01	118.81
Cum disc CF	−1,000.00	−500.00	−117.30	39.71	158.52
	Project L				
Year	*0*	*1*	*2*	*3*	*4*
Cash flow	−1,000	190	270	235	780
WACC	6.0%				
NPV	234.69	<-- =NPV(B18,C17:F17) + B17			
IRR	13.80%	<-- =IRR(B17:F17)			
MIRR	11.74%	<-- =MIRR(B17:F17,B18,B18)			
PB	3.39	<-- =E16 + ABS(E25 / F17)			
DPB	3.62	<-- =E16 + ABS(E27 / F26)			
Cum CF	−1,000	−810	−540	−305	475
Disc CF	−1,000.00	179.25	240.30	197.31	617.83
Cum disc CF	−1,000.00	−820.75	−580.46	−383.15	234.69

Evaluating Capital Budgeting Projects

This section discusses the methods used to evaluate a capital project. Firms continue to grow and thrive by investing in new capital projects that earn more than they cost, so they must constantly be looking out for new products and markets or new production methods. Analyzing capital projects accurately is vital and requires knowledge of both accounting and finance, attention to detail, experience and time. There are many different types of projects available for firms:

- Replacement project: replacing existing assets to continue current operations;
- Efficiency project: usually associated with a change in technology that lowers the firm's production costs;
- Expanding into new products: when the firm is adding to its product line;
- Expanding into new markets: when the firm is trying to capture new market share using its existing product line;
- Safety or environmental projects: these projects are typically required by the government to meet safety or environmental standards;
- General maintenance: things like adding a warehouse or a parking structure.

Different types of projects can require different types of analysis, some more detailed than others. In this chapter, we will look at an expansion project to show how the analysis is performed.

Cash Flow Estimation

Estimating the cash flows for a project is a detailed task, but it follows much of what you have already learned in this course and in the prerequisite accounting course. We start by discussing how to identify which cash flows are to be used in the analysis—the relevant cash flows.

Relevant Cash Flows

One of the most important concepts in determining the cash flows associated with a project is to identify the relevant cash flows, which are not found on one line of a financial statement. In order to identify the relevant cash flows, two things should be kept in mind:

1. Capital budgeting decisions must be based on *cash flows*, not accounting income;
2. Only *incremental cash flows* are relevant to the accept/reject decision.

Accounting income includes profits, which are a return *on* capital, but excludes depreciation, which is a return *of* capital. Both should be considered, and together they comprise the net cash flows for the project. As will be seen in the case analysis, depreciation is deducted in order to get to taxable income, and once taxes are removed, depreciation is added back to obtain the net operating cash flows (net of taxes). Depreciation is an operating expense that requires no payment, so it is cash generated by operations and therefore part of the operating cash flow.

In evaluating a project, we are only concerned with the cash flows that occur *if and only if* we accept the project—these are the incremental cash flows, and they represent the total changes in the firm's cash flows as a result of accepting the project. Four issues relate directly to the incremental cash flows:

1. Sunk cost—an outlay that has already been committed or has already occurred and thus is not affected by the decision relating to the project (not an incremental cost). For example, if the firm owns a piece of property and is considering either selling it or building a warehouse to store inventory. Before building on the property, the land must be tested to see if it can safely be developed. The cost of the test is a sunk cost and should not be included in the cash flows for the project.
2. Opportunity cost—the return on the best alternative use of an asset. For example, if the firm owns a piece of property and is considering either selling it or building a warehouse to store inventory. If the firm chooses to build on the property, they are giving up the opportunity to sell the property. The sale price of the property is an opportunity cost for the project and should be included as an expense in the cash flows.
3. Externalities—effects of the project on other parts of the firm (such as cannibalism). Whenever McDonalds builds a new restaurant, they first determine where the closest McDonalds are to the current site. They know that some of the customers that use the new store will be customers from another McDonalds that find the new one more

convenient. Those customers will be cannibalized by the new store and should not be included in the sales estimates for the new store.

4. Shipping and installation costs—these can be substantial when purchasing fixed assets. The full cost (including both the purchase price and S&I) is used as the depreciable basis when depreciation charges are calculated.

Changes in Net Working Capital

When a firm adds capital assets, there are a number of other changes that go along with the new assets. Normally additional inventories are required to support a new operation, and expanded sales also lead to new accounts receivable, so these new assets will need to be funded. At the same time, accounts payable and accruals will increase spontaneously as a result of the expansion, reducing the amount of funds needed to support the increase in inventories and receivables (this will be discussed in more depth in Chapter 9, "Analyzing and Forecasting Financial Statements"). The difference between the required increase in current assets and the spontaneous increase in current liabilities is called the change in net working capital. If this change is positive (as it usually is), this means that additional funds will be needed to support the increase in current assets. Therefore, most projects have an expense up front (year 0) related to the increase in net working capital, which will be recovered in the project's terminal year (its last year of operation).

Evaluating Capital Budgeting Projects

This example discusses an expansion project—the firm in question is attempting to expand its product line by developing a new product. Wellman Industries has been considering introducing a new solar-powered environmental control system for its line of products intended for mid-size homes. The panels would be used to control the air conditioning, the heating and even the water heater, based on the product's ability to collect and store solar energy. The product would increase the home's energy efficiency, and thereby offer the homeowner a return on their investment.

The product is at a stage where a decision must be made about going into production. Wellman's marketing department is targeting larger homes (> 2,000 SF), where it is most cost-effective; they believe annual sales will be 20,000 units if the price is $2,000, so annual sales revenue is estimated at $40 million. Engineering says that the firm will require additional capacity, and they have looked at a building that costs $12 million, to be purchased at the end of the current year. The building falls into the MACRS 39-year class for depreciation. Equipment would be purchased and installed at that time as well which falls into the MACRS 5-year class. The cost of the equipment is $8 million, including shipping and handling. The project would require an additional investment of $6 million in net working capital, also to be done at the end of the current year.

The project's estimated economic life is four years, after which the building is expected to have a market value of $7.5 million and a book value of $10.908 million, while the equipment will have a market value of $2 million and a book value of $1.36 million. Production estimates that variable manufacturing costs would be 60% of sales, and fixed costs (excluding depreciation) would be $5 million per year. MACRS depreciation amounts for the first four years are as follows:

- Building: year 1, 1.3%; year 2, 2.6%; year 3, 2.6%; year 4, 2.6%;
- Equipment: year 1, 20.0%; year 2, 32.0%; year 3, 19.0%; year 4, 12.0%.

Wellman's marginal tax rate is 40.0%, their cost of capital for this project is 12.0% and for analysis purposes they will assume that all cash flows occur at the end of each calendar year.

The cash flow analysis is done in three parts:

- Initial cash flows: the cash flows involved in getting the project started. They occur in year 0 and are most often cash outflows, such as the cost of the assets and the increase in net working capital.
- Operating cash flows: these are the repetitive cash flows that occur each year associated with using the assets, including such items as sales revenue or expense reduction (cash inflows), operating expenses (fixed and variable), depreciation and taxes.
- Terminal cash flows: the cash flows that occur at the end of the project's economic life that are associated with shutting the project down, such as the return of the net working capital paid up front as well as any net salvage value the new assets may have at the end of the project.

The cash flows for each section of the analysis are discussed separately. Note that the reported cash flows are in thousands (000s).

Initial Cash Flows

There are three cash outflows required to get the project up and running:

- The cost of the building ($12,000);
- The cost of the equipment ($8,000); and
- The increase in NWC ($6,000).

These are the only cash flows required for year 0, so their sum (−$26,000) is the net operating cash flow for year 0 (these cash flows are not affected by the other sections of the analysis). The figures for the building and the equipment are the depreciable basis for each asset (the amount to be depreciated—the amount to multiply by the MACRS percentages).

Operating Cash Flows

This section can be thought of as a modified income statement for each year of the project. The cash flows for this section are determined as follows:

- List all cash inflows—revenue or expense reduction;
- List all operating expenses (cash outflows), including variable and fixed costs and depreciation for all assets;
- Sum the operating cash inflows and cash outflows to arrive at operating (taxable) income for the year;
- Calculate and subtract taxes to obtain net income;
- Add back the depreciation subtracted above to obtain the cash flow from operations.

The calculations for this section are fairly straightforward and can be easily performed in an Excel spreadsheet (see Table 7.3):

- Sales revenue is the same for each year: $20,000 per unit times 2,000 forecasted units equals $40 million per year ($40,000 in thousands);
- Variable costs are 60% of sales, so $40,000 \times -0.6 = -\$24,000$ (negative because it is a cash outflow);
- Fixed costs are $-\$5,000$ each year;
- Depreciation for the building is 1.3% in year 1 and 2.6% in years 2 through 4. These percentages get multiplied by the cost of the building ($-\$12,000$) to arrive at $-\$156$ for year 1 and $-\$312$ for years 2 through 4;
- Depreciation for the equipment changes each year:

  - $-\$8,000 \times 0.2 = -\$1,600$ in year 1;
  - $-\$8,000 \times 0.32 = -\$2,560$ in year 2;
  - $-\$8,000 \times 0.19 = -\$1,520$ in year 3;
  - $-\$8,000 \times 0.12 = -\$960$ in year 4.

Operating income is the sum of the operating cash inflows and the operating cash outflows:

- $OI_1 = 40,000 - 24,000 - 5,000 - 156 - 1,600 = \$9,244$;
- $OI_2 = 40,000 - 24,000 - 5,000 - 312 - 2,560 = \$8,128$;
- $OI_3 = 40,000 - 24,000 - 5,000 - 312 - 1,520 = \$9,168$;
- $OI_4 = 40,000 - 24,000 - 5,000 - 312 - 960 = \$9,728$.

Net income is obtained by calculating taxes (40% of operating income) and subtracting them:

- $T_1 = 9,244 \times -0.4 = -3,697.6$; $NI_1 = 9,244 - 3,697.6 = \$5,546.4$;
- $T_2 = 8,128 \times -0.4 = -3,251.2$; $NI_2 = 8,128 - 3,251.2 = \$4,876.8$;
- $T_3 = 9,168 \times -0.4 = -3,667.2$; $NI_3 = 9,168 - 3,667.2 = \$5,500.8$;
- $T_4 = 9,728 \times -0.4 = -3,891.2$; $NI_4 = 9,728 - 3,891.2 = \$5,836.8$.

Finally, cash flow from operations is obtained by adding back the depreciation for both the building and the equipment:

- $CFO_1 = 5,546.4 + 156 + 1,600 = \$7,302.4$;
- $CFO_2 = 4,876.8 + 312 + 2,560 = \$7,748.8$;
- $CFO_3 = 5,500.8 + 312 + 1,520 = \$7,332.8$;
- $CFO_4 = 5,836.8 + 312 + 960 = \$7,108.8$.

Terminal Cash Flows

At the end of the project's life, two types of terminal cash flows must be accounted for:

1. The return of the net working capital—inventory will be sold off and supplies will not be renewed, so all of the money invested up front will be returned when the project is discontinued;
2. The sale of the assets for salvage value—taxes must be paid if the market value exceeds the book value, while the firm gets a tax credit if the book value exceeds the market value.

The first item (NWC) is simple—just add it as a cash inflow in the final year of the project. Calculating the net (after tax) salvage value of the assets is a three-step process:

1. Subtract the book (undepreciated) value of the asset from the market (salvage) value to obtain the gain (or loss) from the sale;
2. Calculate the amount of taxes due (or the tax credit earned) based on step 1 above;
3. Subtract taxes owed from (or add the tax credit to) the market value to obtain the net salvage value.

For the building, only $1,092 of the $12,000 has been depreciated, leaving a book value of $10,908. Since the building is expected to sell for only $7,500, the firm expects a loss of $3,408. This loss offers the firm a tax credit of $1,363.20 (3,408 × 0.4), so the net salvage value for the building is 7,500 + 1,363.20 = $8,863.20. The equipment has had $6,640 of value depreciated, so the remaining book value is $1,360. Selling the equipment for $2,000 will realize a gain of $640 on the asset. The tax liability for this is 640 × 0.4 = $256, so the net salvage value for the equipment is 2,000 − 256 = $1,744.

Net Operating Cash Flow

These are the numbers used to calculate the project's capital budgeting metrics—the point of the entire exercise. Net operating cash flow (NOCF) for year 0 is the sum of the purchase prices of the building and equipment plus the increase in NWC, or −$26,000. NOCF for years 1 through 3 are the same as the cash flow from operations calculated in the earlier section. For year 4 (the terminal year), NOCF is the sum of the cash flow from operations for year 4 plus the terminal cash flows: 7,108.8 + 6,000 + 8,863.2 + 1,744 = $23,716. The schedule showing all of the calculated figures (in thousands) is shown in Table 7.3.

The net operating cash flows for the project are the numbers that go on the time line for the capital budgeting analysis. The capital budgeting metrics for the project are given below (you should be able to obtain these numbers yourself using Excel):

*   NPV (WACC @ 12%) = $6,988.58 (positive, so the project should be accepted);
*   IRR = 21.89% (IRR > WACC so the project should be accepted);
*   MIRR = 18.87% (MIRR > WACC so the project should be accepted);
*   PB = 3.15 years (< 4 years so the project should be accepted);
*   DPB = 3.54 years (< 4 years so the project should be accepted).

All of the capital budgeting metrics for the project are positive, so it appears to be a good investment.

Paying Attention to Details

It is easy to overlook potential relevant cash flows when analyzing a project, beyond issues like sunk costs and externalities. For example, suppose the firm is considering investing in an efficiency project; they want to replace an active asset with a new asset that will reduce operating costs significantly. Assuming the old asset has salvage value, the net salvage value for the old asset must be included in the initial cash flows (year 0) for the project. In addition, if the old asset had any remaining book value, the depreciation for the old asset is lost because the asset is being sold early. Therefore, the lost depreciation on the old asset must be

Table 7.3 Net Operating Cash Flow Schedule for Wellman Expansion Project (000s)

Wellman Expansion Project Net Operating Cash Flows (000s)					
	0	*1*	*2*	*3*	*4*
Initial Cash Flows					
Building	−12,000.00				
Equipment	−8,000.00				
Increase in Net Working Capital	−6,000.00				
Operating Cash Flows					
Sales Revenue		40,000.00	40,000.00	40,000.00	40,000.00
Variable Costs		−24,000.00	−24,000.00	−24,000.00	−24,000.00
Fixed Costs		−5,000.00	−5,000.00	−5,000.00	−5,000.00
Depreciation—Building		−156.00	−312.00	−312.00	−312.00
Depreciation—Equipment		−1,600.00	−2,560.00	−1,520.00	−960.00
Operating Income		9,244.00	8,128.00	9,168.00	9,728.00
Taxes		−3,697.60	−3,251.20	−3,667.20	−3,891.20
Net Income		5,546.40	4,876.80	5,500.80	5,836.80
Add Back Depreciation		1,756.00	2,872.00	1,832.00	1,272.00
Cash Flow From Operations		7,302.40	7,748.80	7,332.80	7,108.80
Terminal Cash Flows					
Return of Net Working Capital					6,000.00
Net Salvage Value—Building					8,863.20
Net Salvage Value—Equipment					1,744.00
Net Operating Cash Flow	−26,000.00	7,302.40	7,748.80	7,332.80	23,716.00

included in the operating cash flows as a cash inflow. The specifics of the cash flows for each project must be accounted for, which requires attention to details.

The Truth of PR2

PR2 states that the timing of the cash flows affects their present value. This can be seen by simply comparing two projects with identical cash flows that have different timing.

Project X and Project Y both have an initial cost of $800. Project X has cash inflows of $100, $200, $300 and $400 in years 1–4 respectively, while Project Y has cash inflows of $400, $300, $200 and $100 in years 1–4 respectively. Thus, their cash flows are identical, but for X the larger cash flows come later in the project, while for Y the larger cash flows come early. Both projects have an 8.0% discount rate. Using these data to calculate the NPV for each project:

$$NPV_X = -800 + 100 \times 1.08^{-1} + 200 \times 1.08^{-2} + 300 \times 1.08^{-3} + 400 \times 1.08^{-4} = -\$3.78$$
$$NPV_Y = -800 + 400 \times 1.08^{-1} + 300 \times 1.08^{-2} + 200 \times 1.08^{-3} + 100 \times 1.08^{-4} = \$59.84$$

Project X has a negative NPV because the larger cash flows occur later on the time line, so they are discounted more, making their present values smaller. Project X has a positive NPV because the larger cash flows occur early in the project's life. Thus, the timing of the cash flows has an impact on the present value of the series of cash flows.

Adjusting for Risk in the Capital Budgeting Analysis Process

If the project under consideration is of average risk compared to other projects the firm has invested in over time, then the firm's WACC should be used as the discount rate for the NPV analysis. If the project is of more or less than average risk, then the WACC can be adjusted to take that risk into account:

- For projects of above average risk, increase the WACC, which will in turn decrease the NPV of the project;
- For projects of less than average risk, decrease the WACC, which will increase the NPV of the project.

How much to change the WACC is a matter of judgment, and getting input from other analysts is helpful in this decision. Note that this adjusting of the WACC will only affect the DPB, NPV and MIRR, as they are the only capital budgeting metrics that use the WACC in the calculation.

The Investment Opportunity Schedule

The point of valuing the potential investment projects goes beyond merely determining which ones are worthwhile; the firm needs to estimate its capital investment budget for the coming year, in order to establish their financing needs (determine how much new debt and/ or new equity must be raised to fund the new capital projects). The investment opportunity schedule (IOS) is a tool used to compare the returns from the potential projects to the firm's cost of capital. As will be seen, this tool is used to determine which of the potential projects will be included in the next year's capital budget (just because a project has a positive NPV doesn't automatically mean that it will be funded; it just means that it makes the first cut). The following example will show how the IOS is used to help determine the firm's optimal capital budget.

A firm has six potential capital projects for the upcoming fiscal year. The initial cost and IRR for each project being considered is given below, listed in descending order of IRR:

- Project A has a cost of $3.5 million and an IRR of 11.25%;
- Project B has a cost of $4.8 million and an IRR of 10.9%;
- Project C has a cost of $3.1 million and an IRR of 10.2%;
- Project D has a cost of $2.4 million and an IRR of 9.95%;
- Project E has a cost of $2.9 million and an IRR of 9.5%; and
- Project F has a cost of $2.6 million and an IRR of 9.25%.

The following facts are relevant to analyzing the optimal capital budget:

- The firm's WACC is 9.0% using retained earnings and 9.4% if the firm must float new common equity (when they run out of retained earnings);
- All of the projects under consideration are of average risk, so there is no need to adjust the WACC for any project;
- The firm's optimal capital structure consists of 35% debt, 10% preferred equity and 55% common equity, meaning that the funds on the liabilities and equity side of the balance sheet consist of 35% debt, 10% preferred equity and 55% common equity;
- The firm estimates that the addition to retained earnings for the year (the amount of RE that will be available to invest for next year) will be $8.8 million.

Each project in the table was included because its NPV is positive and its IRR is greater than the firm's cost of capital (using retained earnings). Before we construct the IOS, we need one more calculation: the retained earnings break point (REBP). The REBP is defined as the total amount of capital investment that can be supported with retained earnings (meaning that the firm will not need to issue new common equity) and is calculated as the current year's addition to retained earnings divided by the weight of common equity in the capital structure. Therefore, this firm's REBP = $8.8M ÷ 0.55 = $16 million. This means that the firm can finance up to $16 million in capital projects at the WACC of 9.0% (using retained earnings), but as soon as they invest more than $16 million, the cost of capital increases to 9.4%, because then they are forced to float new common equity.

Now we are ready to construct the IOS. The IOS can be created in two ways:

- A graph that has the projects' IRRs on the vertical (Y) axis and the sum of the projects' costs on the horizontal (X) axis; or
- A table that lists the projects by IRR and cost.

While the graph is visually clearer and easier to understand, the table is simpler and easier to construct. Figure 7.3 offers both for your comparison.

The graph is in the top panel of the figure, while the table in in the bottom panel. In the graph, the projects are marked on the schedule at the height of the project's IRR and for the length of the project's initial cost. The resulting stair-step graph shows the expected return for the capital invested. Once that part of the graph is complete, a line for the marginal cost of capital is added to the graph to make sure that all of the projects' IRRs exceed the marginal cost of capital—those that do not are cut. Note that the marginal cost of capital line has a break at the capital budget amount of $16 million, which is the REBP—at that amount, the marginal cost of capital increases from 9.0% to 9.4%. The graph makes it clear that projects A–E are all expected to return more than they cost, but that project F does not.

The table in the lower panel shows how the IOS schedule can be created in Excel. The projects are listed in descending order of IRR, just as in the graph above. The second column (column B) has the cost for each project, while the fourth column (column D) cumulates the costs, so the cumulative cost for Project C, $11.4 million, is the sum of the $3.5 million for A plus the $4.8 million for B plus the $3.1 million for C (see the text box with the sum function below the table). Column E shows the WACC to be used based on the cumulative cost. The IF statement in the text box below the table shows how Excel compares the cumulative cost to the REBP to determine which WACC to use for each level of cumulative cost: the WACC using retained earnings (9.0%) or the WACC using new equity (9.4%). The WACC increases from 9.0% to 9.4% once the cumulative cost reaches or surpasses the REBP. Column F (Accept?) uses an IF statement to compare the WACC to the IRR, and only accepts those projects for which WACC < IRR. The words "Yes" and "No" are in quotes in the IF statement because they are text, and so will be displayed exactly as shown in the quotes. The functions in the text boxes are used in each cell of the column in question; the items that are anchored (i.e., have a $ in the cell reference) are the same in each cell of the column, while the items that are not anchored change when the function is copied to new cells down the column.

The analysis of both the graph and the table provide the same conclusions:

- Projects A–E should be accepted but project F should be rejected;
- The optimal capital budget for the firm for next year is $16.7 million;
- Since the optimal capital budget exceeds the retained earnings break point, the firm will need to issue new common equity to fund next year's capital budget.

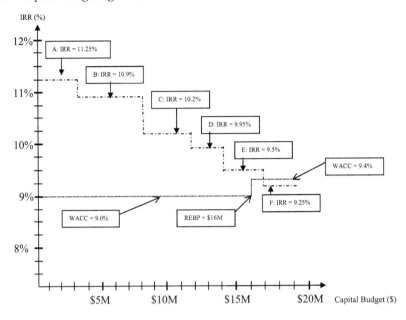

Project	Cost	IRR	Cum Cost	WACC	Accept?		Retained Earnings	8,800,000
A	3,500,000	11.25%	3,500,000	9.00%	Yes		Weight of Equity	0.55
B	4,800,000	10.90%	8,300,000	9.00%	Yes		REBP	16,000,000
C	3,100,000	10.20%	11,400,000	9.00%	Yes			
D	2,400,000	9.95%	13,800,000	9.00%	Yes		WACC(RE)	9.00%
E	2,900,000	9.50%	16,700,000	9.40%	Yes		WACC(NE)	9.40%
F	2,600,000	9.25%	19,300,000	9.40%	No			

=SUM(B2:B7)   =IF(D7>I3,I6,I5)

=IF(E7<C7,"Yes","No")

Figure 7.3 Investment Opportunity Schedule Graph and Table

Summary of the Principles and Precepts Applied in This Chapter

The First Fundamental Principle (FP1): The value of any asset is equal to the present value of the cash flows the asset is expected to produce over its economic life.

The NPV valuation model shows how a project's operating cash flows are used as the basis of the project's value. All of the capital budgeting metrics are based on the projects' expected future cash flows.

The Third Fundamental Principle (FP3): There is an inverse relationship between price and yield; if an asset's price increases, its return will decrease (and vice versa), holding other things constant.

The NPV model uses the firm's WACC as the discount rate, which is the weighted average return to the firm's investors. Increasing the return to one or more groups of the firm's investors will increase the discount rate, which will decrease the NPV. This was made clear in the discussion on the NPV profile.

> **The Second Fundamental Principle (FP2): There is a direct relationship between risk and return; as perceived risk increases, required return will also increase (and vice versa), holding other things constant.**

In capital budgeting, differences in risk among the prospective investments are addressed by adjusting the discount rate (the WACC) for the project. Since the WACC represents the return to the firm's investors, increasing the discount rate means increasing the return to the firm's investors.

> **The First Precept (PR1): The present value of a cash flow (or an asset) is inversely related to its discount rate; increasing the discount rate decreases the present value (and vice versa), holding other things constant.**

Since the firm's WACC is used as the discount rate, increasing the required return to the firm's investors will decrease the present value of the projects' cash flows, and in turn their NPVs. This was made clear in the discussion on the NPV profile.

> **The Second Precept (PR2): The timing of the cash flows of an asset is important; sooner is better (later cash flows are more heavily discounted, reducing their present value).**

The comparison of projects X and Y showed that the timing of the cash flows has a direct impact on their NPV.

> **The Third Precept (PR3): The present value of a cash flow (or an asset) is inversely related to its perceived risk; the higher the risk, the higher the discount rate, and therefore the lower the present value.**

In capital budgeting, the way to account for projects of higher risk is to increase their discount rate (adjust the WACC). Increasing the WACC will decrease the NPV.

End of Chapter Problems

1. The payback period is best defined as:
   a. The time period required for total revenue to equal the initial investment.
   b. The time period required to receive cash flows sufficient to cover the initial investment.
   c. The time period required for the present value of all cash flows to equal the initial investment.
   d. The time period required for the NPV to equal zero.

2. What is the difference between the payback period and the discounted payback period?

    a. The discounted payback period accounts for the time value of money.
    b. The discounted payback period takes into account the expected economic life of the project.
    c. The discounted payback period discounts the taxes on expected cash flows.
    d. The discounted payback period ignores the time value of money.

3. The internal rate of return is best described as the discount rate that:

    a. Equates the NPV and the IRR.
    b. Equals the required rate of return.
    c. Makes the net present value equal to zero.
    d. Equates all cash flows to the current market rate.

4. Independent projects:

    a. Always have negative NPVs.
    b. Do not compete with each other for resources.
    c. Can be mutually exclusive under certain conditions.
    d. Compete with each other for resources.

5. The net present value represents:

    a. The percentage return on the project.
    b. The dollar profits added to the firm discounting at the cost of capital.
    c. The percentage change represented by the project.
    d. The dollar change in the firm's value resulting from undertaking the project.

6. Which of the following items would *not* represent an incremental cash flow?

    a. Salvage value of the new asset required for the project.
    b. Purchase price of the new asset required for the project.
    c. Interest payments for the debt used to finance the project.
    d. Salvage value of an existing asset sold to make room for the new asset required for the project.

7. An externality can best be described as:

    a. An impact, positive or negative, that a new project would have on existing operations.
    b. An example of an opportunity cost.
    c. Something that always has a negative impact.
    d. Something that should not be included in the capital budgeting process.

8. A cost that has been incurred, or will be incurred, whether a project is accepted or rejected, is known as:

    a. An incremental cash flow.
    b. An externality.
    c. A sunk cost.
    d. A terminal cash flow.

9. A project has an initial cost of $45,000. The incremental inflows associated with the project are $20,000 in year 1, $15,000 in year 2, $10,000 in year 3 and $8,000 in year 4.

All cash inflows are at the end of the year. The appropriate discount rate for this project is 8.0%. What is the project's payback period?

10. A project has an initial cost of $45,000. The incremental inflows associated with the project are $20,000 in year 1, $15,000 in year 2, $10,000 in year 3 and $8,000 in year 4. All cash inflows are at the end of the year. The appropriate discount rate for this project is 8.0%. What is the project's discounted payback period?

11. A project has an initial cost of $45,000. The incremental inflows associated with the project are $20,000 in year 1, $15,000 in year 2, $10,000 in year 3 and $8,000 in year 4. All cash inflows are at the end of the year. The appropriate discount rate for this project is 8.0%. What is the project's net present value?

12. A project has an initial cost of $45,000. The incremental inflows associated with the project are $20,000 in year 1, $15,000 in year 2, $10,000 in year 3 and $8,000 in year 4. All cash inflows are at the end of the year. The appropriate discount rate for this project is 8.0%. What is the project's internal rate of return? Calculate to two decimal places.

13. A project has an initial cost of $45,000. The incremental inflows associated with the project are $20,000 in year 1, $15,000 in year 2, $10,000 in year 3 and $8,000 in year 4. All cash inflows are at the end of the year. The appropriate discount rate for this project is 8.0%. What is the project's modified internal rate of return? Calculate to two decimal places.

Use the following data to answer questions 14–26.

Your firm needs a new machine for producing a specific product, as the old machine is no longer viable. Rather than simply replace the old machine with the same model, your production manager wants to try a new machine using a new technology. The new machine will cost $115,000 and will require another $15,000 to ship it and install it in place. It will also require an increase in net working capital of $8,000 up front. The new machine falls under the MACRS 5-year schedule for depreciation (20.00% in year 1, 32.00% in year 2, 19.20% in year 3, 11.52% in years 4 and 5 and 5.76% in year 6).

The production manager expects that the new technology will decrease operating costs by $38,000 per year for the five years it will be in operation. At the end of five years, the project will end and the asset will be sold. It is estimated that the new machine will have a salvage (market) value of $12,000 at the end of five years. The appropriate discount rate for the new machine is 8.5%. The firm's tax rate is 35.0%.

14. What is the depreciable basis of the new machine?

15. What is the net operating cash flow for year 0? Round your answer to the nearest dollar.

16. What is the net operating cash flow for year 1? Round your answer to the nearest dollar.

17. What is the net operating cash flow for year 2? Round your answer to the nearest dollar.

18. What is the net operating cash flow for year 3? Round your answer to the nearest dollar.

19. What is the net operating cash flow for year 4? Round your answer to the nearest dollar.

20. What is the total of the terminal cash flows for the project? Round your answer to the nearest dollar.

21. What is the net operating cash flow for year 5? Round your answer to the nearest dollar.

22. What is the project's NPV, using the 8.50% discount rate? Round your answer to the nearest dollar.

23. What is the project's IRR? Report your answer to two decimal places.

24. What is the project's MIRR, using the 8.50% as the reinvestment rate? Report your answer to two decimal places.

25. What is the project's PB? Report your answer to two decimal places.

26. What is the project's DPB, using the 8.50% discount rate? Report your answer to two decimal places.

Excel Project

Replacement Project Analysis

This case discusses a replacement project—the firm is considering replacing an existing asset that is still productive with a new asset that uses a new technology that will save on production costs. Since the old asset is still productive, the cash flows from that old asset must be considered in the analysis (they are an opportunity cost).

Peterman Plastics uses a lathe for trimming molded plastics. The lathe was purchased ten years ago at a cost of $7,500. It has an expected economic life of 15 years, and the salvage value at the end of that 15 years is expected to be zero. The current lathe has been depreciated on a straight-line basis (@ $500 per year) and currently has a book value of $2,500. The firm's engineers report that a new machine can be purchased for $12,000 (including S&H), and over its five-year economic life it will reduce labor and material costs by $3,000 per year. The new machine falls into the MACRS 3-year depreciation class, which depreciates the equipment over four years (33% in the first year, 45% in the second, 15% in the third and 7% in the fourth year). Salvage value for the new machine at the end of five years is expected to be $2,000. The old machine's current market value is $1,000 and it will be sold if the new machine is purchased. Net working capital will need to increase by $1,000 (for parts and supplies) if the new machine is purchased. The firm's marginal tax rate is 40.0%. The appropriate cost of capital for the new machine is 11.5%.

Do a complete incremental cash flow analysis and capital budgeting analysis for this project. Use the capital budgeting analysis as the basis for a recommendation to your boss on the project. Write a one-page memo to your boss giving your recommendation and supporting it with the capital budgeting analysis.

Bibliography

Fundamentals of Corporate Finance, 12th edition. S. Ross, R. Westerfield and B. Jordan. McGraw-Hill Education, 2019.

Financial Management: Principles & Practice, 8th edition. T. Gallagher. Textbook Media Press, 2019.

Foundations of Financial Management, 17th edition. S. Block, G. Hirt and B. Danielsen. McGraw-Hill Education, 2018.

8   Capital Structure and the WACC

Capital structure refers to the mix of debt and equity the firm uses to fund its assets. There are some large firms that use little or no long-term debt, like Facebook (with zero long-term debt 2013–2017), and others that make much more use of debt, like Tesla (with only 15% of their assets funded by equity in 2017). The different sources of funds have different costs and different levels of risk, and firms typically use the mix of debt, preferred equity and common equity that minimizes their weighted average cost of capital (WACC)—the average cost from all sources of funds, weighted according to how much of each source the firm uses to finance its operations. The overall cost the firm pays for the money it raises will be a function of the amount of money raised via each source (the weights of each source in the capital structure) and the required return associated with each source (the component costs of capital).

In this chapter, we discuss the sources of funds available to the firm and the methods used to determine the cost of funds from each of those different sources. We will review how to determine the weights for each source of capital used in the capital structure, and then put it all together to calculate the weighted average cost of capital. Since the WACC is used as the discount rate for valuing projects as well as for the CFFA model for valuing the firm, this subject is closely tied to all three of the fundamental principles.

The Fundamental Principles in Action

FP1 says that the value of an asset is the present value of the cash flows the asset is expected to produce. For production projects, as well as for the free cash flow model for valuing the firm, the present value is calculated using the WACC as the discount rate. FP2 states that risk and return are directly related, and so riskier assets require higher returns. In the capital budgeting process, projects of higher than average risk are discounted using the WACC increased to adjust for risk. Since the WACC is the weighted average return to the firm's investors, this method assumes that investors will be compensated for taking on higher than average risk with a higher than average return, which is consistent with both PR1 and PR3. FP3 indicates the negative relationship between yield and value; adjusting the WACC up for above-average risk projects will cause the present value of the project's cash flows (and therefore its value) to decrease.

Understanding Capital Structure and Its Effects

When a firm borrows money (issues new debt), both its financial leverage and its financial risk increase. When a firm issues new common equity, its financial leverage decreases. If the firm issues both new debt and new equity, keeping the ratio of debt and equity relatively constant, then financial leverage remains fairly stable. As will be seen, each source of funds (debt vs. preferred equity vs. new common equity vs. retained earnings) has different costs.

Therefore, firms are motivated to (A) use the mix of sources that results in the lowest overall cost of funds and (B) maintain that relationship between the sources over time to stabilize both their costs and their financial leverage. The overall cost of funds, weighted according to the firm's use of the sources of funds, is known as the weighted average cost of capital, or WACC. The formula for calculating the WACC is:

$$WACC = W_d\,k_d\left(1-T\right) + W_p\,k_p + W_e\,k_{e\,or\,n}$$

where: W_d is the percentage of debt used in the capital structure;
W_p is the percentage of preferred equity used in the capital structure;
W_e is the percentage of common equity used in the capital structure;
k_d is the component cost of debt (the appropriate interest rate);
k_p is the component cost of preferred equity;
k_e is the component cost of common equity using retained earnings;
k_n is the component cost of new common equity (floating new shares); and
T is the firm's marginal tax rate.

Notice that the cost of common equity is given in two different forms: the cost of retained earnings (k_e) and the cost of issuing new common equity (k_n). As will be seen, these two sources have different costs, and therefore need to be treated separately.

Two important things to understand about this model:

1.   For the cost of common equity, k_e is used in the model before k_n because retained earnings are cheaper than new common equity (k_n is used when the firm runs out of retained earnings); and
2.   The weights (W_d, W_p and W_e) must sum to 100%.

The firm's capital is supplied by its shareholders (owners and preferred shareholders) and its bondholders (creditors). The firm owes its investors a reasonable return—reasonable by the investors' standards, not the firm's. At the same time, the returns paid to the investors have a direct impact on the value of the firm's investments, as well as the value of the firm itself. Therefore, it is in the firm's best interests to minimize the cost of the money it receives. It is also in the investors' best interests for the firm to minimize its costs; the lower the cost of the debt used, the more likely the firm will be in a position to pay the debt on time and in full. Likewise, the lower the cost of the funds used, the higher the present value of the firm's cash flows, and therefore the higher the intrinsic value of the firm's stock. So, minimizing the firm's cost of capital is in the best interests of the firm and its stakeholders.

The Component Costs of Capital

Each source of funds has a different cost, and the costs reflect the risks being borne by each type of investor. Debt typically has the lowest cost for two reasons:

1.   The risk of default (and possible bankruptcy) is borne by the firm's common shareholders, not the bondholders—the bondholders are protected by the bond's contract and are more likely to be repaid during a bankruptcy proceeding than the shareholders; and
2.   Since interest is paid out of pre-tax earnings, the use of debt allows firms to reduce their taxable income. Debt is the only component cost that receives a tax break.

While the cost of debt increases as the firm borrows more and more money, it is the common shareholders that will lose the most if the firm goes into default. Since the risk of bankruptcy is higher for the common shareholders than for the bondholders, the cost of common equity is usually higher than the cost of debt.

Preferred equity (which is being used less and less over time) also typically has a lower cost than that of common equity, but higher than the cost of debt. There are also two reasons for this:

1. Preferred shareholders have a greater claim against the firm's assets in the case of bankruptcy than the firm's common shareholders; and
2. Preferred dividends are paid before common dividends. If a firm stops paying dividends for several years in order to get the firm through rough times, before the firm can renew paying a dividend to its common shareholders, it may pay all of the unpaid preferred dividends for the time period in which the dividends were halted.

Both of these factors make the preferred shares less risky than the common shares, and therefore the preferred shares tend to earn a lower return than the common shares.

One significant point must be kept in mind when determining the component costs of funds: the relevant rate is the rate on the next amount of funds obtained, not on the last. It does not matter if the firm's most recent bond issue paid 5.5% annual interest; what matters is the interest rate the firm must pay for the next bond issue.

The After-Tax Cost of Debt

As discussed in previous chapters, the cost of debt is interest. Firms take on (or increase) long-term debt by issuing bonds. Thus, the cost of debt is the interest rate the firm will pay for the next issue of bonds. While firms must use the services of a financial intermediary to float new bonds, the flotation costs for the bonds are negligible, and so flotation costs are not included in the calculation of the cost of debt. Flotation costs will be a factor in the cost of issuing new preferred or common equity.

The firm pays its creditors (bondholders) by making regular interest payments over the life of the bond contract, and the final interest payment is combined with the return of the principal borrowed. The interest rate the firm pays is determined by the market (the potential bondholders), which considers the amount of debt the firm already has, the firm's liquidity, the current economic conditions and anything else regarding the firm that they deem relevant to the issue. If the market perceives the new debt as riskier than the outstanding debt, or if the market's tolerance for risk has shifted, the firm may be required to pay a higher interest rate for the new issue of bonds.

The formula for the after-tax cost of debt is as follows:

$$\text{After-Tax Cost of Debt} = k_d(1-T)$$

where: k_d is the coupon interest rate the firm will pay on the next bond issue; and
T is the firm's marginal tax rate.

Example. Buford Industries will issue new bonds that have ten years to maturity and that pay 6.60% annual interest. Buford's marginal tax rate is 25%. What is Buford's after-tax cost of debt?

Solution. After-Tax Cost of Debt $= .066(1-.25) = .0495$ or 4.95%

Thus, while Buford will be paying 6.6% annual interest on its bonds, the fact that they get to pay that interest from pre-tax dollars reduces their taxable income, and this tax avoidance reduces the firm's cost of debt by the percentage of that tax avoidance.

The Cost of Preferred Equity

Preferred equity is raised by issuing new preferred shares. Issuing new preferred shares means using the services of an investment banking house, which will require the firm to pay flotation costs (the costs the investment banking house charges for floating new shares). The model used for calculating the cost of preferred equity is a form of the dividend discount model:

$$k_p = \frac{D_p}{P_n}$$

where:　k_p is the required return on the firm's preferred equity;
　　　　D_p is the annual preferred dividend; and
　　　　P_n is the market price of the preferred stock, net of flotation costs.

As discussed in Chapter 6, the preferred dividend is fixed, which changes two things on the dividend discount model:

- The dividend is no longer time-dependent ($D_1 = D_2 = D_3$), because
- $g = 0$.

This is the first of the three scenarios regarding the DDM considered in Chapter 6.

Example. Zephyr Manufacturing intends to issue new shares of preferred stock that will pay a $6.00 annual preferred dividend. Zephyr's current outstanding preferred shares are selling for $83.00 per share. Floating new shares will cost the firm $3.00 per share. What is Zephyr's cost of preferred equity?

Solution. The net price for Zephyr's new shares is $83 – 3 = $80, and $k_p = 6 \div 80 = .075$, or 7.5%.

The Cost of Internal Common Equity

Internal equity is another name for retained earnings. Since the common shareholders take on the risk of default associated with the firm's debt, the cost of internal equity is typically higher than the cost of preferred equity. But why should retained earnings have a cost? The firm already owns them—nothing to float, nobody looking for a fee. Why aren't they free? Because retained earnings belong to the common shareholders. The firm needs to pay the shareholders for the use of the money.

We will look at two approaches to estimating the firm's cost of retained earnings: the CAPM approach and the DDM approach. Both approaches are grounded in financial theory, and having two perspectives on the metric can be useful, but it can also be confusing. If these two approaches do not agree, resolving discrepancies between them becomes a matter of judgment. However, if they are close together in value, it adds confidence to the estimate.

The CAPM Approach

To estimate the cost of retained earnings using the Capital Asset Pricing Model (from Chapter 3), use the following steps:

1. Determine the risk-free rate (r_{RF});
2. Determine the current market risk premium, which is the expected market return minus the risk-free rate ($r_M - r_{RF}$);
3. Determine the stock's beta coefficient (β_i);
4. Plug these figures into the Security Market Line (SML) equation to calculate the required return on the firm's retained earnings.

For steps 1 and 2, proxies are used to estimate these rates. A common proxy for the risk-free rate is the yield on 10-year Treasury notes, and the market return can be estimated using the yield on a market index fund such as the S&P 500 index fund. For step 3, betas for most publicly traded firms are available on websites like finance.yahoo.com or reuters.com. Once these inputs are determined, they are used to calculate the cost of internal equity using the SML model:

$$k_e = r_{RF} + \left(r_M - r_{RF}\right)\beta_i$$

where: k_e is the firm's cost of retained earnings;
 r_{RF} is the nominal risk-free rate of return;
 r_M is the return to the market; and
 β_i is the beta for stock i.

Example. The current yield on 10-year T-notes is 3.25%, and the S&P 500 index fund is currently returning 8.50%. If Sherman Inc.'s beta is 1.32, what is the estimate for the Sherman's cost of retained earnings?

Solution. $k_e = 3.25 + (8.5 - 3.25)1.32 = 10.18\%$. Since this firm is perceived as riskier than the market (as indicated by its beta of 1.32), the firm's cost of internal equity is higher than the market return of 8.50%.

The DDM Approach

Assuming the firm's dividend is expected to grow at a constant rate for the foreseeable future, this is the second DDM scenario from Chapter 6:

$$k_e = \frac{D_1}{P_0} + g$$

where: k_e is the cost of internal common equity (retained earnings);
 D_1 is the common dividend expected one year in the future ($D_1 = D_0 \times \{1 + g\}$);
 P_0 is the current market price of the firm's common stock; and
 g is the expected future growth rate in dividends.

Note that $D_1 \div P_0$ is the dividend yield (the percentage return on the stock price paid as a dividend), and that if g is expected to be constant in the future, then g also represents the expected growth rate in the firm's stock price. Therefore, this version of the DDM supports theory by calculating the cost of common equity as the combined costs of dividends and capital gains.

Example. Sherman Inc. just paid an annual dividend of $1.20, and the dividend is expected to grow at a constant rate of 5%. If the firm's common stock is currently selling for $24 per share, what is Sherman's cost of internal equity?

Solution. $D_1 = 1.20(1.05) = 1.26$; $k_e = (1.26 \div 24) + .05 = .1025$ or 10.25%.

The Cost of External Common Equity

External equity is another name for issuing new common stock. Issuing new common shares means using the services of an investment banking house, which will require the firm to pay flotation costs (the costs the investment banking house charges for floating new shares). The model used for calculating the cost of external equity is the same one used for internal common equity, but adjusted for flotation costs:

$$k_n = \frac{D_1}{P_n} + g$$

where: k_n is the cost of external common equity (floating new common shares);
D_1 is the common dividend expected one year in the future ($= D_0 \times \{1 + g\}$);
P_n is the current market price of the firm's common stock, net of flotation costs; and
g is the expected future growth rate in dividends.

Example. Sherman Inc. just paid an annual dividend of $1.20, and the dividend is expected to grow at a constant rate of 5%. Flotation for new common shares will be 6% of the stock price. If the firm's common stock is currently selling for $24 per share, what is Sherman's cost of external equity?

Solution. $D_1 = 1.20(1.05) = 1.26$; $k_n = + .05 = .10585$ or 10.59%.
$k_n = 1.26 \div 24(1 - .06) + .05 = .10585$.

Issuing new shares will cost the firm 6% of the new share price—the fee charged by the investment banking house. The flotation costs raise the cost of the firm's common equity from 10.25% (for retained earnings) to 10.59% (for issuing new common shares). The cost goes up because the firm's common shareholders require their 10.25% return, while the investment bank requires an additional 6% of the shares issued. Thus, at the point that the firm runs out of retained earnings, the cost of common equity increases, due to the flotation costs associated with a new issue of common equity. That point, we learned in Chapter 7, is the retained earnings break point (REBP).

Determining the Weights for the Component Costs

The weights of debt (W_d), preferred equity (W_p) and common equity (W_e) to be used in the WACC calculation are not difficult to determine. The weights are calculated as the value of each source of funds divided by the total value of all sources of funds, so that the weights add up to one (100%). It is preferable to use market values rather than book values for calculating the weights. For equity (both common and preferred), this is simple enough: it is the market price of the stock multiplied by the number of shares outstanding. This value for the common stock is known as the market capitalization (or market cap), which represents the current market value of all of the publicly traded shares of the firm's common stock.

For debt, however, determining the market value can be challenging. It may be difficult to estimate how much of the firm's outstanding debt was issued at which time and at which rate, because debt is repaid over time. Under these conditions, it is permissible to use the book value of debt (the total of the long-term and short-term debt amounts on the balance sheet) as the value of debt.

The sum of the values of all sources of funds is the total value of the firm. The weights are then calculated as the value of each source of funds divided by the total value. If done properly, the sum of the weights will be 100%.

Example. Hiram Industries has $500,000 in short-term debt and $2 million in long-term debt. Their preferred shares sell for $40 per share, and there are 250,000 preferred shares outstanding. Hiram's common stock sells for $45 per share, and there are 600,000 shares outstanding. Calculate Hiram's total value and the weights of debt, preferred stock and common stock in their capital structure.

Solution. Total Debt = $500,000 + $2 million = $2.5 million; Total Preferred Equity = $40 × 250,000 = $1 million; Total Common Equity = $45 × 600,000 = $27 million; Total Value = 2.5 + 1 + 27 = $30.5 million. W_d = 2.5 ÷ 30.5 = 0.08196 or 8.20%; W_p = 1 ÷ 30.5 = 0.03278 or 3.28%; W_e = 27 ÷ 30.5 = 0.88524 or 88.52%; 8.2% + 3.28% + 88.52% = 100.00%.

Putting It All Together

Once you have calculated the weights, you can plug the component costs and the weights into the WACC equation and compute the firm's cost of capital. If a firm does not use preferred equity in their capital structure, then both the cost of preferred and the weight of preferred are zero, and so the term representing preferred equity in the WACC equation is zero.

Example. Hiram Industries will pay 6.8% on any new debt that they issue, 9.4% on any new preferred equity and 11.6% for retained earnings. Hiram's marginal tax rate is 30.0%. Use these data and the weights in the prior problem to calculate Hiram's weighted average cost of capital (WACC).

Solution. WACC = 0.082(6.8)(1 − 0.3) + 0.0328(9.4) + 0.8852(11.6) = 0.39032 + 0.30832 + 10.26832 = 10.96696% or approximately 10.97%.

Example. Simpson International has $2 million in short-term debt and $8 million in long-term debt on their balance sheet. Their common stock is currently selling for $30, and there are 500,000 shares of their common stock in the market. Any new debt issued will have to pay a 7.5% coupon rate, and the firm's marginal tax rate is 25%. The firm's retained earnings have a cost of 10.6%, and any new common equity will cost 10.9%. Calculate Simpson's WACC twice: once using retained earnings, and again using new common equity.

Solution. Total Debt = $2 million + $8 million = $10 million; Total Common Equity = $30 × 500,000 = $15 million; Total Value = 10 + 15 = $25 million; W_d = 10 ÷ 25 = 0.4 or 40%; W_e = 15 ÷ 25 = 0.6 or 60%.

$WACC_{RE}$ = 0.4(7.5)(1 − 0.25) + 0.6(10.6) = 2.25 + 6.36 = 8.61%. $WACC_{NCE}$ = 0.4(7.5) (1 − 0.25) + 0.6(10.9) = 2.25 + 6.54 = 8.79%. The cost of capital increases when the firm floats new common equity. Since Simpson does not use preferred equity, that term was left out of the WACC calculation.

Example. The following data reflect the expected future costs and current value metrics for Munson Manufacturing.

- Any new debt issued, short-term or long-term, would require a 7.50% interest rate for up to $10 million in new debt, and 7.85% for up to $20 million in new debt. The firm currently carries $2 million in short-term debt and $11 million in long-term debt on its balance sheet.
- Munson's preferred equity is currently selling for $52.00 per share, and pays a $3.00 annual dividend. Flotation costs for new preferred equity are $2.00 per share. Currently there are 300,000 preferred shares outstanding in the market.
- Munson's last annual common dividend, paid last week, was $1.60, and the common dividend is expected to grow at an annual rate of 5.0% for the foreseeable future. Their common shares currently sell for $45.00, and there are 1.5 million shares out-standing in the market. Flotation costs for new common equity are 6% of the market price.
- Munson has forecasted that they will have $15,371,400 in retained earnings at the end of the year to fund new investment projects. Their capital budget for next year (the amount they intend to invest in new capital projects) is $21,750,000.
- The firm's marginal tax rate is 30.00%.

Use these data to calculate Munson's WACC using both retained earnings and new common equity, and calculate the retained earnings break point to see if it will be necessary to float new common equity to fund next year's capital budget.

Solution. A problem this comprehensive should be dealt with as a series of smaller prob-lems. Calculate each component cost individually, then the values of each source of funds, and then the weights for each component cost, and finally plug them all into the WACC formula. The REBP can be calculated last.

First, we calculate the component costs.

- After-tax cost of debt: $k_d(1 - T) = 0.075 \times (1 - 0.3) = 0.0525$ or 5.25%;
- Cost of preferred equity: $k_p = 3 \div (52 - 2) = 0.06$ or 6.00%;
- Cost of retained earnings: $k_e = \{(1.6 \times 1.05) \div 45\} + .05 = 0.0873$ or 8.73%;
- Cost of new common equity: $k_n \{(1.6 \times 1.05) \div [45 \times (1 - .06)]\} + .05 = 0.08971$ or 8.97%.

Next, we calculate the values of the sources of funds and the total value of all sources.

- Value of debt: $2 million + $11 million = $13,000,000;
- Value of preferred equity: $52 \times 300,000 = $15,600,000;
- Value of common equity: $45 \times 1,500,000 = $67,500,000;
- Total value: 13,000,000 + 15,600,000 + 67,500,000 = $96,100,000.

Now we use the value of each source divided by the total value to calculate the weights of each source of funds.

- Weight of debt: $W_d = 13,000,000 \div 96,100,000 = 0.13527$ or 13.53%;
- Weight of preferred equity: $W_p = 15,600,000 \div 96,100,000 = 0.16233$ or 16.23%;
- Weight of common equity: $W_e = 67,500,000 \div 96,100,000 = 0.70239$ or 70.24%.

Next, we plug the component costs and the weights into the WACC formula to calculate the cost of capital. We do it twice: once using the cost of retained earnings, and again using the cost of new common equity.

$$WACC_{RE} = 0.1353 \times 5.25\% + 0.1623 \times 6.0\% + 0.7024 \times 8.73\% = 0.07818 \text{ or } 7.82\%$$
$$WACC_{NCE} = 0.1353 \times 5.25\% + 0.1623 \times 6.0\% + 0.7024 \times 8.97\% = 0.07984 \text{ or } 7.98\%$$

So, when Munson runs out of retained earnings, their WACC will increase by 16 basis points (0.16%) due to the costs of floating new common equity. Next, we calculate the REBP to see if the firm will need to float new common equity in order to fund their capital budget.

$$REBP = RE \div W_e = 15,371,400 \div 0.7024 = \$21,884,112$$

Munson will be able to fund a capital budget of \$21,884,112 using retained earnings. Since the next year's capital budget is \$21,750,000, Munson will not need to float new common equity.

Summary of the Principles and Precepts Applied in This Chapter

The First Fundamental Principle (FP1): The value of any asset is equal to the present value of the cash flows the asset is expected to produce over its economic life.

For production projects, as well as for the free cash flow model for valuing the firm, the present value is calculated using the WACC as the discount rate.

The Second Fundamental Principle (FP2): There is a direct relationship between risk and return; as perceived risk increases, required return will also increase (and vice versa), holding other things constant.

In the capital budgeting process, projects of higher than average risk are discounted using the WACC adjusted up for risk.

The First Precept (PR1): The present value of a cash flow (or an asset) is inversely related to its discount rate; increasing the discount rate decreases the present value (and vice versa), holding other things constant.
The Third Precept (PR3): The present value of a cash flow (or an asset) is inversely related to its perceived risk; the higher the risk, the higher the discount rate, and therefore the lower the present value.

Since the WACC is the weighted average return to the firm's investors, the method assumes that investors will be compensated for taking on higher than average risk with a higher than average return, which is consistent with both PR1 and PR3.

The Third Fundamental Principle (FP3): There is an inverse relationship between price and yield; if an asset's price increases, its return will decrease (and vice versa), holding other things constant.

Adjusting the WACC up for above average risk projects will cause the present value of the project's cash flows (and therefore its value) to decrease.

End of Chapter Problems

1. Explain in your own words the logic of using the weighted average cost of capital as the discount rate for capital projects.
2. List the component costs of capital in ascending order (all four of them). Justify your ranking with an explanation for each component cost.
3. Calculate the after-tax cost of debt for firms with the following yields to maturity for their new bonds. Assume the firm's marginal tax rate is 25.00%.

   a.   YTM = 6.40%.
   b.   YTM = 7.80%.
   c.   YTM = 9.90%.

   Repeat parts a–c using a marginal tax rate of 35.00%. What effect does raising the tax rate have on the component cost of debt?
4. Tandem Industries can sell new shares of preferred stock for $28.00 per share, but flotation costs will run them $1.00 per share. Tandem's preferred stock currently pays a $3.00 dividend. What is the component cost for Tandem's new preferred equity?
5. Your boss is the treasurer of the company, and she expects the firm will grow at 4.00% annually in the future. She also believes that issuing bonds is less expensive than the cost of retained earnings. Your firm's debt securities have a yield to maturity of 8.50%, and the firm's marginal tax rate is 30.00%. The current market price of your firm's common stock is $19.00, and the annual dividend expected next year is $1.50 per share.
   Calculate the component costs of both debt and retained earnings to see if your boss is right.
6. Empire Capital Enterprises has a beta of 1.36. The current yield on 10-year US T-notes is 4.25%, and the return to the S&P 500 index fund is 9.60%. Given these data, what is Empire's cost of retained earnings?
7. Gallagher Industries' common stock currently sells for $20.00 per share. The common dividend just paid was $1.20, and the dividend is expected to increase at a rate of 5% annually. Floating new common shares will cost Gallagher 5% of the market price of the stock. What is Gallagher's component cost of new common equity?
8. Newman International has an optimal capital structure that consists of 35.00% debt, 15.00% preferred equity, and 50.00% common equity. Their new bond issue will have a coupon rate of 7.20%. Their preferred stock currently sells for $40 per share, and floating new shares would cost $2.00 per share. The preferred dividend is fixed at $2.60 annually. Newman's common stock has a current market price of $33.00, and floating new common shares would cost Newman 6.00% of the share price. The most recent annual common dividend paid was $2.50, and the dividend is expected to grow at an annual rate of 4.00%. The firm's marginal tax rate is 30.00%. Use these data to calculate Newman's WACC using both retained earnings and new common equity.

9. The most recent data for Harper Housewares is given below:

Balance Sheet Data

Cash	250,000	Accounts Payable	480,000
Marketable Securities	150,000	Notes Payable	425,000
Receivables	350,000	Long-Term Debt	1,465,000
Inventory	800,000	Preferred Equity	430,000
Net Fixed Assets	3,450,000	Common Equity	1,400,000
Total Assets	5,000,000	Retained Earnings	800,000
		Total Liabilities and Equity	5,000,000

Market Data

	Price	Shares Outstanding
Preferred Equity	$60.00	50,000
Common Equity	$35.00	100,000

What are Harper's weights for debt, common equity and preferred equity?

10. Daytona Dairies has preferred stock that pays a dividend of $3.25. Their preferred stock currently sells for $34.21. Flotation costs for new preferred stock are expected to be 5% of the share price. What is the component cost of Daytona's preferred equity?

11. T-bonds are currently paying 5.5%, while the S&P 500 is paying 8%. Sentry Electronics has a beta of 1.5. What is the component cost of Sentry's retained earnings?

12. Fairweather Pharmacies' component costs of capital and their weights are given below:

$$k_d = 10\% \quad w_d = 45\%$$
$$k_p = 5\% \quad w_p = 10\%$$
$$k_e = 8\% \quad w_e = 45\%$$
$$T = 40\%$$

Given these figures, what is Fairweather's weighted average cost of capital?

13. Anspagh Automobiles just paid a common dividend of $2.50 at the end of last year, and that dividend is expected to grow at an annual rate of 10%. Their common stock currently sells for $101.85, which is what they expect to get for newly issued shares at this time. Flotation costs on newly issued shares are 5% of the stock price. What is Anspagh's component cost of new equity?

14. The CEO of Harlem Hardware Supplies has submitted together a capital budget of $48,500,000 for the following year's investment opportunities. He expects to have $19,000,000 in retained earnings at the end of the year. Harlem's target capital structure calls for 45% equity. Based on these figures, will Harlem be able to meet their capital budget needs with retained earnings?

Comprehensive Excel Problem

Maggie Nelson, CFO for Sanders Industrial, is preparing to submit the capital budget for the next fiscal year to CEO Jonathon Sanders. Before she can submit the capital budget, she needs you to double-check her calculations for the firm's weighted average cost of capital, to make certain that the capital budget reflects the correct cost of funds. Given that her proposed capital budget for next year is $14.6 million, she wants you to confirm (or refute) all of the associated costs in your own spreadsheet.

You are given the following data to work with:

- The book values of short-term and long-term debt are $1.2 million and $5.55 million respectively;
- The firm has 130,900 shares of preferred equity that have a market price of $55.00 and pay an annual dividend of $3.30 per share;
- The firm has 750,000 shares of common stock that currently sell for $21.40, and just paid an annual dividend of $0.60;
- The firm's common dividend is expected to grow at a constant rate of 5.00% annually for the foreseeable future;
- Any new debt issued by the firm, short-term or long-term, will pay an annual coupon rate of 6.60%;
- Issuing new preferred stock will cost the firm $3.40 per share in flotation costs;
- Issuing new common stock will cost the firm 6.00% of the market price in flotation costs;
- Sanders Industrial has a beta of 1.28;
- The annual yield on 10-year T-notes is 4.60%;
- The annual yield on the S&P 500 index fund is 7.20%;
- The firm is expected to have $6.45 million in retained earnings available for the capital budget;
- The firm's marginal tax rate is 20.00.

Your assignment is to address the following issues:

- Calculate the values for debt, preferred equity and common equity, and use those values to calculate the weights of each source of funds in the capital structure (the weights to use in the WACC calculation);
- Calculate the component costs of all four sources of funds, including any tax benefits as well as any flotation costs for issuing new securities (calculate the cost of retained earnings in two ways—using the DDM and the CAPM approaches—and then use these data to determine what cost to assign for retained earnings);
- Plug the weights and component costs into the WACC equation and calculate the firm's WACC using both retained earnings and new common equity;
- Calculate the retained earnings break point for the level of retained earnings indicated, and determine if funding the capital budget of $14,600,000 will require issuing new common stock;
- Based on the relationship between the REBP and the total capital budget, identify Sanders' marginal cost of capital.

All calculations are to be done in an Excel spreadsheet, using formulas or Excel functions—hard-coded calculations will earn no credit; you must make Excel do the work. Format all dollar values as dollars, and all percentages with a percent sign. Format all percentages to two decimal places (0.023485 = 2.35%), but do not round the calculation—just change the format of the number, not its value. Format all dollar figures to the dollar (no cents).

Turn in a one-page paper addressing the five issues indicated above. Format your spreadsheet so that all of your analysis can be printed on one page, and attach it to your one-page write-up. Email your spreadsheet to the instructor before turning in the hard copy.

Bibliography

Fundamentals of Corporate Finance, 12th edition. S. Ross, R. Westerfield and B. Jordan. McGraw-Hill Education, 2019.

Financial Management: Principles & Practice, 8th edition. T. Gallagher. Textbook Media Press, 2019.

Foundations of Financial Management, 17th edition. S. Block, G. Hirt and B. Danielsen. McGraw-Hill Education, 2018.

9 Analyzing and Forecasting Financial Statements

The financial statements of a corporation contain data regarding the many transactions the firm has been involved in over the period of time the statements represent (in either quarterly or annual reports). These data are a roadmap of how the firm's managers have been making decisions on behalf of the firm's stakeholders, and serve as the basis of the firm's value. Ratio analysis offers tools to determine what the firm is doing well and where it needs to improve, and helps to give an overall picture of the firm's current and future prospects. The one skill all corporate managers need is to be able to read, understand and analyze an income statement and a balance sheet.

In this chapter, we discuss how to analyze the firm's financial statements, as well as how to forecast them. We will perform an organized analysis of an income statement and a balance sheet, and use the analysis to determine the firm's strengths and weaknesses. We will also learn how to create pro forma, or forecasted, financial statements, in order to determine the firm's funding needs for the future. We will start by reviewing the structure of the basic financial statements.

This chapter does not make use of the principles or precepts, since it is not strictly a chapter on financial theory. Most of the material is accounting theory, but all of it is used by financial analysts for understanding the firm's strengths and weaknesses, as well as for forecasting the impact of future decisions on the firm's financial performance.

Understanding the Financial Statements

There are four financial statements published by corporations: the balance sheet, the income statement, the statement of cash flows and the statement of retained earnings. The first two will occupy most of our time and attention in this chapter, while the third will be utilized for one purpose only, and the fourth will only be mentioned in passing. For analytical purposes, the cash flow statement offers little, while the statement of retained earnings offers nothing.

The balance sheet and the income statement are distinctly different in structure and offer different types of data. Each has its own individual use, while the two together offer even more, as will be seen in the ratio analysis.

The Balance Sheet

Table 9.1 contains the balance sheets and income statements for the period 2014–2018 for Marquardt Manufacturing, a fictitious firm that we will be using in the analysis section of this

Table 9.1 Financial Statements for Marquardt Manufacturing 2014–2018

Income Statement FY2014–2018 ($Millions except per share data)

	2014	2015	2016	2017	2018
Sales	6,282.4	6,621.6	6,946.1	7,300.4	7,694.6
Cost of Goods Sold	2,638.6	2,754.6	2,910.4	3,080.8	3,177.9
Gross Profit	3,643.8	3,867.0	4,035.7	4,219.6	4,516.7
Operating Expenses	1,445.00	1,496.5	1,590.7	1,693.7	1,754.4
Depreciation	212.3	208.4	211.1	217.9	223.4
EBIT	1,986.5	2,162.1	2,233.9	2,308.0	2,538.9
Interest	193.1	193.6	202.8	211.4	211.8
EBT	1,793.4	1,968.5	2,031.1	2,096.6	2,327.1
Taxes	581.1	628.0	654.0	670.9	751.7
Net Income	1,212.3	1,340.5	1,377.1	1,425.7	1,575.4
Dividends Paid	614.7	645.4	686.4	737.6	788.9
Shares Outstanding	1,024.5	1,024.5	1,024.5	1,024.5	1,024.5
Dividend per Share	0.60	0.63	0.67	0.72	0.77
Retained Earnings	597.6	695.1	690.7	688.1	786.5
Tax Rate	32.40%	31.90%	32.20%	32.00%	32.30%
Required Return	12.00%	12.00%	12.00%	12.00%	12.00%
WACC	10.70%	10.80%	10.80%	10.90%	10.90%

Balance Sheet FY2014–2018 ($Millions except per share data)

	2014	2015	2016	2017	2018
Cash	125.6	132.4	138.9	146.0	153.9
Marketable Securities	43.2	46.9	41.7	44.3	42.2
Accounts Receivable	973.8	1,006.5	1,083.6	1,160.8	1,177.3
Inventory	1,130.8	1,105.8	1,326.7	1,263.0	1,423.5
Total Current Assets	2,273.4	2,291.6	2,590.9	2,614.1	2,796.9
Fixed Assets	11,699.0	12,609.3	13,353.4	14,339.9	15,191.8
Less Accumulated Depreciation	(3,683.5)	(3,891.9)	(4,103.0)	(4,320.9)	(4,544.3)
Net Fixed Assets	8,015.5	8,717.4	9,250.4	10,019.0	10,647.5
Total Assets	10,288.9	11,009.0	11,841.3	12,633.1	13,444.4
Accounts Payable	201.0	205.3	232.7	233.6	244.7
Accruals	266.5	281.4	293.8	301.3	310.4
Notes Payable	295.6	301.4	303.2	298.5	303.1
Total Current Liabilities	763.1	788.1	829.7	833.4	858.2
Long Term Debt	1,850.0	1,850.0	1,950.0	2,050.0	2,050.0
Total Liabilities	2,613.1	2,638.1	2,779.7	2,883.4	2,908.2
Capital Stock	1,024.5	1,024.5	1,024.5	1,024.5	1,024.5
Retained Earnings	6,651.3	7,346.4	8,037.1	8,725.2	9,511.7
Total Common Equity	7,675.8	8,370.9	9,061.6	9,749.7	10,536.2
Total Liabilities and Equity	10,288.9	11,009.0	11,841.3	12,633.1	13,444.4
Common Stock Price 12/31	10.60	11.13	11.84	12.72	13.60

chapter. The balance sheet is a snapshot of the firm's financial position at a point in time (the end of a year or a quarter). It shows the value of the asset accounts, as well as the liability and owners' equity accounts, as of a specific date. The name refers to the fact that the report has two sides—the asset side on the top, the liabilities and equity side on the bottom—that have equal total value. The top half of the statement shows where the firm is utilizing its capital, while the bottom half shows the sources of the funds being utilized. Many of the account values change on a daily basis; inventories are bought and sold, receivables are incurred or collected, checks are written or cashed. Seasonal issues also affect many firms, so that the financial position can look quite different at different times of the year. Firms generally choose to end their fiscal year during a slow season, when monthly sales and inventories should be at their lowest.

The top half of the balance sheet describes the firm's assets—things the firm owns and utilizes in producing their product or service—listed in descending order of liquidity. In finance, liquidity refers to the ability to turn an asset into cash quickly at a fair market value. The more liquid an asset is, the more likely you are to be able to sell it quickly if necessary, and therefore the lower the asset's risk. The bottom half of the statement contains the claims against those assets, listed in the order in which they must be paid. The structure of both sides of the report goes from short-term to long-term:

- Current assets and current liabilities are short term accounts; current assets are expected to turn over (be consumed and replenished) in one year or less (e.g., the inventories should be sold off in less than one year);
- Fixed assets, long-term debt and owners' equity are long-term accounts; fixed assets are expected to be in service for years, long-term debt may not be paid off for decades and owners' equity is listed last for two reasons:

   1.   Shareholders' claims represent ownership and need never be paid off; and
   2.   Shareholders have a residual claim; i.e., other claimants (the firm's bondholders and the government) get paid first.

The amounts in the balance sheet accounts are known as book values; the total common equity line on the balance sheet is known as the book value of common equity. For many accounts, book values may differ from market values (market values are current, determined in the marketplace, while book values are historic, determined at the point of sale).

Current Assets

Cash and cash equivalents, short-term investments (also known as marketable securities), accounts receivable and inventories are current assets—i.e., they are expected to be converted to cash within one year. All of these accounts are denominated in dollars, but only cash represents actual money that can be spent. Cash equivalents are marketable securities that mature very quickly and are highly liquid, and for that reason are sometimes included with cash. Included in cash equivalents are checks received but not yet deposited, checking accounts, petty cash, savings accounts, money market accounts and short-term, highly liquid investments with a maturity of three months or less such as US T-bills and commercial paper. Cash is held to support operations: in case a machine breaks down or in case a supplier offers a great deal on a part but requires a purchase much larger than your usual order. Many firms have a policy for how much cash to hold that is based on sales (e.g., 2% of annual sales). Because cash is held in support of operations and tends to vary with sales, it is an operating account (as per the discussion in Chapter 6).

Other investments have somewhat longer time to maturity and are less liquid, and these are designated as short-term investments. These will include marketable stocks and bonds that are only slightly less liquid than cash equivalents, and it is where the firm puts excess cash it does not require for operating purposes. For this reason, the short-term investments account is not an operating account.

Accounts receivable are credit sales to customers that have not yet been collected. These are typically monitored by the firm's credit department and reported in what is referred to as an aging report, which shows the amount of current and past due store credit. Assuming the firm's credit policies do not change, the level of accounts receivable will tend to vary with the level of sales. Therefore, the receivables account is an operating account.

Inventories represents the amount invested in raw materials, work in process and finished goods available for sale. The value of the inventories depends partially upon whether the firm uses a FIFO (first in first out) or a LIFO (last in first out) valuation system; if prices are rising, FIFO gives a higher inventories value (as well as a lower Cost of Goods Sold on the income statement) than LIFO. So, the inventory method used can have a large effect on the firm's financial statements—this is important to know when comparing firms. Beyond the impact of the valuation method, the level of inventories is also driven by the level of sales; when sales increase, inventories should increase as well. Therefore, the inventories account is an operating account.

Long-Term Assets

The firm's long-term physical assets (buildings, trucks, machines or the like) are reported net of depreciation. Depreciation is the spreading of the purchase amount of long-term assets over their economic life, to match the expense of using them to the revenues they generate over time. The federal government allows the deduction of depreciation to permit the firm to be in a position to replenish assets when they expire, so that the firm can continue to operate and offer the economy jobs as well as their products or services.

Fixed (or long-term) assets are typically listed as plant, property and equipment (PP&E) or some similar name, and the value is given based on the purchase price of the assets. Accumulated depreciation is removed from gross PP&E, and so net PP&E is the value recorded on the balance sheet. While the long-term assets are clearly used for producing the products or services, their value often does not change in response to a change in sales. This is because many long-term assets have capacity issues, in that they are able to produce a large amount of product. For example, if the fixed assets are capable of producing 100,000 items per quarter, but the firm is selling only 80,000 items per quarter, then sales could increase by 25% (100,000 ÷ 80,000 = 1.25) without needing additional fixed assets. Since fixed assets with capacity issues do not tend to move with sales, they are not designated as operating assets. However, a firm that uses fixed assets without large capacity issues may have a closer relationship between their long-term assets and sales, and they may very well deserve to be designated as operating assets. The significance of this designation will be apparent when we discuss forecasting pro forma financial statements later in this chapter.

Some firms have intangible assets, which are other long-term assets not used in operations. These may include such things as patents or copyrights, or another form of intellectual property, or even Good Will, which is the amount an acquiring firm pays above market value for a firm it acquires. These accounts are not operating accounts.

Finally, total assets are the sum of current assets and long-term assets. Thus, the total assets account is the sum of the top half of the balance sheet, or the total book value of the firm's assets.

Current Liabilities

Accounts payable, notes payable (or short-term debt) and accrued expenses are current liabilities—liabilities that the firm is expected to pay within one year. Accounts payable represent the firm's credit purchases from their suppliers for such things as inventories or supplies. Changes in sales are expected to be reflected by changes in payables; if sales increase, more inventories and supplies will be needed, so more will be purchased on credit. Therefore, accounts payable is an operating account.

Accruals include accrued wages and accrued taxes. Since wages are paid biweekly, and taxes are paid quarterly, the firm accrues these expenses until they are due to be paid. Increases in sales are likely to include increases in wages (temporary workers or overtime, or even adding a shift) as well as increases in accrued taxes. Thus, accrued expenses are also an operating account. The liability accounts that increase in value with an increase in sales are referred to as spontaneous liabilities. This is because their value spontaneously increases with an increase in sales revenue.

Notes payable are short-term debt instruments that must be repaid in less than one year. Raising funds through debt is a strategic choice, not an operating choice, so notes payable is not an operating account.

Long-Term Liabilities

Long-term debt represents bonds issued by the firm that are still in circulation. This is a long-term liability, but the use of debt is a strategic choice, and therefore long-term debt is not an operating account. In fact, there are no debt or equity operating accounts. Other long-term liability accounts, such as pension obligations, are also non-operating accounts.

Equity

Preferred stock is a hybrid security—it has features similar to both debt and common equity. For example, the preferred dividend is fixed, so if the firm grows, preferred shareholders do not share the wealth. In this way, the preferred dividend is similar to an interest payment on a bond. At the same time, the firm can interrupt (stop paying) preferred dividends without the risk of bankruptcy, which is similar to the common dividend. Preferred dividends must be paid before common dividends; in bankruptcy, preferred shareholders rank below debtholders but above common shareholders in their claim against the firm.

Common equity includes both the value of common stock and retained earnings. The common stock account reflects funds acquired by selling common shares, whereas retained earnings are net income that has been plowed back into the firm (not paid to shareholders as dividends). Common equity is sometimes called net worth; if the firm's assets could be sold at book value and used to pay off the liabilities, debt and preferred equity, the remaining cash would belong to the common shareholders. Again, the use of debt, preferred equity and common equity are strategic choices, and so these accounts are not operating accounts.

The sum of current liabilities, long-term debt and liabilities, preferred equity and common equity is known as total liabilities and equity. This half of the balance sheet shows the sources of the funds used to invest in the assets. And because it is the balance sheet, total assets are equal to total liabilities and equity.

Analyzing the balance sheet reveals changes in the nature of the assets the firm is utilizing, as well as changes in the sources of funding for the assets. The analyst's job is to determine which of these changes are good for the firm and which changes require attention. A thorough ratio analysis offers insights into the impact of the decisions made by the firm's managers and therefore into the operational and financial strength of the firm.

The Income Statement

The income statement shows the results of the firm's operations over a period of time (a year or a quarter). Starting with sales, and subtracting the costs of sales and operations (except depreciation and amortization), what remains is known as EBITDA (earnings before interest, taxes, depreciation and amortization). Depreciation was discussed earlier in the section on the balance sheet. Amortization is essentially depreciation for intangible assets. Since depreciation and amortization are non-cash expenses, some analysts think EBITDA is a better measure of financial strength than net income. In either case, depreciation is important because it is part of operating cash flow (see Chapter 6 on the cash flow from assets model). Subtracting depreciation and amortization from EBITDA leaves earnings before interest and taxes (EBIT), or operating earnings.

Net income (also called profit or earnings) is EBIT minus interest and taxes; it is what is available to distribute among the firm's stockholders. If a firm uses preferred equity in its capital structure, then net income available to common shareholders is calculated as net income less preferred dividends. Finally, earnings per share (EPS) are calculated as net income available to common shareholders divided by the number of common shares outstanding.

Analyzing the income statement reveals changes in the firm's revenues and expenses and therefore changes in the firm's overall profitability.

The Statement of Cash Flows

Table 9.2 contains the cash flow statements for Microsoft for the period 2015–2018. The statement of cash flows is exactly what it sounds like—a record of how cash flows through the firm over a period of time. The firm's ability to produce and utilize cash effectively is important, and a good analyst pays close attention to the firm's cash flows. Understanding how cash flows through a business is an important skill for any good businessperson.

Net income can only go in two directions: dividends or retained earnings. Dividends are cash payments to the firm's shareholders; since net income is the shareholders' money, the firm is obligated to return it to the shareholders unless it is able to earn a higher return by reinvesting it into the firm's operations. Retained earnings may be used to purchase new assets, pay interest or retire debt, buy back common stock, increase inventories, finance accounts receivable, invest in short-term securities or be kept as cash.

There is no direct relationship between net income and cash; the year-end cash balance may be higher or lower than the beginning balance, regardless of the amount of net income.

Many factors have an effect on the cash balance:

- Net income before preferred dividends: positive net income generates cash, all other things held constant (which they never are);
- Changes in working capital: increases in inventories and receivables decrease cash, as do decreases in payables and accruals (and vice versa);
- Fixed assets: purchasing fixed assets uses cash while selling them is a source of cash;
- Security transactions and dividend payments: floating stocks or bonds increases cash, while retiring bonds or buying back stocks decreases cash.

Table 9.2 Microsoft Corporation Statement of Cash Flows 2015–2018

Microsoft Corporation (MSFT)

Cash Flow

All numbers in thousands

Period Ending	6/30/2018	6/30/2017	6/30/2016	6/30/2015
Net Income	**16,571,000**	**25,489,000**	**20,539,000**	**12,193,000**
Operating Activities				
Depreciation	9,900,000	7,800,000	5,878,000	5,400,000
Adjustments to Net Income	-3,108,000	1,287,000	6,229,000	10,483,000
Changes in Accounts Receivables	-3,862,000	-1,216,000	562,000	1,456,000
Changes in Liabilities	7,070,000	3,901,000	2,653,000	-1,054,000
Changes in Inventories	-465,000	50,000	600,000	-272,000
Changes in Other Operating Activities	-459,000	349,000	-2,907,000	1,383,000
Total Cash Flow From Operating Activities	**43,884,000**	**39,507,000**	**33,325,000**	**29,668,000**
Investing Activities				
Capital Expenditures	-11,632,000	-8,129,000	-8,343,000	-5,944,000
Investments	6,557,000	-12,511,000	-14,417,000	-12,868,000
Other Cash Flows From Investing Activities	-98,000	-197,000	203,000	-466,000
Total Cash Flows From Investing Activities	**-6,061,000**	**-46,781,000**	**-23,950,000**	**-23,001,000**
Financing Activities				
Dividends Paid	-12,699,000	-11,845,000	-11,006,000	-9,882,000
Sale Purchase of Stock	—	—	—	—
Net Borrowings	-10,201,000	31,459,000	18,283,000	13,661,000
Other Cash Flows From Financing Activities	-971,000	-190,000	-369,000	362,000
Total Cash Flows From Financing Activities	**-33,590,000**	**8,408,000**	**-8,393,000**	**-9,668,000**
Effect of Exchange Rate Changes	50,000	19,000	-67,000	-73,000
Change in Cash and Cash Equivalents	**4,283,000**	**1,153,000**	**915,000**	**-3,074,000**

Each of these activities is reflected in the statement of cash flows, which summarizes the change in the firm's cash position. In the report, activities are separated into three categories and then combined in a summary section:

1. Operating activities: net income, depreciation, changes in current assets (other than cash) and current liabilities, short term investments and short-term debt;
2. Investing activities: the purchase or sale of fixed assets;
3. Financing activities: buying or selling short-term investments, issuing or retiring debt, issuing or repurchasing stocks or paying dividends.

From an analyst's perspective, the most important item on the cash flow statement is the total line at the bottom of the first section (on cash flow from operating activities). If that line is positive, it means that the firm is producing cash from its operations. If a firm is struggling with strategic issues, like fighting for market share or trying to compete with a competitor's new product, as long as the firm is producing cash from operations, the firm will be able to ride out any difficult times. As long as the firm can continue to pay its bills, its suppliers will continue shipping inventory, and they will be able to continue delivering products. However, if the total cash flow from operations line is negative, that means that the firm is burning cash by producing their products, and new sources of cash will be necessary in order to keep producing their products.

A firm that is burning cash through operations will not be in a position to raise funds through issuing new debt or equity. Since the cash flow statement is publicly available, the market will know that the firm is burning cash, and few investors (if any) will be interested in helping to save a struggling firm. The only other source of cash would be to sell off some assets, and no firm in history ever saved themselves by selling off their assets.

Statement of Retained Earnings

This simple statement is also exactly what it sounds like: it indicates changes in the level of retained earnings. The report includes the following data:

- The amount of retained earnings at the beginning of the year;
- The amount of net income available to common shareholders at the end of the year;
- The amount paid out as dividends over the year;
- The amount added to retained earnings over the year; and
- The amount of retained earnings at the end of the year.

There is nothing to analyze on this statement, so it holds no interest for us.

Analyzing the Financial Statements

This chapter discusses how the data obtained from the firm's financial statements are used to uncover strengths and weaknesses in the firm's performance over time. This type of analysis is done by all parties who have a stake in the firm's success: creditors and potential creditors, shareholders and potential shareholders, stock brokers and the firm's managers. Creditors want to make sure the firm is going to be able to pay back its debts. Shareholders want to determine if they should continue to own the stock or sell it and buy another stock. Brokers use the information to sell the stock to potential shareholders. The firm's managers use the information to see where they need to focus their attention to improve performance.

There are five categories of financial ratios discussed here: liquidity, asset management, debt management, profitability and market value ratios. In addition, there are a number of value and growth metrics that will be reviewed. We will also discuss the Du Pont system of analysis. For this analysis, we will use the data in Table 9.1, which contains five years of financial statements on the fictitious firm Marquardt Manufacturing.

Marquardt manufactures a number of recreational items relating to water sports, from water skis to bass boats. They are one of the smaller competitors in a large and growing industry, and the CEO is unsatisfied with the results of their attempts to increase sales and profitability over the past several years. The firm issued $100 million in new long-term bonds in both 2016 and 2017 and used the funds to add additional capacity to production as well as new technology to their product line. Their engineers have developed a number of new products, and while sales have increased, the overall results have not changed much. The CFO has been charged with determining what is driving the disappointing results, as well as a new strategic plan for increasing profitability.

Your charge is to do a thorough financial analysis of Marquardt's financial statements over the five-year period, using all of the metrics included in Figure 9.1. The metrics themselves, using Marquardt's data, can be found in Figure 9.2. Those metrics, as well as the trend analysis of the metrics for Marquardt, are discussed below.

Liquidity Ratios

Liquidity is defined as the ability to turn an asset into cash quickly at a fair market value. Therefore, the liquidity ratios discussed in this section are intended to determine if the firm will be able to pay its short-term obligations (those that are due within the next year) using its short-term assets (those that will be expended within the next year). The liquidity ratios focus on the current assets and current liabilities from the balance sheet. The two liquidity ratios given, the current ratio and the quick ratio, differ only in the case of inventory (it is included in the current ratio but not in the quick ratio). This is because inventory is generally the least liquid of all the current assets. Most firms' inventory is specific to its products, and therefore not of use to other firms (with the possible exception of some raw materials that are of general use, such as screws, washers, lumber, etc.). Because the only difference between these two ratios is inventory, differences in the trends between the two of them can often be tied to changes in the level of inventory.

For Marquardt, the current ratio for 2014 was $2,273.4 \div 763.1 = 2.98$. Over the five-year period, the ratio stayed close to 3.0, falling in 2015 but rising steadily thereafter. The quick ratio, on the other hand, stayed virtually the same for 2014–2016, and then rose slightly for 2017 and 2018. For 2018, Marquardt's quick ratio was $(2,796.9 - 1,423.5) \div 858.2 = 1.60$. Note that for the entire period all metrics are over one, which means that if they had to, Marquardt could cash out current assets to pay for current liabilities and still have assets left over. Thus, the liquidity ratios indicate Marquardt's liquidity is solid and increasing. No concerns there.

Asset Management Ratios

These ratios are used to determine how effectively the firm's managers are utilizing the assets. The inventory turnover ratio points out excessive or slow-moving inventories. Inventory that sits on the floor (rather than getting shipped to customers) is susceptible to damage, pilferage or obsolescence. Therefore, it is in the firm's best interest to minimize the amount

Liquidity Ratios

$$\text{Current Ratio} = \frac{\text{Current Assets}}{\text{Current Liabilities}}$$

$$\text{Quick Ratio} = \frac{\text{Current Assets} - \text{Inventory}}{\text{Current Liabilities}}$$

Asset Management Ratios

$$\text{Inventory Turnover Ratio} = \frac{\text{Sales}}{\text{Inventory}}$$

$$\text{Days Sales Outstanding} = \frac{\text{Accounts Receivable}}{\text{Sales} \div 365}$$

$$\text{Fixed Asset Turnover Ratio} = \frac{\text{Sales}}{\text{Net Fixed Assets}}$$

$$\text{Total Asset Turnover Ratio} = \frac{\text{Sales}}{\text{Total Assets}}$$

Debt Management Ratios

$$\text{Debt Ratio} = \frac{\text{Total Liabilities}}{\text{Total Assets}}$$

$$\text{Equity Multiplier} = \frac{\text{Total Assets}}{\text{Total Common Equity}}$$

$$\text{Times Interest Earned} = \frac{\text{EBIT}}{\text{Interest}}$$

$$\text{Cash Coverage Ratio} = \frac{\text{EBIT} + \text{Depreciation}}{\text{Interest}}$$

Profitability Ratios

$$\text{Gross Margin} = \frac{\text{Sales} - \text{COGS}}{\text{Sales}}$$

$$\text{Operating Margin} = \frac{\text{EBIT}}{\text{Sales}}$$

$$\text{Net Margin} = \frac{\text{Net Income}}{\text{Sales}}$$

$$\text{Return on Assets} = \frac{\text{Net Income}}{\text{Total Assets}}$$

$$\text{Return on Equity} = \frac{\text{Net Income}}{\text{Total Common Equity}}$$

Market Value Ratios

$$\text{Price/Earnings Ratio} = \frac{\text{Stock Price}}{\text{Earnings per Share}}$$

$$\text{Earnings per Share} = \frac{\text{Net Income}}{\# \text{Shares Outstanding}}$$

$$\text{Market to Book Ratio} = \frac{\text{Stock Price}}{\text{Book Value per Share}}$$

$$\text{Book Value per Share} = \frac{\text{Total Common Equity}}{\# \text{Shares Outstanding}}$$

Du Pont Equation

$$\text{ROA} = \frac{\text{Net Income}}{\text{Sales}} \times \frac{\text{Sales}}{\text{Total Assets}}$$

$$\text{ROE} = \text{ROA} \times \text{Equity Multiplier}$$

Value and Growth Metrics

Cash Flow = Net Income + Depreciation and Amortization

$$\text{Return on Invested Capital} = \frac{\text{NOPAT}}{\text{Net Operating Capital}}$$

$$\text{NOPAT} = \text{EBIT} \times (1 - \text{Tax Rate})$$

Net Operating Capital = Net Operating Working Capital + Net Fixed Assets

Net Operating Working Capital = Operating Current Assets – Operating Current Liabilities

Market Value Added = Market Capitalization – Book Value of Equity

Market Capitalization = Stock Price × # Shares Outstanding

Economic Value Added = NOPAT − (Net Operating Capital × WACC)

Figure 9.1 Financial Ratios and Metrics

Marquardt Manufacturing
Financial Ratio Analysis
FY 2014–2019PF

	2014	2015	2016	2017	2018	2019PF
Liquidity Ratios						
Current Ratio	2.98	2.91	3.12	3.14	3.26	3.28
Quick Ratio	1.50	1.50	1.52	1.62	1.60	1.62
Asset Management Ratios						
Inventory Turnover	5.56	5.99	5.24	5.78	5.41	5.58
Days Sales Outstanding	56.58	55.48	56.94	58.04	55.85	54.75
Fixed Asset Turnover	0.78	0.76	0.75	0.73	0.72	0.74
Total Asset Turnover	0.61	0.60	0.59	0.58	0.57	0.59
Debt Management Ratios						
Debt Ratio	25.40%	23.96%	23.47%	22.82%	21.63%	
Equity Multiplier	1.34	1.32	1.31	1.30	1.28	
Times Interest Earned	10.29	11.17	11.02	10.92	11.99	13.05
Cash Coverage Ratio	11.39	12.24	12.06	11.95	13.04	14.11
Profitability Ratios						
Gross Profit Margin	58.00%	58.40%	58.10%	57.80%	58.70%	58.20%
Operating Profit Margin	31.62%	32.65%	32.16%	31.61%	33.00%	32.66%
Net Profit Margin	19.30%	20.24%	19.83%	19.53%	20.47%	20.42%
Return on Assets	11.78%	12.18%	11.63%	11.29%	11.72%	11.98%
Return on Equity	15.79%	16.01%	15.20%	14.62%	14.95%	
Market Value Ratios						
P/E Ratio	8.96	8.51	8.81	9.14	8.84	
Market to Book Ratio	1.41	1.36	1.34	1.34	1.32	
Value and Growth Metrics						
Market Value Added	$3,183.9	$3,031.8	$3,068.5	$3,281.9	$3,397.0	
Economic Value Added	$296.5	$341.0	$297.1	$255.6	$318.5	
ROIC	13.73%	14.06%	13.44%	13.02%	13.38%	13.59%
Du Pont Equation						
Net Margin	19.30%	20.24%	19.83%	19.53%	20.47%	20.42%
Total Asset Turnover	0.61	0.60	0.59	0.58	0.57	0.59
Return on Assets	11.78%	12.18%	11.63%	11.29%	11.72%	11.98%
Equity Multiplier	1.34	1.32	1.31	1.30	1.28	
Return on Equity	15.79%	16.01%	15.20%	14.62%	14.95%	

Figure 9.2 Financial Analysis for Marquardt Manufacturing 2014–2019PF

of inventory that is held to only what is needed to support sales. If the firm is in a seasonal industry, it is expected that inventory will be higher during the busy season. However, it is important that after the busy season is over, the inventory levels are sharply reduced. Marquardt is turning their inventory over more than five times per year, so inventory is not sitting for long (around ten weeks on average). The lowest level for the period was in 2016, when the ITO was $6,946.1 \div 1,326.7 = 5.24$.

The days sales outstanding (DSO) is used to determine if the firm is collecting on its credit sales in a timely fashion. Most firms (including Marquardt) have credit policies that expect full payment on credit sales within 30 days. If the firm's DSO is greater than 30, the customers are taking longer than the published policy allows paying for credit sales, and the money is therefore not available for the firm to use. Marquardt is taking more than 55 days (on average) to collect on credit sales, almost twice as long as permitted by policy. The longest was in 2016, when it took on average just less than 57 days to collect ($1,083.6 \div \{6,946.1 \div 365\} = 56.94$). The CFO will want to speak to the credit manager about enforcing the credit policy more effectively in the future.

The fixed asset turnover ratio (FAT) measures how effectively the firm's fixed assets (buildings and machines) are being used to generate sales. If a firm increases its fixed assets by 20.0% in an effort to stimulate sales, it is expected that sales will increase by more than 20% in turn. If sales increase by less than 20.0%, the new sales are not sufficient to pay for the new assets, and therefore the firm is worse off than before. Marquardt's FAT has been declining by small increments over this period, with 2018 being the lowest ($7,694.6 \div 10,647.5 = 0.72$). This indicates that the increase in assets is not generating a greater increase in sales revenue. The CFO may want to consider focusing on sales efforts for the new plan, to make better use of the new assets the firm acquired in the past few years.

The total asset turnover ratio (TAT) is similar to the FAT ratio but includes the current assets as well. As you will see in the section on financial planning, an increase in sales requires an increase in certain current asset accounts, like cash, receivables and inventory, to support the new sales. Once again, the firm wants to make sure that the increase in assets is justified by the subsequent increase in sales. Over this five-year period, Marquardt's TAT has fallen to its lowest level ($7,694.6 \div 13,444.4 = 0.5723$). As with the FAT, the TAT indicates that the firm is not generating sufficient sales from the new assets, and should be focused on increasing the level of sales moving forward.

Debt Management Ratios

The use of debt in the balance sheet has three implications for the firm:

1. Raising money through debt does not erode the control of the firm's current shareholders, which would be the case if new common shares were sold on the open market;
2. The use of debt increases the return to the firm's shareholders (as will be seen in the section on the Du Pont system of analysis), while also increasing the firm's risk of bankruptcy;
3. As the proportion of debt used in the balance sheet increases, it becomes more expensive (and more difficult) for the firm to continue to borrow.

Given these implications, the debt management ratios are used to determine the potential bankruptcy risk for the firm, based on their current level of debt and their ability to pay their current interest obligations.

The debt ratio is defined as Total Liabilities ÷ Total Assets. In this definition, anything that is not equity is included in the numerator. The reason for defining it this way is that it would make the equity ratio, which would be defined as Total Equity ÷ Total Assets, the complement of the debt ratio (meaning that the two together would add to 1). Thus, if the firm had $10 million in total liabilities and $5 million in total equity (implying that total assets = $15 million), the debt ratio would be 67% and the equity ratio would be 33%. Marquardt's debt ratio has fallen over time to its current level of 21.63% (2,908.2 ÷ 13,444.4 = 0.21631).

Technically speaking, there are liabilities used in the ratio that are not strictly debt: accounts payable (also known as trade credit) is not debt, and neither is accrued expenses. However, there are types of liabilities that are not debt per se, but that are in fact sizeable commitments for the firm (such as pension obligations), and as such are capable of creating financial difficulties for the firm. For that reason, we treat all liabilities as debt for purposes of this particular ratio.

The times interest earned ratio (TIE) measures the firm's ability to pay its interest obligations from operating earnings. Creditors would prefer that this figure be above one, preferably far above one, so that they are very confident that the firm will be able to pay its interest obligations on time and in full. Marquardt's TIE was a solid 10.29 in 2014 (1,986.5 ÷ 193.1 = 10.287), indicating that is was quite able to pay its interest from operating income, and the ratio has increased in the following years.

The cash coverage ratio is similar to the TIE ratio, but includes depreciation in the numerator. In this way, the calculation includes cash available that is not included in the TIE ratio. For Marquardt, the ratio started at 11.39 ({1,986.5 + 212.3} ÷ 193.1 = 11.386) and has risen to 13.04 in 2018. Creditors have little to fear with regard to Marquardt's ability to pay its interest on time.

Profitability Ratios

These ratios are used to determine the effectiveness of the firm's operations in generating profit for its shareholders. While the prior ratios show how effectively the firm's operations are run, these ratios show the impact of those prior ratios on the firm's operating results.

Sales less cost of goods sold is also known as gross profit, so the ratio of that difference to sales is called the gross margin. This ratio measures the percentage of sales that remains after the firm pays for the goods they sell; it is therefore a measure of the firm's purchasing function. If the cost of the goods the firm sells increase over time, the net margin will decrease (all other things held constant). So, it makes sense to monitor the firm's materials management function through the use of this ratio. Marquardt's gross margin has been either just above or just below 58% for the entire five-year period, with its lowest margin occurring in 2017 (4,219.6 ÷ 7,300.4 = 0.57799). Without a competitor's data to compare this ratio to, we cannot say for certain if this result is good or bad on its own. However, we can conclude that the ratio is consistent, and therefore not getting worse over time.

The operating margin measures the percentage of sales remaining after the firm pays its operating expenses (as well as its COGS). Increases in the firm's operating expenses will also decrease the net margin. By monitoring the level of operating expenses, management can respond to increases quickly and take actions that will positively impact profitability. Marquardt's operating margin was at its lowest in 2017 (2,308.0 ÷ 7,300.4 = 0.31614) and at its highest in 2018 (2,538.9 ÷ 7,694.6 = 0.32995). Again, we cannot state definitively if these results are good or bad, as we have no competitor data with which to compare. We can, however, state that the ratio is fairly steady over the period in question.

The net margin measures the percentage of sales that are available to return to the shareholders after paying the expenses of the materials sold, the cost of running operations, the depreciation and amortization expense, the interest expense and taxes. Since net income can only go in one of two directions (either paid directly to shareholders in the form of a dividend or reinvested in the firm as retained earnings), this ratio measures the rate of shareholder profitability from sales revenue. In other words, it measures the percentage of each dollar of sales that is made available to the firm's shareholders.

For Marquardt, this ratio has also been fairly steady, from a low of 19.30% in 2014 (1,212.3 ÷ 6,282.4 = 0.19296) to a high of 20.47% in 2018. While we can't say how this compares to their competitors, we can say that Marquardt's net margin has been relatively stable during this period.

Return on assets (ROA) measures the percentage of total assets that is returned to the shareholders in the form of earnings. Increases in assets should preferably increase the return to shareholders over time, but certainly not decrease it. Marquardt's ROA has been as high as 12.18% in 2015 (1,340.5 ÷ 11,009.0 = 0.12176), but has fallen since that year, ending at 11.72% in 2018. This result indicates that the additional assets the firm has acquired since 2015 have not sufficiently driven an increase in sales to pay for them, which is consistent with the results discussed above.

Return on equity (ROE) measures the percentage of common equity that is returned to the shareholders in the form of earnings. This is the rate of return paid to the firm's owners. If new shares are issued (which would increase the Common Equity line on the balance sheet), it is expected that the ROE would also increase, or at the very least not decrease. Here we see a similar pattern as that with the ROA: the ROE was highest in 2015 (1,340.5 ÷ 8,370.9 = 0.16013), but has fallen since then, and in 2018 was at 14.95%. Thus, earnings have decreased relative to common equity over the past few years, and during this time no new equity was sold. This indicates that the growth in the level of earnings is not keeping up with the growth in total common equity: another indicator that the firm needs additional sales revenue to maintain its level of profitability.

Market Value Ratios

These ratios measure the investors' opinions of the firm's past performance and future prospects. If the liquidity, asset management, debt management and profitability ratios are all favorable, then the market value ratios will also be favorable, and the firm's stock price is likely to be at or near its maximum for the current state of the business.

The price/earnings ratio (P/E) indicates how much the market is willing to pay for each dollar of reported earnings. Firms with higher P/E ratios are seen by the stock market to have higher growth potential, while firms with lower P/E ratios are seen as riskier because they have lower growth prospects. For comparison purposes, the stock market's mean P/E ratio is usually around 15.0, so stocks with P/E ratios below 15 are seen to be growing slower than the market overall, while stocks with P/E ratios above 15 are seen as growing faster than the market overall. Marquardt's P/E ratio was as low as 8.51 in 2015 (11.13 ÷ {1,340.5 ÷ 1,024.5} = 8.506), and as high as 9.14 in 2017, but settled at 8.84 in 2018. So, while the P/E ratio is fairly steady, it is well below the market average. Therefore, Marquardt can be viewed as a low growth stock based on this result.

The market to book ratio (M/B) compares the market price of the stock to the book value per share of the firm's stock, calculated as the common equity line on the balance sheet divided by the number of shares outstanding. If this figure is above one, the market believes the firm's managers have added value to the firm over time, whereas if it is less than one, the market believes value has been destroyed over time by management. While Marquardt's ratio is consistently over one (for 2018 it is 13.60 ÷ {10,536.2 ÷ 1,024.5} = 1.322), it is currently at its lowest for the five-year period. The M/B ratio has fallen over the past four years, indicating that the market sees less value in the firm's stock (relative to its book value) than it did back in 2014. This is another indication that the market sees this as a low growth stock.

Value and Growth Metrics

These metrics are used to determine if the decisions made by the firm's managers have been adding value to the firm. Several are used as the basis for determining bonuses for the firm's operating managers. Some are calculated in order to use them in calculating another metric. All add to our understanding of the firm's true value.

Cash flow represents the amount of cash available to the firm at the time that the income statement is published. Cash flow differs from earnings because some revenues and expenses are non-cash:

Cash Flow = Net Income − Non-Cash Revenues + Non-Cash Expenses

Some revenues may not be collected during the year as cash; many smaller firms make use of barter, for which no cash changes hands. For most firms, the largest non-cash expenses are depreciation and amortization. In addition, deferred taxes are a non-cash expense. However, because of the rarity of non-cash revenues and other non-cash expenses, some analysts define it thusly:

Cash Flow = Net Income + Depreciation and Amortization

This is how we will define it as well. While net cash flow is not a value metric per se, it is a useful measure of the firm's operational liquidity and therefore worth monitoring over time. Using the data for Marquardt, for 2014 net cash flow is 1,986.5 + 212.3 = 2,198.8. The net cash flows for 2015–2018 are 2,370.5, 2,445.0, 2,525.9 and 2,762.3 respectively. Marquardt's operating liquidity is increasing over time.

Return on invested capital (ROIC) measures the net return from operations as a percentage of operating capital. The way to determine if an investment in operating assets is profitable is to compare the ROIC to the WACC; if ROIC > WACC (i.e., if the return is greater than the cost), the growth in assets is adding value to the firm, whereas if ROIC < WACC, the increase in assets is costing more than it is earning. Calculating ROIC is a multi-step process:

$$ROIC = \frac{NOPAT}{Net\ Operating\ Capital}$$

$$NOPAT = EBIT \times (1 - Tax\ Rate)$$

$$Net\ Operating\ Capital = Net\ Operating\ Working\ Capital + Net\ Fixed\ Assets$$

$$NOWC = Operating\ Current\ Assets - Operating\ Current\ Liabilities$$

Using our knowledge of operating accounts from Chapter 6, we can determine Marquardt's ROIC for the period in question. For 2014, the calculation is as follows:

- Net Operating Working Capital = 125.6 + 973.8 + 1,130.8 − 201.0 − 266.5 = 1,762.7;
- Net Operating Capital = 1,762.7 + 8,015.5 = 9,778.2;
- NOPAT = 1,986.5(1 − .324) = 1,342.874;
- ROIC = 1,342.874 ÷ 9,778.2 = 0.13733 or 13.73%.

Using this same approach, Marquardt's ROIC for 2015–2018 is found to be 14.06%, 13.44%, 13.02% and 13.38% respectively. Marquardt's WACC for the period 2014–2018 is given in Table 9.1; for the entire five-year period Marquardt's ROIC > WACC, indicating that the growth in assets is adding value to the firm.

Market value added (MVA) measures the extent to which the stock market recognizes the value added to the firm through the decisions made by the firm's managers. If the market approves of management's decisions, the market price of the stock will rise above its book value, creating market value added.

Market Value Added = Market Capitalization − Book Value of Equity
Market Capitalization = Stock Price × # Shares Outstanding

For 2014, Marquardt's market capitalization was $10.60 × 1,024.5 = $10,859.7 million, and their book value was $7,675.8 million. Therefore, their MVA for 2014 was 10,589.7 − 7,675.8 = $3,183.9 million.

This figure measures the value added *over the life of the firm*, and so does not offer a direct measure of the value added during the most recent year. To determine this, subtract the previous year's MVA from the current year's MVA; a positive number indicates that MVA has increased during the year, while a negative number means that MVA has fallen during the year. Based on this, Marquardt's MVA fell in 2015, but has risen each year since then. This would indicate that the stock market views Marquardt positively over the past three years. This metric can be used in determining management bonuses.

Economic value added (EVA) is a metric created by Stern Stewart & Co that once again compares returns to costs. In this case, it subtracts the cost of operations from the return to operations:

Economic Value Added = NOPAT − (Net Operating Capital × WACC)

Since it is comparing returns and costs for a given year, EVA is a measure of value added over the year in question. For this reason, it is commonly used as a metric for determining bonuses for operating managers. For 2014, Marquardt's EVA was 1,342.8 − (9,778.2 × 0.107) = 296.5, indicating that after the cost of funding operating assets was accounted for, there remained $296.5 million available to be shared with the firm's investors. As can be seen in Figure 9.2, Marquardt has positive EVA for each year during the five-year period.

The Du Pont Equation

The Du Pont equation is so called because it was developed by financial analysts at the Du Pont Corporation, and it is useful because it helps us to understand the drivers of returns to the firm's assets and to its shareholders.

Notice that if a firm uses no debt whatsoever, its total assets would be equal to its common equity (i.e., the entire bottom half of the balance sheet would be equity). Therefore, the return on assets (ROA) would also be equal to the return on equity (ROE), since both returns use net income in the numerator.

Next, notice that the ROA can be broken down into two other ratios: the net margin and the total asset turnover ratio.

$$ROA = \frac{Net\ Income}{Total\ Assets} = \frac{Net\ Income}{Sales} \times \frac{Sales}{Total\ Assets} = Net\ Margin \times TAT$$

This works because the net margin has sales in the denominator while the TAT has sales in the numerator. These two cancel out, leaving net income divided by total assets. In this way, the return the firm earns on its assets can be seen as being driven by the firm's ability to derive profit from sales (the net margin) and the firm's ability to use its assets to generate sales (the TAT).

If a firm does use debt in its capital structure (as all firms do), then ROA will not be equal to ROE. This is because there is one more ratio included in the ROE formula; in addition to the net margin and the TAT, the equity multiplier (EM) is included.

$$ROE = \frac{\text{Net Income}}{\text{Total Common Equity}} = \frac{\text{Net Income}}{\text{Sales}} \times \frac{\text{Sales}}{\text{Total Assets}} \times \frac{\text{Total Assets}}{\text{Total Common Equity}}$$

$$= \text{Net Margin} \times \text{TAT} \times \text{EM}$$

$$= \text{ROA} \times \text{EM}$$

The EM is defined as Total Assets ÷ Common Equity. Notice that this is the inverse of the equity ratio discussed previously (Common Equity ÷ Total Assets). If there is no debt in the firm's balance sheet, then total assets are equal to common equity, and the EM is equal to 1. However, once debt is introduced into the balance sheet, common equity is less than the value of total assets, and the EM increases. This means that introducing debt into the firm's capital structure causes the ROE to be greater than the ROA. This is why debt is referred to as leverage; adding debt to the balance sheet leverages up the return to the firm's shareholders.

Why does this happen? Adding debt to the balance sheet increases the risk of bankruptcy; slightly at first, and more as additional debt is incurred. This risk, however, is not borne by the debtholders, as they have a guaranteed return, guaranteed by the bond contracts. Instead, the risk is borne by the firm's common shareholders, who are at the bottom of a long list of claimants if the firm should file for bankruptcy. Therefore, the increased ROE serves as payment for the increase in bankruptcy risk borne by the common shareholders.

The value of the Du Pont analysis lies in the insight that the return earned by the firm's shareholders is a function of three different activities:

- The ability of the managers to control expenses (reflected in the net margin);
- The ability to use the firm's assets to generate sales (reflected in the TAT); and
- The judicious use of debt in the capital structure (reflected in the EM).

The last column of Figure 9.2 contains the available financial ratio and value metric analysis for the pro forma statements that will be created later in the chapter.

Trend Analysis, Benchmarking, Common Size Analysis and Percent Change Analysis

As mentioned previously, these ratios do not all have target numbers to show if they are good or bad. It is certainly possible to compare the firm's ratios to the average of the industry they are in, but this could lead to the belief that being at the industry average is good. Instead, the firm's ratios should be compared to the industry leader, or for that matter, to any business performing well that the managers wish to emulate. This is called benchmarking, and it is discussed in the next section.

In any case, it is just as important to follow the trends in these ratios over time. While a ratio may be good or bad at any given time, if it is heading in the right direction, the managers appear to be driving positive change. It is usually best to analyze no fewer than three years of financial statements to see how a firm is doing, and 5–10 years is even better.

Trend analysis for Marquardt, based on the metrics in Figure 9.2, shows a typically mixed set of results. Liquidity ratios are solid and increasing. The turnover ratios are decreasing, reflecting the fact that assets are growing faster than sales, while the DSO indicates that the firm's credit policy is not being adhered to by its credit customers. Debt management ratios are solid. Profitability margins fluctuate but show solid profitability, while returns to assets and common shareholders are struggling to stay at recent highs. MVA and EVA show value added consistently over the five-year period, while the Du Pont analysis indicates that the recent decline in ROE is being driven mostly by insufficient growth in sales (indicated by the falling TAT) and the decline in the level of debt (indicated by the falling equity multiplier). Based on these results, Marquardt's top management should focus on three things:

1. Increasing sales aggressively;
2. Speed up collections on credit accounts to bring the DSO down to 30 days; and
3. Make more use of debt.

Benchmarking

Benchmarking is the practice of comparing your firm's results to those of a competitor or another unrelated firm whose performance you aspire to emulate. Rather than comparing the firm's ratios to an industry average (who aspires to be average?), it is better to compare them to a firm you respect for how it operates. If the firm you are analyzing is not the top competitor in its industry, it makes sense to do the same analysis for some of the other top competitors, to see what they are doing differently.

If some competitors use different technology to produce an equivalent product or service, they will have different types of assets, and are therefore likely to have differences in metrics that relate to the assets (like the FAT and TAT, as well as the EVA and ROIC). Some competitors may have different capital structures, making more or less use of debt or preferred equity, which could result in differences in component costs of capital and WACC. These are things to keep in mind when comparing different firms' metrics.

Having data on competitors makes it easier to put the firm's metrics into perspective. For example, if Marquardt were not one of the top competitors in its industry, you would expect it to have lower market value ratios than the better performing firms. While it is possible to benchmark against a firm outside of the industry, that may make some comparisons difficult. When comparing an airline to a firm outside the air transportation industry, for example, the debt management ratios are likely to be different, since airlines use higher levels of debt due to the nature of the assets used (jet airplanes are expensive).

Common Size Analysis and Percent Change Analysis

Common size analysis looks at the financial statements on a relative basis; the balance sheet accounts are all divided by total assets, while the income statement accounts are all divided by sales. In this way, you can compare the structure of the financial statements over time and pinpoint changes in the structure. For example, if a firm's cost of goods sold is increasing over time, it will be seen in the fact that the common size income statement will show the COGS increasing as a percentage of sales over that period of time.

Figure 9.3 contains the common-size financial statements for Marquardt Manufacturing. The figure shows that, for the balance sheet, the asset accounts have been fairly consistent as a percent of total assets, while long-term debt is consistently falling and total common equity is consistently rising. These changes in the capital structure could explain the slight increase in the firm's WACC over the past few years. The income statement shows no real trends in any of the accounts as a percent of sales.

Similar to the common-size analysis, the percent change analysis calculates growth rates in each financial statement account based on the prior year (which means that there are no

	2014	2015	2016	2017	2018
Sales	100.0%	100.0%	100.0%	100.0%	100.0%
Cost of Goods Sold	42.0%	41.6%	41.9%	42.2%	41.3%
Gross Profit	58.0%	58.4%	58.1%	57.8%	58.7%
Operating Expenses	23.0%	22.6%	22.9%	23.2%	22.8%
Depreciation	3.4%	3.1%	3.0%	3.0%	2.9%
EBIT	31.6%	32.7%	32.2%	31.6%	33.0%
Interest	3.1%	2.9%	2.9%	2.9%	2.8%
EBT	28.5%	29.7%	29.2%	28.7%	30.2%
Taxes	9.2%	9.5%	9.4%	9.2%	9.8%
Net Income	19.3%	20.2%	19.8%	19.5%	20.5%

	2014	2015	2016	2017	2018
Assets					
Cash	1.2%	1.2%	1.2%	1.2%	1.1%
Marketable Securities	0.4%	0.4%	0.4%	0.4%	0.3%
Accounts Receivable	9.5%	9.1%	9.2%	9.2%	8.8%
Inventory	11.0%	10.0%	11.2%	10.0%	10.6%
Total Current Assets	22.1%	20.8%	21.9%	20.7%	20.8%
Fixed Assets	113.7%	114.5%	112.8%	113.5%	113.0%
Less Accumulated Depreciation	−35.8%	−35.4%	−34.6%	−34.2%	−33.8%
Net Fixed Assets	77.9%	79.2%	78.1%	79.3%	79.2%
Total Assets	100.0%	100.0%	100.0%	100.0%	100.0%
Liabilities and Equity					
Accounts Payable	2.0%	1.9%	2.0%	1.8%	1.8%
Accruals	2.6%	2.6%	2.5%	2.4%	2.3%
Notes Payable	2.9%	2.7%	2.6%	2.4%	2.3%
Total Current Liabilities	7.4%	7.2%	7.0%	6.6%	6.4%
Long Term Debt	18.0%	16.8%	16.5%	16.2%	15.2%
Total Liabilities	25.4%	24.0%	23.5%	22.8%	21.6%
Capital Stock	10.0%	9.3%	8.7%	8.1%	7.6%
Retained Earnings	64.6%	66.7%	67.9%	69.1%	70.7%
Total Common Equity	74.6%	76.0%	76.5%	77.2%	78.4%
Total Liabilities and Equity	100.0%	100.0%	100.0%	100.0%	100.0%

Figure 9.3 Common-Size Statements for Marquardt Manufacturing 2014–2018

growth rates for the first year). This analysis will indicate which accounts are growing faster than others and help pinpoint areas of concern. For example, it will show when accounts receivable are growing faster than sales, which means that the firm's money is not being collected on a timely basis from its credit customers.

Figure 9.4 shows the percent change analysis for Marquardt Manufacturing for the years 2015–2018. Calculating the growth in the cash account for 2015 is as follows

$$\frac{132.4}{125.6} - 1 = 0.0541 \; or \; 5.4\%$$

	2015	2016	2017	2018
Sales	5.4%	4.9%	5.1%	5.4%
Cost of Goods Sold	4.4%	5.7%	5.9%	3.2%
Gross Profit	6.1%	4.4%	4.6%	7.0%
Operating Expenses	3.6%	6.3%	6.5%	3.6%
Depreciation	−1.8%	1.3%	3.2%	2.5%
EBIT	8.8%	3.3%	3.3%	10.0%
Interest	0.3%	4.8%	4.2%	0.2%
EBT	9.8%	3.2%	3.2%	11.0%
Taxes	8.1%	4.1%	2.6%	12.0%
Net Income	10.6%	2.7%	3.5%	10.5%

	2015	2016	2017	2018
Assets				
Cash	5.4%	4.9%	5.1%	5.4%
Marketable Securities	8.6%	−11.1%	6.2%	−4.7%
Accounts Receivable	3.4%	7.7%	7.1%	1.4%
Inventory	−2.2%	20.0%	−4.8%	12.7%
Total Current Assets	0.8%	13.1%	0.9%	7.0%
Fixed Assets	7.8%	5.9%	7.4%	5.9%
Less Accumulated Depreciation	5.7%	5.4%	5.3%	5.2%
Net Fixed Assets	8.8%	6.1%	8.3%	6.3%
Total Assets	7.0%	7.6%	6.7%	6.4%
Liabilities and Equity				
Accounts Payable	2.1%	13.3%	0.4%	4.8%
Accruals	5.6%	4.4%	2.6%	3.0%
Notes Payable	2.0%	0.6%	−1.6%	1.5%
Total Current Liabilities	3.3%	5.3%	0.4%	3.0%
Long Term Debt	0.0%	5.4%	5.1%	0.0%
Total Liabilities	1.0%	5.4%	3.7%	0.9%
Capital Stock	0.0%	0.0%	0.0%	0.0%
Retained Earnings	10.5%	9.4%	8.6%	9.0%
Total Common Equity	9.1%	8.3%	7.6%	8.1%
Total Liabilities and Equity	7.0%	7.6%	6.7%	6.4%

Figure 9.4 Percent Change Analysis—Marquardt Manufacturing 2015–2018

Certain numbers stand out in this exhibit: in the balance sheet, the 11% drop in marketable securities in 2016, the increases in receivables in 2016 and 2017, the increases in inventory in 2016 and 2018 and the increase in accounts payable in 2016 are noticeable. In the income statement, the fact that COGS grew faster than sales in 2016 and 2017, as did operating expenses, is worthy of attention.

There is one thing the percent change analysis points out that we already suspected: both net fixed assets and total assets are growing faster than sales over this period. This is solid evidence in support of a focus on sales growth in the upcoming strategic plan.

Forecasting Financial Statements—The Percent of Sales Method

The percent of sales method is exactly what it sounds like: forecasted accounts are calculated as a percentage of sales, so that changes in forecasted sales will result in changes in the forecasts of the supporting accounts. Certain asset accounts increase to support the increase in sales, and certain liability accounts increase due to the increases in the asset accounts. This is where we will make the most use of our understanding of operating accounts, as was discussed in Chapter 6.

The entire financial forecasting endeavor begins with the sales forecast, and therefore an accurate sales forecast is essential. If the forecast is too high, the firm as at risk of over-investing in production assets that will not be fully utilized, increasing the firm's operating costs without a sufficient increase in revenue. Turnover ratios will be low, depreciation and inventory costs will be high and spoilage is likely to increase. If the forecast is too low, the firm will not be in a position to compete on volume and possibly even cost (loss of economies of scale) and thus may lose market share. In either case, the result is likely to be decreased profits, low ROE, and a depressed stock price. The finance department is not usually included in the sales forecasting process (it is typically done in the marketing department), but since finance must work with the forecast, they must believe in it. Therefore, it is up to the financial analysts to make certain that the sales forecast is neither overly optimistic nor pessimistic.

Once sales have been forecasted, we are ready to begin building pro forma financial statements in an Excel spreadsheet. The most commonly used method is the percent of sales method, where forecasted accounts are calculated as a percent of the sales figure based on past history. Those past percentages are applied to the sales forecast to estimate future levels of those accounts.

There are two basic approaches to applying the percent of sales method: using the mean value of the percentage over the time period being studied, or using any notable trend in the percent of sales over the time period. Which approach to use is a judgment call. If the percent of sales is hovering around some figure (going above and below it, back and forth), then there is no obvious trend, and it makes sense to use the mean percentage. If the data are showing a consistent increase or decrease in the percentage, then using that trend needs to be considered in the analysis. Note that these approaches both require multiple years' worth of data as inputs. If your data are for a lesser period of time, you may alternatively use the most recent year's percent of sales multipliers. However, this will ignore any trends that may be occurring with the variables in question.

The accounts that are forecasted are the operating accounts, which by definition are the accounts that are known to have a relationship with the level of sales. For the income statement that includes the cost of goods sold and the operating expenses, and for the balance sheet it includes cash, accounts receivable, inventory, accounts payable and accrued expenses. One operating account that varies in behavior, based on the industry the firm is in, is net fixed assets.

While fixed assets are operating assets, they often do not need to increase in response to an increase in sales. This is because many operating assets have large capacity. For example, if a machine is capable of producing 100,000 items per month, but sales are only 80,000 items per month, then sales can increase by 25% before the machine reaches its monthly capacity. For this reason, fixed assets are typically not forecasted as a percent of sales. Instead, they are usually forecasted with regard to their current capacity in order to determine when additional capacity will be needed (e.g., at what level of sales will the firm need to buy another machine).

Non-operating accounts are typically forecasted to remain at their most recent level. Unless you have specific information regarding these accounts, your best move is to hold these accounts at their current level. One non-operating account that differs in this regard is the retained earnings account on the balance sheet. The forecast for retained earnings will be the sum of the level of retained earnings in the most recent year and the addition to retained earnings forecasted on the pro forma income statement. This will be seen in the following example, in which we will forecast the 2019 financial statements for Marquardt Manufacturing.

We must start with the sales forecast. For this exercise, we are going to use an aggressive sales forecast for 2019, assuming that sales will increase by 10.0%. This forecast is an aggressive target being considered by the CFO as part of the new strategic plan.

Two final details: first, Marquardt has contracted to purchase $775 million in net fixed assets in early 2019. Therefore, the net fixed assets will increase by $775 million in the pro forma model. Second, the annual common dividend will be increased to $0.83 per share in 2019. This will be used in the analysis after the pro forma income statement to determine the addition to retained earnings.

Forecasting the Income Statement

To start with, the 2019 sales forecast is derived by increasing 2018 sales by 10% (per the CFO's wishes):

$$7,694.6 \times 1.1 = 8,464.06$$

The perfect tool for forecasting the income statement is the common-size income statement (see Figure 9.3). Note that Marquardt's COGS has either dipped slightly below 42% of sales or risen very slightly above 42% of sales, throughout the period. Since there is no clear trend in this variable, it makes sense to consider using the mean, which is 41.8%. The forecasted level of COGS is calculated below:

$$8,464.06 \times 0.418 = 3,537.9771$$

Similarly, the operating expenses as a percent of sales vary from as low as 22.6% to a high of 23.2%. Since there is no clear trend to the percentages (they rise and fall), it makes sense to use the mean, which is 22.9%. This is used to calculate the forecasted level of operating expenses:

$$8,464.06 \times 0.229 = 1,938.2697$$

Depreciation is not an operating account; for most large corporations, there are people that can provide an estimate of the next year's depreciation expense within the accounting department. If you have no data on what to expect for depreciation in the coming year, your best estimate is the depreciation amount for the current year. Therefore, the $223.4 million figure for depreciation in 2018 is copied over to 2019. Gross profit and EBIT are subtotals that are calculated after the forecasted figures are determined.

Interest is treated the same as depreciation. Without specific information with regard to the expected amount of interest due in 2019, your best estimate is the amount of interest paid in 2018. Therefore, the $211.8 million in interest paid in 2018 is copied over to 2019, and EBT (earnings before taxes) is calculated in order to determine taxes owed. To estimate taxes, it is necessary to see what has been happening to the firm's tax rate over time. This can be calculated from Table 9.1 by simply dividing taxes by EBT; for 2014, the tax rate was 581.1 ÷ 1,793.4 = .32402, or 32.40%. This same calculation done for years 2015–2018 reveals annual tax rates of 31.90%, 32.20%, 32.00% and 32.30% respectively. Since all of the annual rates are close to each other, we could use the average of all five years for the pro forma analysis. However, since the most recent year (2018) had one of the higher rates, we will use that rate. In this way, we are likely being conservative in our estimate of the taxes (overestimating rather than underestimating them). So, taxes for 2019 pro forma are calculated as 2,552.6 × 0.323 = 824.4898. Subtracting that amount from EBT leaves net income of $1,728.1 million for pro forma 2019.

The last remaining analysis for the pro forma income statement is to determine what part of net income will be paid out as a dividend, and what part will be retained and used for future growth opportunities. We were told that the dividend will increase to $0.83 per share in 2019. Assuming no new shares are issued, that means that the total dividend paid by Marquardt will be 0.83 × 1,024.5 = $850.335 million. Subtracting this amount from net income results in an addition to retained earnings of $877.7 million. This amount will be carried over to the balance sheet pro forma statement. See Figure 9.5 for the finished pro forma income statement.

Forecasting the Balance Sheet

To aid in forecasting the balance sheet, Figure 9.6 shows the balance sheet accounts as a percent of sales; in other words, each balance sheet account value was divided by the amount of sales for that year. This figure shows clearly the relationships between sales and the balance sheet operating accounts. Note that, to the right of the 2018 percentages, there is a column that shows the average of the operating accounts over the five-year period. We will use most, but not all, of these averages in our analysis.

The cash account is kept at a steady 2% of sales—Marquardt's cash policy is to maintain the balance of cash equal to 2% of sales, which is a common policy. With no fluctuation in the variable, the mean will be used in the analysis. Receivables rose and fell to between 15.2% and 15.9% of sales. However, the CFO has directed the credit manager to tighten up on credit policy with the goal of reducing the days sales outstanding metric. For 2019 pro forma, the CFO has directed you to assume that receivables will be limited to 15.0% of sales, so that will be the metric used for accounts receivable. Inventory has no clear trend, rising as high as 19.1% and falling as low as 16.7% of sales. Therefore, the five-year mean of 17.92% is the metric to use. Finally, we recall that net fixed assets are going to increase by $775 million.

For the liabilities, payables have also fluctuated over time, but within a tight range; they have fallen as low as 3.1% and risen as high as 3.4% of sales. With no clear trend, the mean of 3.21% of sales is a reasonable multiplier to use for accounts payable. For accrued expenses, however, the data show a clear trend: falling by ten basis points each year over the last two years, while holding steady prior to the drop in 2017. The range for this variable is tight enough over this period that using the mean would not be out of line. However, using the mean would be the same as assuming a reversal in the short-term trend (going up in 2019 rather than down). Rather than build a reversal into the analysis, it makes more sense to use the most recent percentage (4.0% in 2018) rather than the mean. So, for the 2019 pro forma analysis, the percent of sales multiplier for accruals will be 4.0%.

Income Statement FY2014–2019PF ($Millions except per share data)

	2014	2015	2016	2017	2018	2019PF
Sales	6,282.4	6,621.6	6,946.1	7,300.4	7,694.6	8,464.1
Cost of Goods Sold	2,638.6	2,754.6	2,910.4	3,080.8	3,177.9	3,538.0
Gross Profit	3,643.8	3,867.0	4,035.7	4,219.6	4,516.7	4,926.1
Operating Expenses	1,445.00	1,496.5	1,590.7	1,693.7	1,754.4	1,938.3
Depreciation	212.3	208.4	211.1	217.9	223.4	223.4
EBIT	1,986.5	2,162.1	2,233.9	2,308.0	2,538.9	2,764.4
Interest	193.1	193.6	202.8	211.4	211.8	211.8
EBT	1,793.4	1,968.5	2,031.1	2,096.6	2,327.1	2,552.6
Taxes	581.1	628.0	654.0	670.9	751.7	824.5
Net Income	1,212.3	1,340.5	1,377.1	1,425.7	1,575.4	1,728.1
Dividends Paid	614.7	645.4	686.4	737.6	788.9	850.3
Shares Outstanding	1,024.5	1,024.5	1,024.5	1,024.5	1,024.5	1,024.5
Dividend per Share	0.60	0.63	0.67	0.72	0.77	0.83
Retained Earnings	597.6	695.1	690.7	688.1	786.5	877.7

Balance Sheet FY2014–2019PF ($Millions except per share data)

	2014	2015	2016	2017	2018	2019PF
Assets						
Cash	125.6	132.4	138.9	146.0	153.9	169.3
Marketable Securities	43.2	46.9	41.7	44.3	42.2	42.2
Accounts Receivable	973.8	1,006.5	1,083.6	1,160.8	1,177.3	1,269.6
Inventory	1,130.8	1,105.8	1,326.7	1,263.0	1,423.5	1,516.8
Total Current Assets	2,273.4	2,291.6	2,590.9	2,614.1	2,796.9	2,997.8
Fixed Assets	11,699.0	12,609.3	13,353.4	14,339.9	15,191.8	
Less Accumulated Depreciation	(3,683.5)	(3,891.9)	(4,103.0)	(4,320.9)	(4,544.3)	
Net Fixed Assets	8,015.5	8,717.4	9,250.4	10,019.0	10,647.5	11,422.5
Total Assets	10,288.9	11,009.0	11,841.3	12,633.1	13,444.4	14,420.3
Liabilities and Equity						
Accounts Payable	201.0	205.3	232.7	233.6	244.7	271.7
Accruals	266.5	281.4	293.8	301.3	310.4	338.6
Notes Payable	295.6	301.4	303.2	298.5	303.1	303.1
Total Current Liabilities	763.1	788.1	829.7	833.4	858.2	913.4
Long Term Debt	1,850.0	1,850.0	1,950.0	2,050.0	2,050.0	2,050.0
Total Liabilities	2,613.1	2,638.1	2,779.7	2,883.4	2,908.2	2,963.4
Capital Stock	1,024.5	1,024.5	1,024.5	1,024.5	1,024.5	1,024.5
Retained Earnings	6,651.3	7,346.4	8,037.1	8,725.2	9,511.7	10,389.4
Total Common Equity	7,675.8	8,370.9	9,061.6	9,749.7	10,536.2	11,413.9
Total Liab. and Equity	10,288.9	11,009.0	11,841.3	12,633.1	13,444.4	14,377.3

	AFN	43.0

Figure 9.5 Marquardt Financial Statements 2014–2019 Pro Forma

Marquardt Manufacturing
Percent of Sales Balance Sheet FY2014–2018

	2014	2015	2016	2017	2018	Mean
Assets						
Cash	2.0%	2.0%	2.0%	2.0%	2.0%	2.00%
Marketable Securities	0.7%	0.7%	0.6%	0.6%	0.5%	
Accounts Receivable	15.5%	15.2%	15.6%	15.9%	15.3%	15.50%
Inventory	18.0%	16.7%	19.1%	17.3%	18.5%	17.92%
Total Current Assets	36.2%	34.6%	37.3%	35.8%	36.3%	
Fixed Assets	186.2%	190.4%	192.2%	196.4%	197.4%	
Less Accumulated Depreciation	−58.6%	−58.8%	−59.1%	−59.2%	−59.1%	
Net Fixed Assets	127.6%	131.7%	133.2%	137.2%	138.4%	
Total Assets	163.8%	166.3%	170.5%	173.0%	174.7%	
Liabilities and Equity						
Accounts Payable	3.2%	3.1%	3.4%	3.2%	3.2%	3.21%
Accruals	4.2%	4.2%	4.2%	4.1%	4.0%	4.18%
Notes Payable	4.7%	4.6%	4.4%	4.1%	3.9%	
Total Current Liabilities	12.1%	11.9%	11.9%	11.4%	11.2%	
Long Term Debt	29.4%	27.9%	28.1%	28.1%	26.6%	
Total Liabilities	41.6%	39.8%	40.0%	39.5%	37.8%	
Capital Stock	16.3%	15.5%	14.7%	14.0%	13.3%	
Retained Earnings	105.9%	110.9%	115.7%	119.5%	123.6%	
Total Common Equity	122.2%	126.4%	130.5%	133.6%	136.9%	
Total Liabilities and Equity	163.8%	166.3%	170.5%	173.0%	174.7%	

Figure 9.6 Marquardt Percent of Sales Balance Sheet 2014–2018

We must also remember that the forecasted addition to retained earnings is $877.7 million (from the pro forma income statement), and so the retained earnings account must be increased by that amount.

Using the metrics discussed above, the 2019 pro forma values for the forecasted accounts in the balance sheet are calculated below:

- Cash = 8,464.1 × 0.02 = 169.282;
- Accounts Receivable = 8,464.1 × 0.15 = 1,269.615;
- Inventory = 8,464.1 × 0.1792 = 1,516.7667;
- Net Fixed Assets = 10,647.5 + 775 = 11,422.5;
- Accounts Payable = 8,464.1 × 0.0321 = 271.6976;
- Accruals = 8,464.1 × 0.04 = 338.564;
- Retained Earnings = 9,511.7 + 877.7 = 10,389.4

The 2018 values for marketable securities, notes payable, long-term debt and capital stock are copied over into the 2019 pro forma column, and then all subtotals and totals are calculated. The result is shown in Figure 9.5.

The most notable thing about the 2019 pro forma balance sheet is that it doesn't balance; there are more assets than liabilities and equity. This is typical—it means that the plan for 2019 requires assets that are not currently funded, so the firm will need to raise money to pay for those new assets. This is indicated at the bottom of the balance sheet, by the additional funds needed metric (AFN). The AFN metric is calculated as total assets minus total liabilities and equity. For pro forma 2019, AFN = 14,420.3 − 14,377.3 = 43.0. Thus, Marquardt will need to raise $43 million to fund its 2019 capital budget. These funds will be raised by issuing new debt and/or new common equity. It will be the CFO's decision as to how much of each type of security the firm chooses to issue.

Analyzing the Pro Forma Statements

Figure 9.2 shows the ratio analysis for the 2019 pro forma statements, with certain metrics left blank. Those metrics cannot be calculated without making the pro forma balance sheet balance. Therefore, any metrics that require debt or equity values cannot be calculated. It is certainly possible to make assumptions about the debt and equity added to the balance sheet to make it balance, but that creates new issues. For example, adding new debt will increase the amount of interest to be paid in 2019, which will reduce the level of net income, and in turn the addition to retained earnings. That will unbalance the balance sheet. If new common shares are issued to rebalance it, the number of shares outstanding will increase, and therefore the total dividend paid will increase. This in turn will reduce the addition to retained earnings, which will further unbalance the balance sheet. Any corrections made to rebalance the balance sheet will have the same results—it is a circular problem. While such circularities can be dealt with in an Excel spreadsheet, it is an unnecessary complication. The pro forma statements are estimates, based on assumptions, and therefore attempts at accuracy are inherently futile. The statements are more useful to see the general impact of decisions made rather than to precisely predict the future.

Despite not having all of the metrics available, conclusions can be drawn from those metrics that can be calculated. As Figure 9.2 shows, the liquidity ratios increase slightly, all of the turnover ratios are better and the DSO has decreased to its lowest level in this time period. This last result reflects the tightening of the credit policy requested by the CFO. TIE and CCR are better, but were fine before, so these do not impact the analysis. Margins are just slightly below the 2018 results, while ROA is slightly up. ROIC is slightly up as well. For the Du Pont analysis, the increase in ROA is driven by the increase in sales revenue (reflected in the increase in the TAT). This shows that the focus on increasing sales will increase the return to the firm's assets. And since the only difference between ROA and ROE is the equity multiplier (this is what the Du Pont analysis shows), holding the EM constant, an increase in ROA will result in an increase in ROE. Therefore, the CFO's plan to focus on sales will likely result in an increase in the return to the firm's shareholders.

Summary

This chapter reviews the structure of the major corporate financial statements and shows how they can be analyzed as well as forecasted for future periods. While not strictly finance, the skills developed in this chapter are used by financial analysts every day and will help you to understand what the firm is doing well and what it could be doing better. Understanding and analyzing financial statements is one of the most important skills you can develop during your undergraduate studies.

End of Chapter Problems

1. What is the biggest difference between the income statement and the balance sheet?
2. What purpose does the statement of cash flows serve?
3. Harvest Biotech recently ended their fiscal year by paying $3,000,000 in total dividends and retaining $4,500,000 in earnings. If they have 10 million shares outstanding, what are their earnings per share and dividends per share for the fiscal year just ended?
4. Burger Baron has a DSO of 45 days. Their annual sales are $3.6 million. What is the value of their accounts receivable?
5. Brand X has current assets of $30 million. Their current ratio is 1.5 and their quick ratio is 1.0. What are Brand X's current liabilities and inventory?
6. Bumstead Beauty Products has an ROA of 15%, an NM of 3% and an ROE of 18%. What are their TAT ratio and EM?
7. Ipswich Insurance has an equity multiplier of 2.5. The firm's assets are financed with a combination of long-term debt and common equity. What is their debt ratio?
8. Main Street Motors has $600,000 of debt on its balance sheet, on which it pays 15% interest annually. Their sales are $5 million per year, and the net margin on those sales is 4%. The corporate tax rate for Main Street is 35%. Their debt agreement requires them to maintain a times interest earned (TIE) ratio of 4, or else their loans will not be renewed and they will face bankruptcy. Should the managers be concerned?
9. A firm has a current ratio of 2.0 and a quick ratio of 1.6. If the firm doubles their inventory and intends to pay for it within 30 days of receipt, what will be their new current ratio?
10. The controller of the firm where you work has determined that the firm's return on equity (ROE) is 15%. The president is interested in the various components that went into this calculation. You are given the following information: Total Debt / Total Assets = 0.35, and the total assets turnover ratio (TAT) is 2.8. What is the net margin (NM)?
11. You are given the following data for the Susquahanna Hat Company:

    • Sales / Total Assets = 1.5;
    • Return on Assets = 3%;
    • Return on Equity = 5%.

    Calculate Susquahanna's net margin and equity multiplier.

12. Scranton Rubber has $1.5 million in current assets and $650,000 in current liabilities. Their present inventory level is $350,000. They want to increase inventory, and they intend to raise the funds by issuing short-term notes payable. How much can they increase their short-term debt (notes payable) without pushing their current ratio below 2.0?
13. Hang Ten Surfing Supplies have annual sales of $25 million, of which 3% goes to net margin. Their balance sheet indicates that they carry $7.5 million in debt, on which they pay interest of 10%. They pay corporate taxes of 40%. What is their EBIT?

Comprehensive Excel Problem

Imperial Packaging, Inc. is a producer of custom packaging, everything from sturdy cartons and cases for protecting fragile items on long trips to artistic displays and coverings for products and their packaging. Their clientele are high-end producers of custom products that are marketed for their unique style and sophistication. You are a financial analyst for the firm, and the CFO has assigned you to help him explain the 2018 results as reflected in the financial statements given in Table 9.3.

Table 9.3 Financial Statements for Imperial Packaging, Inc. 2014–2018

Income Statement FY2014–2018 ($Millions except per share data)

	2014	2015	2016	2017	2018
Sales	157.2	166.6	176.3	187.4	198.8
Cost of Goods Sold	59.7	62.8	67.3	70.1	76.1
Gross Profit	97.5	103.8	109.0	117.3	122.7
Operating Expenses	30.7	32.8	34.0	36.0	39.4
Depreciation	3.1	3.2	3.4	3.4	3.5
EBIT	63.7	67.8	71.6	77.9	79.8
Interest	1.0	1.4	1.4	1.6	1.6
EBT	62.7	66.4	70.2	76.3	78.2
Taxes	18.80	19.90	21.10	22.90	23.50
Net Income	43.9	46.5	49.1	53.4	54.7
Dividends Paid	40.0	42.0	48.6	51.0	55.7
Shares Outstanding	20.0	20.0	22.0	22.0	24.0
Dividend per Share	2.00	2.10	2.21	2.32	2.32
Retained Earnings	3.9	4.5	0.5	2.4	(1.0)
Tax Rate	29.98%	29.97%	30.06%	30.01%	30.05%
Required Return	11.30%	11.30%	11.30%	11.30%	11.30%
WACC	8.85%	8.85%	8.85%	8.85%	8.85%

Balance Sheet FY2014–2018 ($Millions except per share data)

	2014	2015	2016	2017	2018
Cash	3.1	3.3	3.5	3.7	4.0
Marketable Securities	0.4	1.1	0.7	0.6	1.2
Accounts Receivable	13.1	13.9	14.7	15.6	16.6
Inventory	10.0	10.5	11.2	11.7	12.7
Total Current Assets	26.6	28.8	30.1	31.6	34.5
Fixed Assets	126.40	137.60	142.90	150.90	153.90
Less Accumulated Depreciation	(70.7)	(73.9)	(77.3)	(80.7)	(84.2)
Net Fixed Assets	55.7	63.7	65.6	70.2	69.7
Total Assets	82.3	92.5	95.7	101.8	104.2
Accounts Payable	5.0	5.2	5.6	5.8	6.3
Accruals	7.7	8.2	8.5	9.0	9.9
Notes Payable	1.2	1.2	1.2	1.2	1.2
Total Current Liabilities	13.9	14.6	15.3	16.0	17.4
Long Term Debt	15.0	20.0	20.0	23.0	23.0
Total Liabilities	28.9	34.6	35.3	39.0	40.4
Capital Stock	20.0	20.0	22.0	22.0	24.0
Retained Earnings	33.4	37.9	38.4	40.8	39.8
Total Common Equity	53.4	57.9	60.4	62.8	63.8
Total Liabilities and Equity	82.3	92.5	95.7	101.8	104.2
Common Stock Price 12/31	39.96	42.12	44.06	46.11	46.48

The firm has been growing steadily, with sales growth at around 6% per year since 2014. Imperial issued new long-term debt in 2015 and again in 2017, and they also issued new common equity in 2016 and 2018. During the period 2015–2017, the firm was able to increase the common dividend by 5% each year and still have a positive addition to retained earnings.

However, in 2018, the firm was unable to increase the dividend, and yet also had a negative addition to retained earnings (i.e., retained earnings on the balance sheet fell in 2018). The CFO would like to increase the dividend by 5% in 2019, and so she needs you to analyze the firm's financial statements over the past five years, and to forecast the pro forma financial statements for 2019 and analyze them as well.

You are to recreate the financial statements in Table 9.3 in an Excel spreadsheet, then do a complete ratio and metrics analysis, similar to what was done for Marquardt Manufacturing. Include all the ratios included in the chapter and the value metrics MVA, EVA and ROIC. Create common-size statements and do a percent change analysis as well. The CFO needs you to determine two things:

1. What drove the results that made it impossible to increase the dividend in 2018?
2. Are we on track to be able to afford growing the dividend by 5% in 2019?

Make the following assumptions during the analysis:

- In 2019, sales growth will be in line with growth in 2015–2018;
- No new net fixed assets will be required to meet the 2019 sales forecast;
- The 2019PF dividend will be $2.44 per share.

Use the percent of sales method as taught in the chapter to forecast the 2019 pro forma statements. Write a concise (one page) paper outlining the results of your analysis and answering the two questions posed to you by the CFO.

Bibliography

Fundamentals of Corporate Finance, 12th edition. S. Ross, R. Westerfield and B. Jordan. McGraw-Hill Education, 2019.

Financial Management: Principles & Practice, 8th edition. T. Gallagher. Textbook Media Press, 2019.

Foundations of Financial Management, 17th edition. S. Block, G. Hirt and B. Danielsen. McGraw-Hill Education, 2018.

10 Finance Within the Firm

This chapter is intended as an overview of how finance is used both in the economy and within the corporate structure. We will discuss the role finance plays in different industries as well as within a company. We will review the different forms of organization a business can take, along with the benefits and shortcomings of each form. Finally, we will discuss the goals financial managers should pursue in the decisions they make.

The Role of Finance

Within a business, the role of finance is to determine how money is to be raised, spent and invested. Funds raised from different sources have different costs and different associated risks. The chief financial officer decides whether to issue new bonds, for what maturity and paying what interest rate, or to issue equity, preferred or common, and what dividend to pay the shareholders. The ability to raise money quickly and at a reasonable cost directly impacts other decisions the firm will make, from what markets to enter to how many people to hire. The CFO will help to decide what products to make and how to make them, based on the costs associated with the production processes and the cash flows realized from the products. The CFO determines how much cash to make available for operations and where to invest any leftover cash. Credit policy, inventory valuation and dividend policy all fall under the responsibility of the head of the finance department.

Within a corporation, money is followed carefully through the system, and it is managed both for the short term and the long term. In the short term, the firm must decide how much cash to keep on hand, how much inventory to keep on the shelves, how much credit to extend and to whom and whether to pay the bills quickly to get a discount or pay them later at full price. In the long term, decisions include which production assets to purchase, whether to use manual or automated processes, whether to build a production facility or rent one, whether to pay a trucking company to ship their goods or to purchase their own fleet of trucks, or any number of other decisions that will determine the nature of the firm's cash flows for years to come.

Finance Is a Strategic Discipline

Any major decision, such as the choice of which technology to use in the production process, whether to build, purchase or rent a facility, where to set up the corporate offices or even what product lines to pursue, commits the firm to a long-term plan. Each year, managers throughout the company, from the production floor to the corporate offices, promote different investment options for top management to consider: an automated inventory retrieval system, a product intended to take market share from a competitor or a new technology that will manufacture a current product at a lower cost. The finance department analyzes those options using the methods discussed in this book in order to determine the value of each option. The CEO, CFO and other top managers choose which options to invest in, based on the firm's strategic plan as well as the value of each option. For this reason, finance is a strategic discipline. The techniques learned in a course like this one allow the firm's analysts to value each option available and estimate the impact of each option on the firm's intrinsic value. It is every manager's responsibility to maximize the intrinsic value of the firm.

The Intrinsic Value of the Firm

Most finance textbooks teach that it is the responsibility of the firm's managers to maximize shareholder wealth, which is generally translated as meaning to maximize the firm's common stock price. However, this is short-sighted; the stock price can be manipulated in many ways, and those ways generally do not add long-term value to the firm. For this reason, this book promotes maximizing the intrinsic value of the firm, or the intrinsic common stock price.

The intrinsic stock price is the true value of the stock, based on all available information. This includes information known only by the firm's managers (i.e., insider information) and includes any impacts the decisions have on any and all of the firm's stakeholders:

- Customers, who come to depend on the firm for its products or services;
- Suppliers, who in some cases live or die based on the success or failure of the businesses they supply;
- Employees, who devote the better part of each week to the firm's success, and who take pride in the work that they perform on the company's behalf;
- The community in which the business operates, which is invested in the firm's success; and
- Investors, including bondholders, preferred shareholders and common shareholders, who supply the firm with the funds they need to continue in business.

Customers offer more than revenue to a firm; they offer loyalty to their products or services. In the spring of 1985, the Coca Cola Company introduced Coke II (otherwise known as New Coke), its newest product that was intended to help them compete with the Pepsi Company. As far as loyal Coke drinkers were concerned, the company made two huge mistakes:

1. They changed a product that did not need changing; and
2. They took the original product off of the market.

The new product was an instant flop, and within three months the original product, labeled "Coke Classic," hit the shelves. Coke II was discontinued seven years later, and since then has been the subject of a number of business cases that discuss developing and introducing new products.

Businesses choose their suppliers based on a number of characteristics, such as the quality of their product or service, the price they charge and the customer service they offer during and after purchase. Some suppliers dedicate assets and even manpower to specific customers in order to be able to address their needs promptly. This type of loyalty is offered without expectations of loyalty in return, because it is good business. When President Obama chose to bail out GM shortly after taking office, he did so for many reasons, but one specific reason was the impact it would have on the local community; numerous local businesses made virtually all of their revenue from supplying the local GM plant.

Employees are assets to businesses and deserve to be treated as such, but unfortunately that is not always the case. Newsweek[1] reported that in 2017, the same year Jeff Bezos, CEO of Amazon, was named the richest man in the world, more than 10% of the over 6,000 Amazon employees in Ohio were receiving food stamps. In September 2018, Senator Bernie Sanders of Vermont introduced the Stop BEZOS Act, which required such large employers as Amazon and Wal-Mart to pay the government for the various forms of public assistance (e.g., food stamps, public housing, Medicaid) received by their employees. The bill was not intended to pass Congress—there was virtually zero chance of that happening—but rather to begin a national conversation about corporate subsidies paid for with taxpayer funds. Wal-Mart claims that its strategy is low prices, but in fact it is low wages, which is why so many Wal-Mart employees are on public assistance. In 2012, the six people that make up the Walton family had a combined wealth of $90 billion—more than the bottom 30% of earners in the United States.[2] There has also been a push by state governments, aided by the courts, to bust unions through the so-called right to work laws. Governments represent the people, not the business community. Such inequality cannot exist without at least tacit approval by the federal government.

The community in which a firm produces its product or service benefits from the firm's success, and most communities realize this. The community, in turn, offers many things to firms that are often unappreciated. For example:

- An ongoing source of labor;
- Restaurants for meals or outings;
- Local businesses as customers or suppliers; and
- Retail stores for employees' convenience.

Efforts made and money spent on supporting the local community often pay dividends for the firm in terms of good public relations and support from the local government.

There is a large and growing interest among investors in firms that produce with socially or environmentally friendly processes; it is referred to as socially responsible investing. For example, so-called green funds are mutual funds that limit investment to firms that limit their carbon footprint and contribute to environmental protection, or firms developing alternative energy sources, or even firms that practice ethical corporate governance. The market is attempting to tell corporate executives that how they choose to operate their business matters to investors.

Thus, all managers of a business, financial or otherwise, are obligated to make decisions for the firm that will maximize the intrinsic value of the firm. Such decisions take into account all of the firm's stakeholders and not just its common shareholders. The current focus on shareholder wealth is short-sighted and can have dire consequences. A perfect example of why maximizing the market price of the stock is not sufficient is Enron.

Enron Corporation was an energy and energy services firm located in Houston, Texas that was founded in 1985 as a merger between two smaller, Texas-based energy firms. In the latter half of the 1980s, Enron grew by developing genuinely creative ways to offer their services. However, the firm eventually had difficulty continually finding the means to buoy its stock price, and during the 1990s the firm used fraudulent accounting practices to transfer liabilities off of its balance sheet, making the firm appear less risky and thus keeping its stock price artificially elevated, while also making the firm seem far more profitable than it actually was. For some time, these practices were successful, and in December of 2000, Enron's common stock hit a high of over $90.50 per share. In August of 2001, market analysts began to question Enron's numbers, and the story unraveled quickly; by the end of November 2001, the stock was worth less than one dollar. Enron employees had invested their pensions heavily in Enron stock, at management's insistence. When the firm filed for bankruptcy, employees lost not only their jobs but also their life savings.

The current financial paradigm for American businesses is to maximize the common stock price, which has resulted in an increase in value-neutral practices such as share buybacks. Prior to 1982, it was illegal for corporations to buy back their own stock, as it was seen as a form of stock price manipulation (which it clearly is). In 1982, the Securities and Exchange Commission (SEC) passed rule 10b-18, making stock buybacks legal. This was a boon to large corporations. The math is simple: the firm's earnings per share (EPS) is calculated as net income divided by the number of shares outstanding. Repurchasing some of the shares reduces the number of shares outstanding, increasing EPS, and a higher EPS causes the market to reprice the stock upward. The buyback does nothing for the firm other than put upward pressure on the stock price; no real value is added. But the increase in the stock price helps top management to meet their goals and achieve their huge bonuses. Therefore, top managers are motivated to continue this practice, which only benefits them. The stakeholder value maximization approach discussed above is in line with the theory on sustainability.

Corporate Sustainability

The theory of corporate sustainability is still in the development stage, but the crux of it is that corporations have an ethical obligation to run the business in a way that is sustainable for all parties involved. The theory does not deny the importance of growth and profitability, but rather recognizes the importance of other societal goals, such as economic and social justice and environmental protection, which aid in sustaining the relationships among the parties (i.e., the stakeholders). True sustainability is sustainability for everyone, not just the shareholders.

The concept of corporate sustainability is essentially an amalgam of four other established concepts:

- Corporate social responsibility—managers have an ethical obligation to address the needs of society as a whole, not just to act solely in the interests of the shareholders or their own self-interest;
- Sustainable development—development that meets the needs of present generations without compromising the ability of future generations to meet their own needs as well;
- Stakeholder theory—the stronger the firm's relationships are with other external parties, the easier it will be to meet the firm's business objectives, while the worse the relationships, the harder it will be; and
- Corporate accountability— the legal or ethical responsibility to provide an accurate account or justification of the actions for which the firm is responsible.

These other concepts provide not only ethical but also business arguments in favor of acting in furtherance of society's needs rather than just the shareholders' needs. At this time, corporate America is not in favor of this paradigm and is actively lobbying to maintain the status quo. Given the amount of money at stake, it is unlikely that the business community will accept such a change without having it forced upon them.

How to Maximize the Intrinsic Stock Price

It is easy to measure the market price of the stock—it is published all day long and changes constantly with trades based on new information. The intrinsic price of the stock, however, is nowhere to be found. What actions can management take to optimize the intrinsic value?

The actions the managers can take are those that the fundamental principles indicate will increase the present value of the firm's expected future cash flows:

- Maximize the size of the expected future cash flows;
- Obtain the cash flows sooner rather than later; and
- Reduce the riskiness of the cash flows.

Maximizing the size of the expected future cash flows requires maximizing revenues and/or minimizing expenses. Good businesses work on this every day, and the best firms maintain continual focus on optimizing sales relationships and finding creative ways to reduce costs without affecting quality. For example, a manager could replace a currently utilized production asset with a new asset, one that uses a new technology that will reduce operating costs. This will increase the size of the expected future cash flows associated with that asset.

Managers must be on the lookout for creative opportunities to obtain cash flows sooner rather than later. A simple example would be to depreciate production assets using a MACRS schedule rather than straight line depreciation; the MACRS schedule offers higher depreciation rates early in the asset's life, increasing the early cash flows from the asset. Another example would be that the purchasing department could propose purchasing contracts with its suppliers that reward volume purchases with lower prices or even rebates for meeting certain volume targets. Having good relationships with the suppliers makes this easier to implement.

The riskiness of the firm's cash flows is also linked to the relationships among the stakeholders. Purchasing expenses are managed by managing the relationships with the suppliers; price increases are inevitable, but good relationships make them work for all parties involved. Operating expenses will also increase over time, if for no other reason than salary increases, but again, a good relationship with the employees enables salary increases to work for the firm as well as the employees.

As these suggested managerial actions indicate, the answer can be found in the area of stakeholder theory. Each of the firm's major stakeholders—customers, employees, suppliers, the community and investors—is so designated because they have a stake in the firm's success. With this understanding, the way to optimize the firm's intrinsic value is to optimize the relationships the firm has with its stakeholders:

- For customers, offer a quality product or service at a reasonable price and emphasize the impact of good customer service before, during and after the sale;
- For employees, offer a living wage and decent benefits, along with upward mobility to motivate the best employees to be ambitious;
- For suppliers, show appreciation through loyalty and understanding for their need to be profitable as well, and find new ways for them to provide service to strengthen the relationship;
- For the community, hold open houses or tours to let them see what the firm does and how it does it, and respond to any requests or complaints made to show them that they are being heard; and

- For the investors, besides offering them a return on their investment, show them the ways in which the efforts made to strengthen the relationships with all stakeholders have benefited the firm, and therefore the investors.

The term brain drain is used to describe what happens to a firm when attrition takes their best and brightest employees. While money is sometimes the cause of brain drain, research indicates that the corporate culture is the biggest factor in losing good employees. Research also shows that the costs of brain drain are often underestimated by firms. The techniques offered to firms to help prevent brain drain are based on developing better relationships with its employees. This same approach can be used to develop better relationships between the firm and all of its stakeholders. The better the relationships the firm has with its stakeholders, the smoother the path to achieving the firm's goals.

Types of Financial Decisions

Decisions within the responsibility of the CFO fall into three general areas: capital budgeting, working capital management or capital structure. Questions therefore tend to relate to:

- How do we invest long term to implement our strategic plan?
- How do we manage our funds in the short term to support production?
- How do we obtain the funds that we need?

Capital budgeting decisions involve large initial purchases and large cash inflows from sales revenue over an extended period of time. Each decision of this type commits the firm to utilizing the assets for years, so if the decision works it can be quite profitable, while if it doesn't work it can be quite expensive. Such decisions need to be made carefully, with accurate analysis using reasonable assumptions.

By investing in positive NPV projects, the firm will be able to continue to grow over time. The nature of those projects depends to some extent on the industry the firm is in. For any large retailer, like Wal-Mart or Costco, deciding whether to open a new store would be a typical capital budgeting decision. In the case of Hewlett Packard, the decisions to merge with Compaq in 2002 and to acquire Electronic Data Systems in 2008 were large, complex capital budgeting decisions.

Working capital refers to current assets and current liabilities, the short-term balance sheet accounts used to support day-to-day operations. Managing working capital is necessary to prevent costly interruptions to production, and it involves a number of different activities that impact cash inflows and outflows. Typical working capital issues include:

- How much cash to have available for production (since cash does not earn interest);
- How much credit should be extended to customers, and at what interest rate;
- How much inventory should be kept in stock;
- Should we pay cash for operating purchases or use trade credit (credit extended by suppliers); and
- How much short-term debt should be used to support operations.

Capital structure refers to the mix of debt and equity the firm uses to purchase its assets and support operations. The chosen levels of debt and equity determine the firm's WACC, which is used as the discount rate for capital budgeting decisions. Therefore, the capital structure has an impact on the risk and the value of the firm. Typical capital structure issues include:

- Should we issue bonds, stocks or both?
- What maturity should the bonds be assigned?
- What interest rate is appropriate for the bonds?
- What dividend should we pay the common shareholders?

The Importance of Finance

The value of the firm derives from the cash flows it produces. The stock market sets a price for a firm's common stock based on its expectations regarding the firm's future cash flows. Some investors will have optimistic views on the firm's future cash flows and be willing to pay more for the stock. Other investors will have less optimistic, or even pessimistic, views on the firm's future cash flows and only be willing to pay less, or possibly even want to sell the stock. Investors vote with their wallets; the volume and pricing of buy and sell orders set the bid and ask prices for the stock. When more investors want to buy than to sell, it pushes the stock price up, and when more investors want to sell than to buy, the price will fall. Expectations of future cash flows are shaped by the news published about the firm, such as changes in top management, lawsuits or the annual report with the audited financial statements.

It is the responsibility of all managers in a firm to focus their efforts towards maximizing the intrinsic value of the firm. This means making decisions that are expected to increase the firm's cash flows, speed up their arrival or reduce their risk. It is the CFO's responsibility to determine the value of those decisions, whether they include:

- Introducing a new product;
- Entering a new market;
- Utilizing a new production process;
- Acquiring another firm; or
- Changing the location of the corporate headquarters.

While none of these decisions are purely financial in nature, they all have value, and it is the function of finance to determine the appropriate value. Therefore, analysts that work in finance must be well trained in how to determine value. They must understand the mathematics of finance, be comfortable using statistics to measure risk and be able to build spreadsheet models to analyze decisions.

If the stock market agrees with the decisions the firm's managers implement, it will respond positively, maintaining or even increasing the firm's common stock price. If it disagrees with any decisions, it will respond negatively, pushing the stock price down. In 2017, approximately 80% of the market cap of the S&P 500 was owned by institutional investors,[3] all of whom employ sophisticated and capable analysts. If institutional investors' analysts disagree with the firm's decisions, the investors may decide to sell the stock. If the amount of stock they own is large enough, it could have a strong impact on the market price of the stock. Any significant fall in the stock price could make it difficult (or more expensive) to issue new securities in order to purchase new assets.

These days, institutional investors are using their ownership power to drive change in firms whose top management have made decisions they find questionable. In late 2016, Wells Fargo agreed to separate chairman and CEO positions, formerly both held by one person, in response to a shareholder proposal filed in October by a group of institutional investors. This came about after the bank paid settlements of $190 million for retail banking sales practice abuses committed under the prior CEO/Chairman. In April of 2018, a group of institutional investors used their ownership power to obtain a meeting with Chevron's new CEO. They wanted to discuss changing the firm's legal strategy with regard to a judgment of $9.5 billion by the top Ecuadorian court over pollution. The legal strategy chosen by Chevron's top management was more costly than the institutional investors felt was justified.

Finance is important because value is important; the value of the firm's product or service, the value of the firm's common stock or the value of the firm itself. Since the primary goal of all managers should be to maximize the intrinsic value of the firm, finance has an impact on every important decision made by business managers. The knowledge and skills developed while working in finance can offer many opportunities not offered candidates in other fields.

Careers in Finance

The field of finance offers a number of different career opportunities, most of which fall within one of three main career paths:

- Investments and wealth management;
- Financial markets and institutions; and
- Financial management.

These career paths involve different types of tasks, but utilize the same principles and require basically the same skills. So, the knowledge and skills you obtain from studying for a major in finance will be useful in any of these career paths.

Investments and Wealth Management

Finance majors working in the fields of investments or wealth management will locate, select and either promote or manage income-producing assets, such as stocks, bonds or derivative securities. Jobs within this area include:

- Security analyst, responsible for learning as much about a firm as possible in order to make a recommendation on the firm's securities (e.g., buy, hold or sell). Most analysts are experts in a particular industry or industry segment and specialize in a number of competitors. Good analysts are detail-oriented, organized and creative problem solvers. A security analyst needs a good understanding of the mathematics of finance, the ability to work with and interpret statistics and advanced spreadsheet skills for creating models.
- Investment managers, responsible for either recommending or selecting and purchasing securities on behalf of other investors. A broker at an investment firm offers a selection of possible investments for their clients to choose from, while a mutual fund manager creates a portfolio of securities and markets it to the investing community. Investment managers are basically financially savvy sales people; their job is to get investors to invest in the securities or funds they are offering. In addition to financial math skills, an understanding of statistics and a comfort with spreadsheet models, these positions require good people skills and a desire to sell.
- Wealth managers work with their clients to devise an investment strategy and create a portfolio that meets their long-term needs. Wealth managers work with people preparing for their retirement, helping to meet specific investing goals over time, as well as during

their retirement, helping them to budget their expenditures to maintain their wealth and/ or meet specific goals, such as travel or setting up trusts for family members. In addition to having a working knowledge of financial math, statistics and financial modeling, wealth managers need to enjoy working closely with people, asking lots of questions in order to fully understand their client's needs and creating investment strategies that are in line with the client's return and risk preferences.

While all of these careers offer substantial compensation, the highest compensation is available in the investment management field. However, those jobs are based on commission, which means having to sell in order to earn.

Financial Markets and Institutions

Jobs in this career path are involved in some form of managing the flow of money through financial institutions. The major employers in this career path include:

* Commercial banks, which employ tellers, loan officers, credit analysts and financial managers who supervise other positions and are involved in data collection and reporting;
* Insurance companies, which employ customer service representatives, claims clerks, underwriters, sales agents, claims adjusters and actuaries; and
* Investment banks, which employ analysts to work in mergers and acquisitions, underwriters for debt and equity offerings and private equity analysts.

Positions in any of these institutions require an understanding of financial math and statistics and the ability to build spreadsheet models. Investment banks offer the highest salaries of these institutions, but the jobs are not entry level, and there are far more candidates seeking employment than there are open positions.

Financial Management

Financial managers are responsible for managing the finances of a business. Positions in financial analysis involve analyzing and forecasting financial data, assessing risks and evaluating investment opportunities and determining when, how much and what type of securities to issue to support operations. Financial analysts often interact with managers from other areas of the company:

* Working with accounting managers to obtain data and craft custom reports;
* Working with marketing managers and engineers for new product development projects;
* Providing guidance and recommendations to senior management.

Corporate jobs pay well and offer many opportunities for growth by moving into new areas and taking on more responsibility. They also require an understanding of financial math, statistics and advanced spreadsheet skills.

Forms of Business Organization

There are three basic forms of organization a business can have: a proprietorship, a partnership and a corporation. Proprietorship is the simplest; partnerships can be of different types; and corporations can take on slightly different forms as well. We will look at each in turn.

Proprietorship

This is the form of organization used by most small businesses. A proprietor raises some money, chooses a location for a base of operations and then starts to sell the product or service. A benefit is that the proprietor has total control of how the business operates (within the law), and the business income is the proprietor's income. A disadvantage is that profits or losses are reflected in the proprietor's tax returns, and taxes are paid at the individual rates, which are higher than the corporate rate. Also, since a proprietorship has no formal books to review, raising money is a function of the credit worthiness of the proprietor, and the proprietor bears all liability for borrowed funds. Further, unless the business is passed on or sold, it dies with its owner. However, the largest concern related to proprietorships is liability.

Proprietors have unlimited liability with regard to their business. This means that the owner has sole responsibility for all of the obligations of the business—expenses, taxes, lawsuits, fines, etc. If the proprietor is hit with a large obligation (like a lawsuit), not only can the courts take away the business, they can go after the owner's personal assets (i.e., their home and personal bank accounts). Insurance is often available to help reduce those risks, but they cannot be eliminated.

Partnership

A partnership is essentially a proprietorship owned by two or more people. The partnership can be informal (without a written agreement), or the rights and responsibilities of each partner can be spelled out in a contract. The same benefits (no shareholders to answer to) and concerns (unlimited liability, difficulty raising capital, incomes taxed at personal levels) apply to partnerships as to proprietorships, but the income and liability are shared.

Some partnerships have different classes of partners: general partners and limited partners. Limited partners are limited as to both income and liability—they have limited liability, and for that reason earn less income—while general partners share more in both income and liability. Limited partners typically take a less active role in the running of the business. In either case, the lifetime of the partnership is limited to the lifetimes of the partners.

Corporation

This book focuses on the corporate organization of business. Unlike proprietorships and partnerships, corporations are legal entities, separate from their owners. One of the obligations of being a publicly held corporation (i.e., one whose stock is publicly traded) is that it must publish annual reports that are verified by an accounting firm. These reports include audited financial statements that reflect the results the firm experienced over the year. Having this information public makes it easier for the firm to raise money by issuing bonds or stocks. This is a distinct advantage of the corporate form of organization. Another is that the transfer of ownership is simple: sell the common shares on the market. This makes it possible for the firm to remain in business virtually forever. Yet another benefit of the corporate form is limited liability: the owners are only liable to the degree that they have already invested in the firm; their personal wealth is not at risk.

One major disadvantage of the corporate form of organization is double taxation. The firm pays taxes on operating earnings after interest is deducted, and the balance is net income. Net income only goes in two directions: reinvested in the firm in the form of retained earnings, or redistributed to the owners in the form of a common dividend. The dividend is income to the shareholder and is therefore taxable. So dividends are taxed twice: once when it is income to the firm, and again when it is income to the owners.

There are several types of corporate form in use. Those discussed above, with common shares trading on the stock market, are public corporations. These are the corporations that have financial reporting requirements with audited statements. Private corporations are small, often family owned, corporations that do not offer stock to the general public, and therefore have no public reporting requirements. S corporations are also very small, and the S designation means that the corporations do not pay taxes themselves, but instead pass the profits along to the owners, where the income is taxed at the individual rates. Professional corporations are businesses that offer professional services, such as doctors, lawyers, accountants or podiatrists. They are limited to members within the specific profession. It should be noted that incorporation does not protect the owners of a professional corporation from malpractice claims.

Benefit corporation is a relatively new designation. In a benefit corporation, it is the duty of the directors to consider the firm's impact on society and the environment in their decisions. Not all states recognize benefit corporation status, but the list is growing. Limited liability companies (LLCs) avoid double taxation while also enjoying limited liability: the best of both worlds.

The Secret to a Successful Business

Actually, it's not a secret. It is in fact rather simple: the way to be successful in business is to invest in projects that earn more than they cost. In capital budgeting terms, this means to invest in projects that have positive net present values. Therefore, strategic choices require two essential bits of information: what does it cost, and what will it earn.

It is simple, but not necessarily easy. Estimating cash flows for projects is as much art as it is science, and mistakes are inevitable. But a firm that has a good eye for investments that yield more than they cost will surge ahead of its competition. Companies that can see the value in a new technology, or a new product line, or a new market, will lead their industries rather than follow. Those firms are the ones that have well-trained professionals on their staff that can work effectively across disciplines, that have production workers who see the value in the efforts they make every day to produce the firm's products or services, that have managers that see the value in their production workers and see to it that they have the resources they need to do their jobs and that treat their suppliers, their customers, their investors and their community as an integral part of the firm's success.

Summary

The field of finance has much to offer strong candidates, much more than money. The problem-solving skills learned in financial analysis can make a candidate indispensable, which can lead to promotions and new opportunities within the firm. The best candidates take leadership roles and offer themselves as mentors to newer candidates. It is quite common for the CFO to move into the CEO role when the opportunity arises. With leadership comes the chance to make big decisions that have an impact and make a difference. Candidates with a finance major have an advantage in the job market due to the specialized skills taught in the major, skills like problem-solving and spreadsheet modeling. In addition, the strategic nature of the work is interesting.

End of Chapter Problems

1. Name the three general areas in which financial decisions arise.
2. Why is finance a strategic discipline?
3. Define the intrinsic value of the firm's stock.
4. What is the main point of the Enron example used in this chapter?
5. Why is finance important to a business?
6. Which of the following is a capital budgeting decision:

   a. How many shares of stock to issue.
   b. Whether or not to purchase a new machine for the production line.
   c. How much of a common dividend to pay.
   d. How much inventory to keep on hand.
   e. Whether or not to offer a discounted price to boost sales.

7. Which of the following is a working capital management decision:

   a. How many shares of stock to issue.
   b. Whether or not to purchase a new machine for the production line.
   c. How much of a common dividend to pay.
   d. How much inventory to keep on hand.
   e. Whether or not to offer a discounted price to boost sales.

8. Which of the following is a capital structure decision:

   a. How many shares of stock to issue.
   b. Whether or not to purchase a new machine for the production line.
   c. How much of a common dividend to pay.
   d. How much inventory to keep on hand.
   e. Whether or not to offer a discounted price to boost sales.

9. A firm's short-term assets and short-term liabilities are referred to as the firm's:

   a. Capital structure.
   b. Debt-to-equity ratio.
   c. Working capital.
   d. Net fixed assets.
   e. Additional funds needed.

10. A business owned by a single individual who has unlimited liability for the firm's debt is called a:

    a. Corporation.
    b. S corporation.
    c. General partnership.
    d. Limited partnership.
    e. Sole proprietorship.

11. A business owned by two or more individuals, all having equal liability in the firm's debt, is called a:

    a. Corporation.
    b. S corporation.

c. General partnership.
d. Limited partnership.
e. Sole proprietorship.

12. A business owned by two or more individuals, with some owners having different amounts of liability in the firm's debt, is called a:

a. Corporation.
b. S corporation.
c. General partnership.
d. Limited partnership.
e. Sole proprietorship.

13. Which of the following statements is correct?

a. Corporations can have an unlimited life.
b. Corporate profits are taxable income to the shareholders when earned.
c. Shareholders are protected from all potential losses.
d. The majority of firms in the US are organized as corporations.
e. Retained earnings are double-taxed.

14. Which of the following statements is correct?

a. A limited partnership is legally the same as a corporation.
b. Partnerships are the most complex type of organization to form.
c. Earnings from sole proprietorships and partnerships are taxed at the individual level.
d. Only sole proprietorships have limited lives.
e. Limited partnerships are required to restate the liability to each partner annually when they file their financial reports with the SEC.

Notes

1 Guarnieri, G. "Jeff Bezos Is the Richest Man in the World, But Hundreds of Amazon Employees Are on Food Stamps," *Newsweek*, January 16, 2018.
2 Stiglitz, J. *The Price of Inequality*, 2nd edition, W.W. Norton and Company, 2013.
3 McGrath, C. "80% of Equity Market Cap Held by Institutions," *Pensions & Investments*, April 25, 2017.

Bibliography

Fundamentals of Corporate Finance, 12th edition. S. Ross, R. Westerfield and B. Jordan. McGraw-Hill Education, 2019.
Financial Management: Principles & Practice, 8th edition. T. Gallagher. Textbook Media Press, 2019.
Wilson, M. "Corporate Sustainability: What Is It and Where Does It Come From?" *Ivey Business Journal*, March/April 2003.

11 Legal and Ethical Issues in Finance

In this chapter we will discuss legal and ethical issues faced by both the firm as a legal entity and by the managers who run the firm. We will review cases where the firm's managers failed to follow legal or ethical practices, and understand the outcomes resulting from their decisions. We will discuss at length the 2008 financial crisis as well as the resulting recovery (now known as the Great Recession), and the legal and ethical decisions that preceded them.

While this chapter makes no use of the fundamental principles and precepts, it may very well be the most important chapter in the book. The examples discussed in this chapter represent huge mistakes, grievous lapses in judgment that ended with tragic results. All of us who are even remotely associated with the financial world need to understand and appreciate these cases for what they are: opportunities to learn from the mistakes of others.

Financial and Accounting Scandals

The twentieth and twenty-first centuries so far have seen a remarkable number of financial scandals in the corporate and banking worlds. Most of these scandals involve some sort of accounting trickery, while the scandals regarding investments typically involve Ponzi schemes. The discussion in this section is limited to the post-WWII period and to US-based firms.

WorldCom

WorldCom was the second largest long-distance telephone service provider (behind AT&T) at one point during the 1990s. CEO Bernard Ebbers' aggressive growth strategy, including the 1997 merger with MCI, had driven the common stock price above $60. However, by 2000 the telecommunications industry was in decline, and Ebbers had begun to feel the heat in late 1999, when the Department of Justice prevented the attempted merger with Sprint. He had been using his WorldCom stock to finance his other businesses (including lumber and yachting), and the falling price had resulted in Ebbers receiving margin calls (calls from his broker to put more money in his trading account to cover losses).

Ebbers owned so much WorldCom stock that liquidating his position to cover the margin calls would have driven the stock price down even further, so the board of directors agreed to cover his margin calls. But the falling stock price had also convinced Ebbers and CFO Scott Sullivan to begin using fraudulent accounting to cover the falling earnings and prop up the stock price. They booked certain operating expenses as capital expenditures, and they inflated revenues using bogus accounting entries. Their efforts inflated the value of the firm's assets by $11 billion, making it the largest accounting fraud scandal in US history to date. Both Ebbers and Sullivan spent time in prison for their part in the fraud.

Enron

While Enron has already been discussed in this book, the lessons this case has to offer are worth repeating. Prior to the accounting scandal becoming public, Enron had been named "America's Most Innovative Company" for six consecutive years by Fortune magazine. Enron's managers used a number of deceptive and fraudulent accounting practices to hide the truth. They used special purpose entities (SPEs) to hide significant liabilities, making them seem profitable while earnings were declining. Over time the fraud got bigger and bolder in order to keep driving the stock price higher, while Enron was in fact losing money. Many of their claims regarding profitability could not be confirmed, raising suspicions among stock analysts. In the meantime, like a Ponzi scheme, Enron needed more demand for their stock to maintain the high price at the same time that the officers were disinvesting. CEO Ken Lay strongly encouraged employees to invest their pension money in Enron stock while selling upwards of $100 million of his own shares.

In August of 2001 Enron's stock was selling for more than $90 per share. On November 28, 2001, when the news of Enron's deception was made public, the stock price fell to less than $1. The depth of the scandal was such that Arthur Andersen, at the time one of the leading accounting firms in the world, was found guilty of obstructing justice for destroying documents related to the Enron audit. The conviction forced Andersen to stop auditing public companies, effectively ending their business. CEO Ken Lay, COO Jeff Skilling and CFO Andrew Fastow were all convicted and sentenced to prison, and all served time except Lay, who died before serving his sentence. The scandal also resulted in the passing of the Sarbanes–Oxley Act of 2002, which among other things holds corporate officers responsible for the accuracy of their audited accounting statements.

Towers Financial

In 1995 Steven Hoffenberg, former owner of the *New York Post*, pleaded guilty to selling $475 million in fraudulent bonds and for using profits from new investors to pay returns to earlier investors, a classic Ponzi scheme. As chairman of Towers Financial, Hoffenberg and his associates also used fraudulent accounting methods to maintain the scam. The SEC claimed that in fiscal year 1991, Towers reported earnings of $13.1 million when in fact they had losses of $136.6 million. According to the SEC, Towers bought tens of millions in worthless loans and then simply declared the loans more valuable than they were and reported a profit, while collecting almost nothing on the loans. The fictitious returns on these loans were used to market the bonds Towers sold, which were likewise worthless. Hoffenberg bought the *New York Post* in an attempt to kill the story, but in fact it merely sped up the process, leading to the SEC's lawsuit against him. Hoffenberg was sentenced to 20 years in prison, but was released after 16 years. In 2016, he formed a political action committee (PAC) called Get Our Jobs Back Inc. in support of Donald Trump's bid for the presidency.

Adelphia Communications

Adelphia Communications Corporation was a cable TV provider located in Pennsylvania. Prior to filing for bankruptcy in 2002, Adelphia had been the fifth largest cable company in the US. Founded in 1952 by John Rigas, it was the Rigas family's taste for wealth that drove them to steal $100 million from the company. Among the claims of their excesses, the family had the company buy 3,600 acres of timberland, costing $26 million, in order to be able to preserve the view from the window of their home. Five of the firm's officers were indicted on bank fraud, securities violations and conspiracy, and founder John Rigas and his son Timothy were found guilty and sentenced to lengthy prison terms.

Bayou Hedge Fund

The Bayou Hedge Fund Group was founded by Samuel Israel III in 1996 with $300 million from investors that were told to expect it to grow to over $7 billion in ten years' time, which represents an average annual compound return of over 37% (a truly spectacular claim!). Federal prosecutors determined that Bayou had lied about its operations from the start, over-stating gains and reporting gains when there were in fact losses. All indications are that Bayou never made any real money at all, and that the principals, CEO Israel and CFO Daniel Marino, were running a Ponzi scheme, using new investors to pay earlier investors. In 2008, Israel was sentenced to 20 years in prison for fraud.

Refco

Refco was a financial services company founded in 1969 by Ray Friedman. In August 2005, CEO Phillip Bennett took the firm public, selling over 26 million shares of common stock in its IPO. The IPO shares started at $22, but closed the same day above $27, based on reports that Refco's earnings had grown by an average of 33% per year over the four years prior to the IPO. In October of 2005, the firm announced that Bennett had hidden $430 million in bad debts from the firm's auditors and investors, which caused the stock price to drop to below $1 per share. In 2008, Bennett pleaded guilty to securities fraud and other criminal charges and was sent to prison for 16 years.

Madoff Investment Securities

Bernie Madoff founded Madoff Investment Securities in 1960 and ran it along with several other family members until 2008. Madoff Investments was one of the key players in developing the NASDAQ quotation system, and Bernie Madoff served as chairman of the board of directors for the National Association of Securities Dealers (NASD) and on their board of governors. His firm had a solid track record of returns through the 1980s, but the wealth management division of Madoff Investments may have been a fraud from the beginning.

Madoff himself admitted that he stopped making trades in the early 1990s, and that all of his returns since that point had been falsified. Instead he began using money from new investors to pay off earlier investors, a common story. He was arrested in December 2008, and in 2009 he pleaded guilty to running the largest Ponzi scheme in history. He was sentenced to 150 years in prison and was ordered to pay restitution to his investors totaling $170 billion. In addition, criminal charges related to activities involving Madoff Investments were filed against Aurelia Finance, a private Swiss bank and fund management firm, and Bank Medici, an Austrian bank.

Lessons From Financial Scandals

While each of the scandals discussed above is unique in some way, there are certain patterns that repeat often enough to be singled out. Fraudulent accounting is common in these cases, having been a part of the WorldCom, Enron, Towers and Refco scandals. "Cooking the books" can help bolster a falling stock price for a while, but it requires bigger lies with each new set of financial statements, and eventually a smart analyst will see the inconsistencies. Once a firm starts on this road, there is no turning back, and as we have seen, the consequences can be dire.

Ponzi schemes also played a part in Enron, the Bayou Hedge Fund, Towers Financial and Madoff Investments. A Ponzi scheme, also known as a pyramid scheme, is simple in structure and operation: money invested by new clients is used to pay returns to earlier clients, while large sums are skimmed off and spent or stashed away. Enron's Ponzi scheme was a bit different; top management used the trust put in them by the rank and file workers to get them to invest their pension money in Enron stock, helping to keep up the demand for the stock, and so propping up the price. Any such scheme requires a constant influx of new investors in order to maintain the illusion, and even if no investors pull out, at some point the number of investors required to continue the operation becomes too much, and the pyramid collapses under its own weight.

Enron used a new method that literally changed the way accounting is done: they corrupted the auditors. Arthur Andersen, one of the Big Five accounting firms before the scandal, surrendered its license to practice as certified public accountants after being found guilty in a criminal trial in 2002. However, in 2005 the Supreme Court overturned the conviction.

While greed played a part in all of these scandals, it was the primary driving force for the Adelphia scandal. Members of the Rigas family felt entitled to use the business to finance their chosen lifestyle and worked together to break the law for that purpose. It cost them their freedom.

While all of these cases resulted in legal problems for those concerned, the legal charges all resulted from ethical failures on the part of those involved. For Bernie Madoff, it was his ethical choices that caused all the trouble for his firm. Similarly, Refco's downfall was caused by CEO Phillip Bennett. However, in Enron, Towers Financial, WorldCom and Bayou, it was the corrupt culture that led many to make the disastrously bad choices that brought down their firms. A rogue employee needs a position of power from which to wreak havoc on a firm; a corrupt culture cannot help but destroy itself.

Misusing Risk

Another issue that has created scandals and shuttered businesses is the misuse of risk. There are patterns repeated in these cases as well, such as the attempt to cover one bad bet with another, known as "doubling down," or improper corporate governance. The results can be disastrous. In this section, we include cases that occurred outside the United States.

Lincoln Savings and Loan

Lincoln Savings and Loan Association of Irvine, California was a small, slow-growing institution before Charles Keating took it over in 1983. Over the next four years, Keating quintupled the S&L's assets by making highly risky investments with depositors' money. American Continental Corporation, the parent company of Lincoln Savings, went bankrupt in early 1989, taking with it the savings of its depositors, and initiating the Savings and Loan Crisis of the 1980s and 1990s. This crisis resulted in the failure of more than 1,000 savings and loan institutions across the country.

The crisis came about due to deregulation of the savings and loan industry during the 1980s, and the resulting scandal, known as the "Keating Five" scandal, tarnished the reputations of five powerful politicians: US Senators Alan Cranston, Dennis DeConcini, John Glenn, John McCain and Donald Riegle, Jr. The failure cost the federal government (and so the taxpayers) over $3 billion, and resulted in Keating spending four and a half years in prison for fraud, racketeering and conspiracy.

Proctor & Gamble and Bankers Trust

In the early 1990s, Proctor and Gamble (P&G) entered into two interest rate swaps with Bankers Trust, in an attempt to lower their borrowing costs. The firm chose to use over-the-counter (OTC) derivatives rather than exchange-traded derivatives, based on accounting rules that existed at the time that did not require an initial margin deposit or marking-to-market (settling up losses on a daily basis). They had used derivatives in the past with success. However, this time they included an additional transaction that was designed to speculate on the shape of the yield curve. The structure of this transaction was such that if the yield curve stayed the same or flattened, P&G would either break even or come out ahead, while if the yield curve shifted upward, P&G would lose considerably. If economic conditions did not change much, P&G would be able to purchase a low-priced call option to close the position, locking in their gains. However, since P&G had no idea what would happen with interest rates, they were speculating in an area in which they had no expertise. The results were costly.

Between February and December 1994, the Federal Reserve tightened monetary conditions, causing the yield curve to shift upwards. The interest rate for their speculative transaction rose quickly, and P&G ended up owing Bankers Trust almost $200 million. P&G filed suit against Bankers Trust in an attempt to limit their losses, and an out-of-court settlement did in fact limit their losses to $35 million. But their reputation was tarnished, and they learned a costly lesson about speculating in the derivatives market.

Orange County, California

In December of 1994, Orange County, California filed for bankruptcy. They reported a loss of $1.5 billion on a portfolio worth $7.6 billion, making it the largest municipal bankruptcy in US history. There were a number of factors that led to this result, not the least of which was that the man in charge of Orange County's investments, Robert Citron, had no education in accounting or finance. Prior to 1994, Citron's results were spectacular, so much so that other state entities joined in the investments with Citron, creating the Orange County Investment Pool (OCIP). This resulted in a portfolio consisting of $7.6 billion in investor funds and $12.9 billion in debt in the form of reverse repurchase agreements.

Reverse repurchase agreements involve the sale of an asset (typically a bond) in the spot market with an agreement to buy it back at a future date at a fixed price. They are effectively collateralized loans, but because of the fixed repurchase price, they are also similar to forward contracts. Robert Citron bet on declining interest rates by entering into numerous reverse repurchase agreements. If interest rates fell, Citron gained not only interest returns but also capital gains because the price of the bonds he had to repurchase was fixed at the time of the reverse repo deal. By contrast, the bonds he acquired could be sold at appreciated prices. The combination of falling interest rates plus OCIP's leverage earned Citron large profits when interest rates fell, but they resulted in large losses when interest rates rose.

From 1989 to 1992, US Treasury security yields fell steadily, e.g., the 1-year T-bill rate fell from 9.0% to 3.7%. Citron's strategy was essentially betting that interest rates would fall. In

February 1994, the Federal Reserve tightened credit to reduce the threat of inflation and the risk of the economy overheating. As a result, interest rates started rising; from February to December, the Fed raised interest rates six times, and yields on 1-year T-bills rose from 3.5% to 7.1%. As rates rose and bond prices fell, Citron considered bonds relatively cheap; he borrowed and bought more bonds, essentially using a "doubling down" strategy.

In October–November 1994, it became clear that the OCIP was in major trouble. Investors became spooked, resulting in mass withdrawals and a liquidity crisis. Orange County wanted to notify the public quickly to allay their fears, but they were hampered by the Brown Act of 1953, which required them to give three days' notice prior to holding public meetings. Giving that much prior notice made it likely that more of the investors in the OCIP would withdraw their funds as well, exacerbating the problem. An audit of the books published on December 1, 1994, estimated the losses at $1.5 billion. Three days later, Robert Citron resigned.

A big part of the problem in Orange County was a lack of proper oversight. Only one member of the Board of Supervisors to whom Robert Citron reported had any financial expertise, and hard questions about Citron's borrowing and investment transactions were not asked by any member of the board. Citron reported to the board only once a year, which is relatively seldom for a fund as large as OCIP. As long as results were good, details were unnecessary.

Barings Bank

In 1995 Barings Bank, the second oldest merchant bank in the world, was forced to close its doors after 233 years in business due to the transgressions of one man, Nick Leeson. Leeson began working at Barings' London headquarters in 1989, settling futures and options trades in the back office. He proved to be very good at back office administration, and so he was sent to Barings' Indonesia office in 1990. During his early years there he did very well, and he became the chief trader and head of settlements for Barings Futures (Singapore) in 1992. This situation allowed him to makes trades without supervision, since he was the one reporting on trade activity.

Leeson was allowed to execute orders for Barings' customers and to conduct inter-exchange arbitrage. However, rather than doing inter-exchange arbitrage, Leeson was taking naked speculative positions. In particular, he made a major bet that the Nikkei 225 would rise from June 1994 through February 1995. Leeson was able to hide his speculative positions by using a special trade account that he controlled, and that he used to make unauthorized trades and falsify reports.

As losses mounted, Leeson tried to recoup them by doubling his bets on the Nikkei 225, but the Nikkei kept dropping, and his losses grew even more rapidly. This led to increasing difficulty in funding margin calls. Desperate to fund these calls, Leeson resorted to increasing commission income by trading at non-market prices, booking fictitious trades and falsifying records. In the beginning of 1995, the end was near.

On December 31, 1994, losses had grown to £208 million. On January 17, 1995, there was a massive earthquake in Kobe, Japan, registering 7.3 on the Richter scale. This earthquake led to the Nikkei 225 plummeting even further. By the end of February 1995, losses had increased to £860 million. Rather than face his supervisors, Leeson and his wife fled to Malaysia, leaving a confession for the chairman of the bank. The bank was declared insolvent on February 26, 1995.

While it was Leeson's actions that brought Barings bank down, it was Barings' lack of supervision over his activities that made it possible. The Bank of England investigated the collapse, and in the report they issued on July 18, 1995, the blame for the catastrophe was split between Leeson and his supervisors. Leeson worked without internal controls; he could do whatever he wanted and cover it up in the report. By the time Barings caught wind of the problem, their doors were halfway closed.

Long Term Capital Management

Long Term Capital Management (LTCM) was a hedge fund founded in 1994 by John Meriwether, the former vice chairman of global fixed income trading, arbitrage and foreign exchange at Salomon Brothers. The group that ran the fund included a "Who's Who" list of notable academics and practitioners:

* Robert Merton and Myron Scholes, winners of the Nobel Prize in Economics;
* David Mullins Jr., former member of the Federal Reserve's Board of Governors; and
* Eight former colleagues of Meriwether from Salomon Brothers.

LTCM chose to initially focus on global bond markets, and then rapidly expand into domestic and foreign equity markets. Their strategy was to identify small imperfections in market prices and relations (e.g., spreads between interest rate yields) and to exploit these arbitrage opportunities using relatively little equity capital while leveraging (borrowing) as much as possible. They needed to secure long-term funding to ride out bad times, and to monitor the high level of risk using Value at Risk (VaR). At the same time, LTCM chose to maintain as much secrecy as possible regarding its approach from both clients and competitors.

From 1994 to 1997, assets grew from $20 billion to $130 billion, while equity grew from $1.25 billion to $7.1 billion. During this period, gross returns and net returns (i.e., net LTCM fees) increased by approximately 290% and 180% respectively. It was an impressive performance, yet there was a caveat: the high returns on equity were driven by high leverage. Gross returns on assets ranged from 0.67% to 2.45%. The high returns on equity resulted from multiplying these nondescript gross returns by high leverage ratios.

Many of LTCM's trades were based on a belief (from historical patterns) that certain spreads would narrow over time. During 1997–1998, however, many of these spreads widened. Two major international crises were key factors:

* The Asian Tiger Crisis of 1997—the crisis affected Thailand, Malaysia, Philippines, Indonesia and South Korea;
* The Russian Bond Default—after months of economic and financial unrest, on August 17, 1998, Russia devalued the ruble and announced a moratorium on $13.5 billion local currency debt.

Global markets became increasingly volatile. Historical patterns in financial prices and yield spreads no longer held. Risk assessments based on historical parameter estimates and VAR became problematic, so the true degree of risk was intangible. Liquidity and diversification problems snowballed, outside funding dried up and losses mounted rapidly. By the summer of 1998, LTCM was in deep trouble and looking for a "white knight" to ride in to the rescue.

On September 18, 1998, the president of the New York Fed convened a consortium of major banks to discuss a bailout. On September 23, Warren Buffet (Berkshire Hathaway), AIG and Goldman Sachs made an offer for LTCP (the portfolio managed by LTCM), but it had a one-hour deadline which passed. No deal was struck. On September 28, a bailout agreement was finally reached. Fourteen banks and brokerage houses contributed $3.65 billion—the Federal Reserve System contributed nothing. The consortium received 90% ownership, the principals and investors received 10% ownership.

Reaction to the bailout was mixed. Some thought the bailout prevented a major global financial market meltdown. Others thought the Fed should not have intervened on behalf of rich investors and that the principals should receive nothing after generating such massive losses. Either way, public opinion was not kind; for all involved in LTCM, their legacies have been tarnished.

Lessons From Misusing Risk

Once again, although these cases have major differences, there are certain common factors that can be identified as having contributed to the negative outcomes. For example, Proctor & Gamble–Bankers Trust, Orange County, California and Long Term Capital Management all involved speculating on interest rates; P&G–BT involved speculating on the shape of the yield curve, Orange County involved betting that interest rates would fall and LTCM involved betting on the spread between different interest rates. All three suffered big losses when interest rates turned against them. The principals involved failed to hedge their positions, resulting in disaster.

A lack of oversight led to risky behavior for both Orange County and Barings Bank. Robert Citron did not explain the methods he used to achieve the returns he obtained, and that satisfied his superiors as long as the returns were good. Since only one person on the Board of Supervisors had any financial expertise, no questions were asked. Barings Bank, on the other hand, gave Nick Leeson the opportunity to trade without oversight as well as the ability to cover his tracks administratively; the fox was guarding the hen house. In both cases, results were the only metric of interest to the supervisors.

The use of leverage made things worse for Orange County and LTCM; in both cases, the high use of debt made it virtually impossible to get out of their trading positions in a timely manner. These cases clearly show that while the use of debt can leverage returns up (as the Du Pont formula teaches), it can also drive returns down. Excessive use of debt also makes it more difficult to undo trading positions quickly.

Both Orange Country and Barings Bank saw a difficult situation get worse when the trader involved attempted to correct prior mistakes by "doubling down," or increasing the size of each consecutive bet to "double or nothing." A simple example will show how quickly this strategy can overwhelm the trader. Start with a $100,000 trade that loses, and double the trade with each consecutive bet:

- Bet 1: $100,000 bet loses, position = −$100,000;
- Bet 2: $200,000 bet loses, position = −$300,000;
- Bet 3: $400,000 bet loses, position = −$700,000;
- Bet 4: $800,000 bet loses, position = −$1,500,000.

Starting with a $100,000 loss, it takes only three additional "double or nothing" bets to be well over a million dollars down! Doubling down does not reduce risk; it amplifies it.

The Savings and Loan Crisis revealed one of the newer fears for the economy: contagion. One of the justifications used to bail out Wall Street and the big banks after the 2008 financial crisis was the fear of the kind of contagion seen after Lincoln Savings and Loan went under. This was made clear by the "too big to fail" label that was given to these institutions. The simple fact of the matter is, if a financial institution is too big to fail, it is too big to manage and therefore needs to be downsized.

Another issue that arose in the LTCM case was the ineffectiveness of the VaR metric when the future differs from the past. Value at Risk (VaR) is a statistical measure of market risk that LTCM relied on to measure its market risk exposures. At the 99% level of confidence, LTCM's econometricians assured the principals and investors that the company should lose no more than $105 million per day. The problem was that VaR assumes the future will be like the past, and that all possible future events fit neatly into a normally distributed, bell-shaped distribution function. Both of these assumptions proved to be incorrect in 1998.

The legal issues that arose in these cases stemmed more from arrogance than unethical behavior, although bad ethical choices were made as well. For example, with the Orange County case, the culture of the Board of Supervisors was unprofessional, not corrupt, while Robert Citron's initial activities were misguided but not necessarily unethical (although a case could be made that he had no business having that kind of fiduciary responsibility given his lack of education in the field). However, his efforts to correct his mistakes by doubling down were certainly unethical. While Proctor and Gamble did nothing illegal in setting up their interest rate swap, they chose to take a position in the market, which is not their area of expertise. They manufacture consumer goods, so any positions they take in the market should be for hedging, not speculating. By exposing themselves to risks they did not understand, they put their stakeholders' value at unnecessary risk. That went against their responsibility as managers and was therefore unethical.

The 2008 Financial Crisis

The seeds for the 2008 financial crisis were sown in the real estate and housing construction boom that began in the late 1990s. Following the tech bubble in the stock market in 2000, the Federal Reserve lowered interest rates to stimulate the economy, and more and more families chose to take on debt in order to live a better life. However, even under these conditions, there are only so many families available that have the income and credit needed to qualify for a mortgage. The idea of selling subprime mortgages grew from the push to continue selling houses in both the real estate market and the construction industry: offering mortgages to high risk ("subprime") borrowers at higher interest rates to compensate the lenders for the higher risk. While this idea on its own offered some additional sales, what truly opened the flood gates for the subprime market were two different but concurrent changes: how mortgage lenders changed their business model and the development of mortgage-backed securities (MBSs).

The original business model for mortgage lenders was seen in the movie *It's a Wonderful Life* with Jimmy Stewart. The mortgage lender would manage the relationship with the borrower throughout the life of the loan, helping out if the family needed help and celebrating with the family when the debt was paid and the house was finally theirs. In the early 2000s, the financial industry realized that these mortgages were liquid and could be sold on the market. Financial engineers working for investment banks understood that the monthly payments from mortgages could be used as payments to other lenders, and so they securitized the payments from multiple mortgages to create different types of MBSs, including collateralized debt obligations (CDOs). These CDOs were constructed of different parts of many different mortgages of various degrees of risk, bundled in a way that made understanding the associated risks very difficult to assess. The investment banks then presented the CDOs to the security rating agencies (Fitch's, Standard & Poor's and Moody's) as low risk. When the ratings agencies balked at assigning the CDOs a low risk rating without confirmation, the investment banks threatened to take their business elsewhere, using their considerable revenue stream to coerce the agencies into complying. In this way, the investment banks were able to sell the MBSs as low risk securities, which made them appealing to a much wider market.

Over time, the quality of the mortgages being used for the MBSs declined even further, as mortgages were sold to borrowers of lesser and lesser means. These mortgage loans to high-risk clients were known in the industry as NINJA loans: no income, no job or assets. At the same time, the lenders starting adding numerous "fees" to the closing costs of these mortgages, making it even more profitable to write subprime contracts. They then sold the mortgages within a few days of the closing date. The mortgage lenders realized that when they sold the mortgage, they also sold the risk that went along with it. That fact motivated lenders to sell mortgages to anyone they could, regardless of their credit worthiness. The numerous tricks the mortgage lenders used to get subprime borrowers to sign up are referred to as predatory lending practices, because they targeted these people like predators and talked them into something they couldn't afford. There is evidence that some lenders used "bait and switch" tactics, drawing borrowers in with one rate and then announcing at the closing that the original rate was no longer available, and that the new higher rate was their only choice. The borrowers were faced with either agreeing to a loan they could not afford or walking away from owning a home. Not an easy decision to make under any conditions, more so having to make it at the closing.

The most common subprime mortgages were 5-year ARMs (adjustable rate mortgages). In these contracts, the interest rate is fixed for the first five-year period, after which the interest rate varies with another market rate, such as the LIBOR rate (London Interbank Offer Rate). In the expanding economy at that time, the switch to an adjustable interest rate caused the rate to soar, making the mortgage payments soar as well. The borrowers were told early on that they could use the fixed rate period to clean up their credit and refinance at a lower rate based on their new credit situation. What they were not told is that cleaning up your credit requires time and money, and these borrowers were unable to increase their income sufficiently during the fixed rate period to make refinancing a reality. Therefore, most of these subprime borrowers were faced with the reality of foreclosure due to ballooning mortgage payments. Many of them chose to simply walk away from their new homes, abandoning them and destroying their credit in the process. The mortgage lenders made this decision easier as well by getting these borrowers into homes without any equity.

Standard practice for mortgage lenders is to require the borrower to put a down payment on the mortgage of at least 20% of the value of the house, so that the borrower has equity in the house (something to lose). For many of the subprime loans, however, no down payments were requested, with the loan amount being more than 100% of the price of the house. Borrowers were told they could use the additional funds to update the kitchen or bathroom, or to help clean up their credit, or even to take a vacation. People with insufficient means and poor credit were given houses with no money down. When the payments became too high, they simply packed their things and left the house. Entire housing developments were abandoned and foreclosed upon. In September of 2008, Fannie Mae and Freddie Mac, two government-sponsored enterprises responsible for a good portion of the subprime mortgages sold, were taken over by the federal government in order to cover their MBS obligations.

Once the mortgage payments stopped coming in, the payments for the associated CDOs also stopped, and the owners of those CDOs were looking to sell. There were trillions of dollars' worth of these CDOs being held around the world, and everyone who owned them was looking to sell at the same time. Since no one was interested in buying, their value quickly went to zero.

It became apparent in the spring of 2007 that banks were refusing to do business with other banks due to their losses in the CDOs, and the federal government had to step in to provide assurances of liquidity. In August of 2007, the Federal Reserve Open Market Committee began lowering the federal funds rate (the rate banks charge other banks for overnight deposits), and in December 2007 they instituted the Term Auction Facility (TAF) to provide short-term credit to banks holding subprime mortgages. In March 2008, the Federal Reserve guaranteed the bad debt of the investment bank Bear Sterns in order to enable another investment bank, JP Morgan Chase, to acquire it. In September 2008, the Lehman Brothers' investment bank went bankrupt when the Federal Reserve refused to guarantee its loans. Also in September 2008, the Federal Reserve took over American International Group (AIG), a multinational finance and insurance company, for selling huge amounts of credit default swaps (basically insurance against default) without hedging its investment. On September 29, 2008, the day Congress instituted the Troubled Asset Relief Program (TARP), an attempt to get banks to start lending money again by giving them money to lend, the Dow Jones Industrial Average (DJIA) fell 770 points, its largest one-day decline at that time. In December 2008, the federal funds rate was lowered to 0%, and in January 2009 the three largest US automakers, GM, Ford and Fiat Chrysler, were bailed out at taxpayer expense, victims of the Great Recession.

All parties involved bear responsibility for the results associated with the subprime mortgage market and the mortgage-backed securities market, but a big part of why it happened was due to deregulation. It started with banking deregulation in the 1980s that led to the S&L crisis, and then the Gramm–Leach–Bliley Act in 1999 repealed provisions of the Glass–Stegall Act, which permitted banks to take more risks with depositors' funds. In 2000 the Commodities Futures Modernization Act, which was written with assistance from the financial industry, effectively banned further regulation of the derivatives market. This led to exponential growth in the derivatives industry and caused Warren Buffet to famously refer to derivatives as "financial weapons of mass destruction."[1] In 2004, the SEC relaxed its net capital rule, which allowed investment banks to significantly increase their level of debt, which in turn fueled the growth in mortgage-backed securities.

The Glass–Steagall Act was passed by Congress in 1933 in response to the stock market crash of 1929. Among other things, it prevented banks from investing in, or being in any way involved with, risky securities. While some argue that the Glass–Steagall Act was effectively dead by the time the Gramm–Leach–Bliley Act was passed, Nobel Prize-winning economist Joseph Stiglitz disagrees. He wrote:

> When repeal of Glass–Stegall brought investment and commercial banks together, the investment-bank culture came out on top. There was a demand for the kind of high returns that could be obtained only through high leverage and big risk taking.[2]

Agency Issues

The managers of a corporation act as agents on behalf of the firm's stakeholders. They make decisions to purchase, utilize or liquidate assets that have a direct impact on the firm's cash flows, and therefore its value. Managers, as agents, have an ethical obligation to make decisions that promote the best interests of the firm's stakeholders. It is human nature, however, to make choices that benefit the manager, such as using the company credit card to put gasoline in a personal vehicle, or using the company condominium for personal entertainment.

Agency issues are ways in which conflicts arise between the interests of the firm's managers and its stakeholders, particularly with regard to conflicts with the common shareholders.

The costs associated with trying to reduce agency conflicts are known as agency costs. One example of an agency cost is the cost of auditing a firm's financial statements. A sole proprietor knows what decisions were made to operate the business, and so there is no need to do an audit. When some of the decision-making authority is granted to others, the shareholders are justified in using an outside audit to confirm the numbers reported by the managers. The audit is used to monitor managerial behavior, to make sure the managers are looking out for the owners' interests.

While most agency issues are relatively minor, managers have an impressive ability of finding new ways to take advantage of their positions for personal gain. The value of an independent audit was verified by the Enron scandal. The top managers' behavior was despicable, all the way up to the CEO, but they could not have gotten away with it had they not corrupted Arthur Andersen. In this way, the Enron scandal can be seen as an agency issue at its core.

Summary

There are a number of lessons to be learned from the scandals and debacles discussed in this chapter, lessons relating to managerial responsibility, fiduciary duty, business ethics and corruption. All of these issues are important, but they miss the most essential point of all: this is all typical human behavior. Research in the field of behavioral finance shows what researchers in psychology have known for decades: people will do what they are incentivized to do.

This all falls on the current culture in business in general and on the financial industry in particular. The current cultures for both promote maximizing shareholder wealth (i.e., the common stock price) first and foremost, to the detriment of other issues. The theory of corporate sustainability teaches that this approach ignores all stakeholders other than the common shareholders, which forces the other stakeholders to take the brunt of management's stock price maximizing activities. Profits are increased by denying raises to workers and stealing their wages through unpaid overtime. Operating expenses associated with the disposing of industrial waste are avoided by dumping the materials in a remote location. Margins are increased by using less expensive, substandard materials, lowering the quality of the product being sold.

In the case of Enron, some Wall Street analysts continued to give the stock a buy rating up to a month before they filed for bankruptcy, despite the warning signs in their financial disclosures as early as two years prior, and despite the fact that Enron's officers were obfuscating rather than explaining the complicated nature of their financial positions. Those analysts were in a difficult position; the investment banks they worked for also earned money from Enron by helping them issue new securities. If their analysts were to issue a sell recommendation for Enron's stock, Enron's CFO would move their business to a different investment bank. So, the sales and trading side of the bank put pressure on the research side of the bank to avoid lowering the recommendation on the stocks of their clients. The results were disastrous for all stakeholders other than the officers, but the Enron employees were hurt the most: they not only lost their jobs, they also lost all the money they had invested for their retirement.

The culture of business in general, and that of the financial industry in particular, is at the root of the legal and ethical issues that continue to populate the news. Shareholder wealth maximization is the heart of the problem and needs to change. Businesses and financial firms lobby Congress hard and often to maintain the status quo, donating millions to their reelection campaigns. This necessary change will not be made quickly or painlessly, but will require pressure from within the industries as well as the firms themselves. Business schools must promote the teaching of ethics in business and finance that includes stakeholder theory and corporate sustainability. They must show students the value to society in recognizing the importance of all the stakeholders, so that future generations of new managers can change the culture from within.

End of Chapter Problems

1. What unusual step did the board of directors at WorldCom take to avoid lowering the stock price?
2. What legal accounting tool did Enron's CFO use to make earnings look better than they were?
3. How does a Ponzi scheme work?
4. What other firm did the Enron scandal bring down, and for what reason?
5. What circumstance made it possible for Charles Keating to quintuple Lincoln Savings and Loan's assets in a short period of time?
6. Who were the Keating five?
7. In what way was Proctor and Gamble's interest rate swap deal unethical?
8. What particular form of debt did Robert Citron use to leverage up the returns to the Orange County Investment Pool?
9. What circumstance in the economy made Robert Citron's investment strategy change from a winner to a loser?
10. What circumstance allowed Robert Citron to put the Orange County Investment Pool's funds at risk?
11. What circumstance allowed Nick Leeson to put Barings Bank's funds at risk?
12. What strategy that Nick Leeson tried only made things worse?
13. What part of the strategy made things worse for both Orange County and Long Term Capital Management when returns started going negative?
14. What situation that arose due to the S&L crisis caused the federal government to bail out Wall Street and the big banks in the 2007 financial crisis?
15. What risk metric proved insufficient for Long Term Capital Management?

Notes

1 "Buffet Warns on Investment 'Time Bomb'," *BBC News*, March 4, 2003.
2 Stiglitz, J. "Capitalist Fools," *Vanity Fair*, January 2009.

Bibliography

Fundamentals of Corporate Finance, 12th edition. S. Ross, R. Westerfield and B. Jordan. McGraw-Hill Education, 2019.
Financial Management: Principles & Practice, 8th edition. T. Gallagher. Textbook Media Press, 2019.
Risk Takers: Uses and Abuses of Financial Derivatives, 2nd edition. J. Marthinsen. Pearson, 2009.
The Smartest Guys in the Room: The Amazing Rise and Scandalous Fall of Enron. B. McLean and P. Elkind. Penguin Publishing Group, 2004.
Online archives, www.chicagotribune.com
Online archives, www.washingtonpost.com

12 Financial Markets and Institutions

One of the primary duties of the CFO is to acquire capital for the firm when needed. While firms do have access to capital in the form of retained earnings, for most firms that is not enough to fund all of their capital projects on an ongoing basis; most firms need to raise funds in the capital markets from time to time. An understanding of the financial markets and the institutions within those markets is crucial for determining the options available to the firm in terms of financing.

Just as there are different types of financial institutions, there are also different types of financial markets. Generally speaking, markets exist to bring buyers and sellers together. Financial markets exist to bring together those entities that need funds (such as governments or corporations) with those entities that have excess funds available (such as pension funds or insurance companies). People are motivated to invest when they believe the return from the investment will be worth the risk, so those entities in need of funds vie for the funds available by way of the expected return to their securities. Those securities that are seen as having sufficient return relative to their perceived risk will be in demand, and will be successful in raising funds. Since there are different levels of risk tolerance in the financial markets, many different types of securities, with different levels of perceived risk and expected return, can successfully raise funds in the capital markets at any given time.

In this chapter, we will discuss the different types of financial markets available for those entities in need of funds, as well as the different types of securities used to raise funds. We will discuss the controversial theory of market efficiency and how it can impact financial decision-making. We will also discuss the different types of financial institutions that make up our financial system, including the Federal Reserve Bank, the central bank of the United States.

Financial Markets

As discussed above, financial markets exist to match entities that need funds with entities that have funds available to invest. Markets exist for different types of securities, with different levels of risk tolerance, different maturities and different cash flows. Stocks are issued by corporations, while debt securities (such as bonds) are issued by both corporations and governments.

Primary Markets

Primary market transactions are those in which the corporation is the seller of the securities and the recipient of the funds (minus flotation costs). Primary market transactions can be either public offerings or private placements. Public offerings include initial public offerings (IPOs), in which a firm's common stock is sold to the public for the first time, and seasoned equity offerings (SEOs), in which a firm offers additional shares of a stock that is already publicly traded. A private placement is a negotiated sale to a specific buyer.

All public offerings of debt and equity must be registered with the Securities and Exchange Commission (SEC), the federal body that regulates the stock and bond markets. The registration process requires the issuing entity to disclose a good deal of information about the corporation prior to selling any securities. The costs associated with public offerings can be substantial.

Private placements do not have to be registered with the SEC, avoiding all of the associated regulations. Due to this, private placements do not require underwriters—investment banks that help corporations sell new issues publicly—and therefore do not incur flotation fees. Private placements of debt and equity are typically made with large institutional investors such as insurance companies or mutual funds.

Secondary Markets

Secondary market transactions occur when one owner of a stock sells it to a new owner, or a debtholder sells bonds to a new debtholder. Funds related to secondary market transactions do not flow to the corporation. However, an active secondary market is crucial for success when issuing new securities in the primary market.

Any and all trades of a security after the IPO or SEO take place in the secondary market. This means that the primary market is quite small (there aren't too many IPOs or SEOs) while the secondary market is huge. Prices posted on stock market websites and published in print are secondary market prices.

Secondary markets are either dealer markets or auction markets. Dealer markets are those in which dealers buy or sell stocks or bonds, generally for themselves and at their own risk. Auction markets are where brokers match up buyers and sellers to facilitate transactions. Dealer markets exist electronically, whereas auction markets have physical locations (e.g., the New York Stock Exchange is an auction market).

Dealer markets in corporate stock and long-term debt are referred to as over-the-counter (OTC) markets, a reference to long ago when securities were bought and sold at counters in dealer's offices. Many US stocks and most long-term debt are sold in markets that have no central location, but transact via electronic networks. Auction markets (like the NYSE or the AMEX) exist to connect investors who want to buy with investors who want to sell; dealers only get involved when a counterparty to a transaction is not available (e.g., if an investor wants to buy a stock for which there are no sell orders).

Money Market

The money market exists to trade securities that have maturities of less than one year. This market is a network of dealers connected by phones and computers, making for quick trading among themselves and with the issuing entities. Money market transactions are for large denominations, and they take place between financial institutions and companies, not individuals. Individuals can invest in money market securities through a money market mutual fund.

Capital Market

The capital market exists for long-term debt and equity securities (securities with more than one year to maturity). Corporations as well as governments (at every level) raise money in the capital market. Firms use the proceeds from capital market transactions for purchasing long-term assets such as buildings or production equipment. Local governments may use the proceeds for such projects as infrastructure improvements.

The Efficient Market Hypothesis

What are we referring to when we speak about market efficiency? What exactly is it that financial markets are expected to be efficient at? They are expected to be efficient at processing information effectively and reflecting it in current stock prices. When stories about publicly held corporations first hit the news, the stock market will respond in one of three ways:

- If the news is unexpected and good, the stock price will increase, higher for stories of high impact, less for stories of less importance;
- If the news is unexpected and bad, the stock price will decrease, lower for stories of high impact, less for stories of less importance; or
- Little or no movement if the story is expected.

As an example, on November 1, 2018, Amazon, Facebook and Netflix all reported lower than expected revenue for the quarter. As would be expected, each stock's price fell in subsequent trading. On the same day, however, Apple reported higher than expected earnings, and their stock price fell 4%. Why did this occur? It occurred because at the Apple investor meeting where the results were reported, Apple offered guidance for the following quarter, indicating that revenue projections for the coming holidays were not likely to meet analysts' expectations. This unexpected news drove the stock price down in subsequent trading.

On December 19, 2018, the Food and Drug Administration (FDA) announced that it had approved the drug Olaparib for use in treating patients with ovarian cancer. The commercial name for the drug is Lynparza, and it is produced by AstraZeneca Pharmaceuticals. On the day that the announcement was made, AstraZeneca's common stock price fell by 0.68%. Why was there no increase in the price from the good news? In fact, the news was expected—the drug had been under review for years. Had the drug not been approved, AstraZeneca's stock price would likely have fallen significantly. However, the expected news of its approval had virtually no impact on the firm's stock price because it was expected.

Stock prices change virtually every day, and the more popularly traded stocks change in price all day long. Most news stories have minor impact on stock prices, but a series of minor news stories can have a significant impact over time. When the market's belief regarding the stock's future expected cash flows changes, investors will make trades based on the change in belief, and the trades will cause the stock price to change (since the trades themselves are news). If more investors are looking to sell than buy, demand for the stock will fall, and so will the stock price. If more investors are looking to buy than sell, demand for the stock will increase, driving the stock price up.

In a truly efficient market, assets are priced appropriately, and the return investors earn is therefore appropriate. This implies that earning higher than expected (or excess) returns cannot occur in an efficient market. Practical results do not support this implication, making the theory seem flawed. The occurrence of market corrections that destroy billions of dollars in value in a day makes the theory look ludicrous.

Any theory regarding human behavior must be complex, as we humans are not simple creatures. The nature of market efficiency is more fluid than a first reading of the theory would lead one to believe. Before we discuss the theory itself, we will discuss the existence of excess returns, or what is involved in "beating the market."

Beating the Market

When we speak of "beating the market," what exactly do we mean? We mean earning a higher return than is appropriate for the given level of risk. In Chapter 3 we calculated the 2013 expected return for Amazon using the risk-free rate of 2.35%, the market return of 18.99% and Amazon's beta of 1.27 by plugging these numbers into the Security Market Line (SML) formula:

$$k_{Amazon} = 2.35 + (18.99 - 2.35)1.27 = 23.48\%$$

Based on the data given, the appropriate return for Amazon's common stock for 2013 was 23.48%. In fact, in 2013 Amazon's common stock had a return of 35.10%. However, the fact that Amazon earned a higher return than the market does not in itself mean that it beat the market. Amazon's stock is riskier than the market, as indicated by the beta of 1.27. Therefore, we expect Amazon to have a return higher than the market. If Amazon's return for 2013 had been 20.50%, it would have been a bad year for Amazon investors, even though their return would be higher than the market return, because it would be less than required for the given level of risk.

Excess return is calculated as the realized return minus the expected return. The excess return earned by Amazon in 2013 was 35.10% − 23.48% = 11.62%. This positive excess return means that for 2013, Amazon beat the market. Had Amazon only earned 20.50%, their excess return would be 20.50% − 23.48% = −2.98%, indicating that they had underperformed the market.

The Three Levels of Market Efficiency

Theory recognizes three levels of market efficiency: the weak form, the semi-strong form and the strong form of efficiency. The higher levels of efficiency build upon the lower levels, so that each level includes the level or levels below.

Weak Form Efficiency

The weak form of market efficiency states that all information regarding past stock price movements and volume is already reflected in current stock prices. This implies that analyzing past stock price changes and volume will be of no help in earning excess returns (returns above what is appropriate for the level of risk involved). If the weak form of efficiency is true, then technical analysis (studying past stock prices to find exploitable patterns) is a waste of time. Since less than 10% of Wall Street analysts are technicians, Wall Street generally does not have a problem with the weak form of market efficiency.

Semi-Strong Form Efficiency

The semi-strong form of market efficiency states that all publicly available information—including past prices and volume figures, published financial statements, news reports, blogs, etc.—is already reflected in current stock prices, and attempts to use these data to earn excess returns are therefore pointless. If the semi-strong form of efficiency is true, then fundamental analysis (analyzing the firm's public information to determine the intrinsic value of their common stock) is also a waste of time. Since more than 90% of Wall Street analysts use fundamental analysis to earn their living, the Street has no use for the semi-strong form of market efficiency.

Strong Form Efficiency

The strong form of market efficiency states that all available information, public or private, is already reflected in current stock prices, and therefore attempts to use any information to earn excess returns would be futile. This would imply that having insider information would not help an investor to earn excess returns. If Congress believed that, then insider trading would not be illegal. In 1987, Ivan Boesky, a stock trader running his own New York-based broker-age firm, was found guilty of insider trading. He was fined $100 million, sentenced to prison for three and a half years and banned from ever working in the securities industry again. It would be difficult to find anyone who truly believes in the strong form of market efficiency.

A Way to View Market Efficiency

The financial markets are among the most researched and analyzed human endeavors in world history. Remarkable amounts of data are collected and analyzed every day, both by those working in the financial industry and academics, all working to understand the dynam-ics of market movements. All of this work has led to the following general conclusions:

1. Short-term stock price and market movements are very difficult to predict with any accuracy;
2. The market reacts relatively quickly to new information, and attempts to exploit these reactions consistently fail;
3. If there is a way to consistently beat the stock market, it is elusive.

These results tend to support market efficiency on a general level, despite the seemingly contrary evidence of market corrections. However, since we are discussing a human phe-nomenon, we must allow for the vagaries of human behavior. There is another way to view market efficiency that allows for results like market corrections.

Corrections point out inefficiencies in certain specific markets, not in the stock market as a whole. For example, in 2008 the S&P 500 Index lost more than a third of its value during the financial crisis. However, also during 2008, Wal-Mart Inc. earned a 20% return, while Anheuser Busch earned a 39% return. While the financial and automotive industries were teetering on the brink, firms like McDonalds and Hasbro did just fine. This is evidence that not all industries in the stock market were affected equally by the financial crisis.

There can be pockets of inefficiency in an otherwise efficient system. Corrections occur when certain stock prices are above their intrinsic value, creating a "bubble," or a disconnect between the stock's intrinsic value and its market value. A combination of news stories and trading activities can occasionally drive a stock's market price above its intrinsic price, creat-ing a bubble. The longer the bubble remains, the bigger it has the potential to get. Eventually, when the truth is known, negative news stories will trigger selling of the stock, which will cause the price to fall. When this occurs at the level of a single stock, the shareholders are the ones who are affected by it. When this occurs to an entire industry, like the internet bubble that popped in 2000, it can lead to a recession. And when it occurs in more than one industry at the same time, like the real estate bubble and the collapse of the financial industry in 2007, it can lead to a global recession. Despite these glaring weaknesses in the system, the markets can still be considered to be efficient on a general level. This is because there are forces in the economy working to help keep markets efficient.

Forces That Determine Market Efficiency

There are three economic forces that help lead to market efficiency:

1.   Investors use their information in a rational manner;
2.   There are independent deviations from rationality;
3.   Arbitrageurs exist.

Economists assume that consumers are rational decision makers pursuing self-interest. If investors are similarly rational, they will not systematically overvalue or undervalue financial securities. If in fact all investors make rational investment decisions, it would be difficult indeed to earn excess returns. Therefore, if this assumption were true, the financial markets would be expected to be efficient.

If we do not assume that all investors behave rationally, then perhaps we can assume that those investors that are behaving irrationally are doing so independently (i.e., not working together). If that is the case, then some investors will overvalue securities while others will undervalue them. Since they are not working in concert, they do not push the market in any one direction, but rather tend to work in different directions at the same time, and so cancel each other out. These differences can be viewed as noise that can be minimized through diversification. Therefore, if this assumption were true, the financial markets would be expected to be efficient.

Finally, if we assume that investors can be neither rational nor independent, if we acknowledge that irrational investors could band together to drive prices away from their intrinsic values, we know that arbitrageurs exist. Arbitrage is taking advantage of the mispricing of a financial asset in two different markets. Assets that trade with any volume are constantly monitored for deviations in pricing across markets by traders that use data-driven models to make trading decisions. Any significant deviation will trigger a trade that will buy the asset in the low market and sell it in the high market, thus locking in a risk-free profit. The deviation may be small, but the volume of the trade can make the profit significant. These large trades act as news, and will drive the asset's price towards its intrinsic value.

The combined impact of these three forces helps to maintain general efficiency in the market. Clearly it is not a perfect system; the Great Recession was a painful reminder of that. One of the more recent developments that can drive change in the market is the influence of institutional investors.

Institutional Investors

According to analyst Charles McGrath, in April of 2017 institutional investors held just over 80% of the market value of the S&P 500 Index.[1] Institutional investors include insurance companies, pension funds, mutual funds, endowments and trust departments. These institutions invest in large blocks of stocks in order to be able to influence key decisions such as a merger or acquisition, or an issue of stock options to the executives. Also in April of 2017, of the ten largest US corporations, institutions owned at least 70% of their stock.[2] The executives of these corporations have no choice but to listen to what these investors have to say, as they have tremendous voting power.

An activist investor is an institutional investor (or an extremely wealthy individual) that purchases a controlling share of a firm's stock in order to change the firm's direction, often by obtaining a seat on the board of directors. In 2017, activist investor Nelsen Peltz of Trian Fund Management fought a long, expensive battle with Proctor and Gamble CEO David Taylor for a seat on P&G's board of directors. Once on the board, he argued that P&G needed to improve their product development efforts and increase their margins. Institutional investors are big enough to influence the actions of major corporations.

Financial Securities

Financial securities come in a variety of types and maturities, and are traded in both the money and capital markets. While the biggest difference between the money and capital markets is the maturity of the securities traded, there are also differences in the types of securities offered in each market as well.

Money Market Securities

Money market securities are highly liquid and relatively low risk, as they are generally issued by entities with exceptional credit. Governments, large corporations and financial institutions issue money market securities to handle short-term situations that require more cash than is currently available. Governments, large corporations and financial institutions also purchase money market securities when they want to earn some interest on their money but they require liquidity. There are several options:

- Treasury bills (T-bills) are debt securities issued by the US federal government to finance the federal budget deficit or to refinance previously issued debt. They are issued in one month, three month, six month and one year maturities. T-bills are considered safe because to date the US government has never defaulted on its debt (although it has come very close more than once). Because of this, some researchers consider the annualized return on T-bills to be a proxy for the risk-free rate used in the SML model.
- Commercial paper is effectively an IOU; it is a short-term promissory note issued by a large corporation or financial institution with exceptional credit. The issuer must be creditworthy because the notes are unsecured; no specific assets are pledged as collateral for the debt. Because of the creditworthiness of the borrowers, commercial paper is considered safe and liquid, and in fact it can be traded.
- Negotiable certificates of deposits (CDs) are certificates verifying that funds have been deposited and will be repaid with interest on a specific date. Unlike the CDs offered to consumers, these CDs are of large denominations ($100,000 or more) with maturities between two weeks and one year. They are negotiable in that they can be traded in the secondary market. Large corporations buy negotiable CDs when they have cash to invest in the short term, and they sell negotiable CDs when they need to raise cash quickly.
- A banker's acceptance is effectively a bank's promise to pay. They are used for international transactions so that the firm that is owed is relieved of the need to travel overseas in order to collect on the debt.

There are also money market mutual funds available, which are funds that invest in short-term financial assets for a management fee.

Capital Market Securities

Capital market securities have longer maturities, and in many cases are less liquid and less safe than money market securities. The various forms of stocks and bonds available are all traded in the capital market.

Equity

Equity, or stock, is sold in two general forms: common and preferred. Common equity (or common stock) represents ownership in the issuing firm. Common shareholders have the right to any common dividends that are issued, and they have the right to vote on issues addressed by the board of directors, but only to the degree to which they own shares. Common shareholders also want to see the stock go up in price (a capital gain), so that when they are ready, they can sell the stock for a profit. So the total return to common shareholders consists of the dividend yield and the capital gains yield.

Preferred equity does not represent ownership, but rather preference when it comes to dividends; common dividends only get paid after preferred dividends are paid. If the firm stops paying all dividends for a while in response to some significant hardship, before it can pay any common dividend the firm must pay all back preferred dividends that were skipped. This makes the preferred dividend less risky, and so the return to preferred shareholders is usually less than the return to the common shareholders. The preferred dividend is fixed, while the common dividend is expected to increase over time.

Debt

Debt is exactly what it sounds like: a loan that has to be repaid. Payment for the use of the money comes in the form of interest. The interest rate earned for investing in debt is determined by the risks associated with the debt, as discussed in Chapter 4. Financial debt securities are typically referred to as bonds. In this section, we discuss the different types of bonds that are available to investors.

Treasury Bonds

The US government issues Treasury notes or Treasury bonds when it wants to borrow funds for more than one year. T-notes have maturities of from two to ten years, while T-bonds have maturities of more than ten years. Interest payments for both are made semiannually, and the principal is repaid at maturity with the final interest payment. Some researchers use the yield on 10-year T-notes as a proxy for the risk-free rate, rather than the T-bill rate. The reasoning is that the stock market is a long-term investment, and so when using the risk-free rate to determine the expected return to a stock, a long-term risk-free rate should be used.

Municipal Bonds

Municipal bonds, or "munis," are bonds issued by state and local governments. Investors in high tax rates like munis because their interest payments are not federally taxable. Because of the tax benefit, interest rates on munis are typically lower than for other bonds of similar risk and maturity. Municipal bonds are therefore popular with investors in high tax brackets. State, county or city governments issue bonds to pay for such projects as infrastructure construction or technology upgrades.

Corporate Bonds

Corporate bonds are similar in structure to T-notes and T-bonds, but in this case, they are issued by a corporation. They are riskier than T-notes or T-bonds because, unlike the federal government, corporations do not have the power to print money to cover their debts. Corporations have been known to default. Some corporations are not as popular as others, and their bonds don't get traded as often, so those bonds have some liquidity risk as well. For these reasons, the returns to corporate bonds are typically higher than those of Treasury bonds.

Mutual Funds

In a mutual fund, a money manager pools money from many investors to create a portfolio. Mutual funds can contain stocks, bonds, money market securities or a combination of the three. The nature of the portfolio is designed to appeal to specific clientele; there are equity funds, fixed income (bond) funds, balanced funds that include both equity and debt, money market funds, index funds (designed to track a specific stock index, like the S&P 500 index), funds of funds, which are mutual funds that invest in other mutual funds, and specialty funds.

Specialty funds are designed to focus on specialized clientele. For example, green funds are mutual funds that invest in companies who limit their environmental impact during production. Socially responsible funds invest in firms that promote economic and social justice. These types of funds have become remarkably popular in recent years.

Derivative Securities

Derivatives are financial securities whose value derives from the value of the underlying asset. The underlying asset could be a stock, a bond, a commodity, a currency, an interest rate or a stock index. Derivative securities include forward contracts, futures contracts and options.

A forward contract is an agreement between two parties to undertake a specific transaction at a future date. For example, at the beginning of the season, a farmer can negotiate a forward contract to sell corn to a grocery chain once it is harvested at the end of the season, at a price agreed upon today. This way the farmer guarantees the selling price ahead of time, and the grocery chain locks in its purchase price early on. It is a legal contract; if one party defaults, the other party has legal recourse in the court system. Forward contracts are fully customized, and therefore are not liquid.

Futures contracts are essentially standardized forward contracts. Because they are standardized, they are liquid, and so they are actively traded. Futures contracts specify the underlying asset in great detail, including the amount or quantity, the future price, and the expiration date. Futures contracts exist on commodities like wheat or coffee, precious metals like gold or silver, currencies like the Euro or the Japanese yen, foreign exchange rates, interest rates and even weather. Futures contracts can be used for hedging (managing risk) as well as for speculating. For example, suppose John Deere Inc. agrees to supply a French firm with heavy equipment to be used in construction. The French firm agrees to the quoted price, but insists that it must be able to pay in Euros. This would put John Deere at risk for changes in the Euro-US Dollar exchange rate, which could reduce their profit on the contract. To hedge this risk, John Deere's CEO could sell the Euros for dollars in the Futures market, locking in their price (and their profit).

Options

Financial options are derivative securities that give the buyer the right, but not the obligation, to buy or sell the underlying financial asset at a fixed price over a specified period of time. A call option gives the buyer the right to buy the underlying asset, and a put option gives the buyer the right to sell the underlying asset. Each option contract is for 100 options, and each contract specifies the underlying asset, the exercise price (or strike price), which is the price at which the asset will be bought or sold, and the expiration date of the contract. American-style options can be exercised at any time up to the expiration date, while European-style options can only be exercised on the expiration date. To exercise the option is to complete the transaction (i.e., buy or sell the underlying asset, or settle the difference in cash). The price paid for the option is called the premium.

They are called options because the buyer can choose not to exercise the option—to let it expire without transacting—if circumstances warrant it. For example, suppose you paid $200 for one call option contract on Microsoft stock that lets you purchase 100 shares of MSFT for $100 per share, and that expires on September 1. On September 1, MSFT is selling in the market for $97.65. In this case, you should let the call options expire; you don't need to pay $100 for a stock you can buy in the open market for $97.65. By letting them expire, you would only be out the $200 premium. On the other hand, if on September 1 MSFT is selling for $105, then you would exercise the option, purchasing 100 shares for $10,000 and selling them instantly for $10,500 (or simply collecting the $500 difference). After subtracting the $200 premium, you would have a profit of $300 on an investment of $200—a 150% return!

The "moneyness" of an option refers to its profit and loss position from the long perspective (the buyer). If exercising the option would be profitable, the option is in the money (ITM) because it has intrinsic value. If exercising the option would break even, the option is at the money (ATM), and if exercising would lead to a loss, the option is out of the money (OTM). ATM and OTM options have no intrinsic value.

Intrinsic value is calculated differently for call options vs. put options (which makes sense—they are opposing positions). For a call option, intrinsic value is calculated as the market price minus the exercise price. Conversely, for a put option, intrinsic value is calculated as the exercise price minus the market price. Considering the MSFT call options from above, at the first market price ($97.65), the call options are out of the money, as they have no intrinsic value ($97.65 − $100 = −$2.35 per option or −$235 for the contract, so exercising would lose money). At the second market price, however ($105), the calls are in the money ($105 − $100 = $5 per option × 100 = $500 per contract).

Note that the moneyness of an option does not take into account the premium; it can happen that an ITM option is not profitable. For example, on January 10, 2019, Exxon Mobil (XOM) was selling for $71.44. On the same day, call options on XOM with a strike price of $70.00 and that matured on January 11 were selling for $1.60. The call is in the money—its intrinsic value is $1.44, or $144 for the contract—but exercising the options would still end up costing $0.16 per option, or $16 per contract, due to the premium paid. It is worth exercising the option to reduce the loss on the trade, but the trade is still a loss. Moneyness and profit are not the same thing.

Like with futures contracts, options can be used for hedging or for speculating. Buying options (known as being long the options) allows the investor to limit their potential losses to the premium paid. Selling options (known as writing the options, or being short the options), however, can be quite risky. The long position is able to limit risk because the risk is shifted to the short position. For example, using the MSFT options above, at the $105 market price the long position is up $500 and the short position is down $500—it is a zero-sum game, meaning that for one side to win the other side has to lose. If on September 1 MSFT rises to $200, the long position is up $10,000 and the short position is down $10,000. Since there is no limit to how high the stock price can go, there is no limit to how much the short position can lose. At the same time, the long position can only lose up to the initial investment of $200, no more.

Financial Institutions

The financial system is designed to provide liquidity and aid in the flow of funds throughout the economy. Financial institutions exist to assist in these endeavors. In this section, we discuss the numerous types of financial institutions available, starting with the central bank of the United States, the Federal Reserve.

The Federal Reserve System

The Federal Reserve Bank (the Fed) regulates the money supply, makes loans to member banks as well as other financial institutions and oversees the nation's financial system. The Fed has a mandate to maximize employment, control inflation and manage long-term interest rates. It uses open-market sales and purchases of T-bills and adjustments to the discount rate as tools to slow down or jump start the economy when needed.

The Federal Reserve System consists of 12 district Federal Reserve banks throughout the country, a board of governors that oversees the 12 district banks and helps to implement monetary policy, and the Federal Open Market Committee (FOMC) that meets regularly to set monetary policy. The Fed also conducts research in the economy, regularly publishing papers and maintaining data for professional and academic use in the Federal Reserve Economic Database (FRED).

The Fed was created in 1913 in response to a series of banking panics around the turn of the twentieth century. It was intended to add some stability to the banking system, but over time its responsibilities have increased to include:

- Supervising and regulating banking institutions;
- Protecting the credit rights of consumers;
- Managing systemic risk in the financial markets; and
- Providing financial services to depository institutions.

The Fed also serves as the lender of last resort to financial institutions that can't obtain credit, and whose collapse would be detrimental to the economy.

The Fed uses the FOMC to control the money supply. The FOMC uses open-market operations (the buying or selling of Treasury securities or foreign currencies) to make adjustments to the money supply:

- When the FOMC wants to increase the money supply, it instructs its traders to buy Treasury securities on the open market. Increasing the supply of money increases liquidity and decreases the cost of money, both of which will stimulate economic activity and thus speed up the economy.

- When they want to decrease the money supply, the FOMC instructs its traders to sell Treasury securities on the open market. Decreasing the money supply decreases liquidity and increases the cost of money, which will dampen economic activity and slow the economy down. This is how the Fed helps to manage inflation.

Commercial Banks

Commercial banks exist mainly to make loans to businesses; banks also make loans to other entities, but most of their income comes from business loans. Banks make money by charging more for the money they lend than the money they pay their depositors to use their funds; the difference is known as the interest rate spread. Banks require a charter—an authorization from the government to operate—before they can take deposits. This is because banks are a part of the money supply system, and because deposits are federally insured. So opening a bank is not as simple as opening a business—as it should be.

Commercial banks are not permitted to lend out 100% of their depositors' money; the Fed requires banks to maintain a minimum amount of reserves on hand to manage the withdrawal requests of their depositors and fund their operations. This is known as the required reserve ratio, and it is set by the Fed, based on the size of the bank. The Fed also uses the reserve requirement ratio to help control the money supply; increasing the reserve requirement ratio reduces the amount banks can loan out, which will slow down the economy, while decreasing the reserve requirement will increase the amount the banks can loan, which will increase economic activity.

Savings and Loan Associations

Savings and loans (S&Ls) are similar to banks in that they take in deposits and lend a percentage of the deposits out, but the loans they make are primarily mortgage loans. Mortgage loans are loans that are collateralized by real estate; if the borrower defaults, the lender takes possession of the real estate and sells it to recoup their funds. Like banks, S&Ls make their money by charging more for the loans than they pay to their depositors (the interest rate spread). Also like banks, S&Ls require a charter before they can begin operations.

Credit Unions

Credit unions are financial institutions owned by their members, who are usually associated with an industry. For example, Alliant Credit Union, which has its headquarters in Chicago, Illinois, is associated with the airline industry. Credit unions loan out money to members at rates typically lower than available elsewhere. Since members own the institution, residual income from operations is paid out as a dividend to the members. Like banks and S&Ls, credit unions also require a charter before they can open their doors.

Finance Companies

Finance companies are nonbank institutions that make short- and intermediate-term loans to businesses and consumers that don't qualify for loans with other financial institutions. Like banks and S&Ls, they make their money through the interest rate spread. However, they differ from banks and S&Ls as to the source of their funds; while banks and S&Ls get their money from depositors, finance companies get their funds from bank loans or by selling commercial paper.

Consumer finance companies make small loans to consumers for such things as car purchases, vacations or medical expenses. Consumer finance companies generally make loans to consumers with less than perfect credit; because the customers are of higher risk, they charge a higher interest rate. LendingTree, a division of IAC, is a well-known consumer finance company.

Commercial finance companies are firms that provide credit to other businesses. For example, a factor is a commercial finance company that lends money to businesses who in turn pledge their accounts receivable or inventory as collateral on the loan. Some factors will buy a firm's accounts receivable at a reduced price, making money through collection efforts while offering an injection of cash into the business.

Insurance Companies

Insurance companies assume their clients' risks for an ongoing fee known as a premium. They use the pool of premiums paid by all clients to cover damage claims submitted by clients, and invest the rest to earn interest. The two main types of insurance companies are life insurance and property and casualty insurance.

Life insurance companies pay benefits to their clients' survivors when they die. Life insurance companies use actuaries to help them assess the risks for their clients. Actuaries are people who use applied mathematics to forecast likely claims for insurance companies and pension funds. The actuaries calculate the premium necessary for a client, based on their age and their current state of health, to cover insurance benefits and expenses while still earning a profit.

Property and casualty insurance companies offer insurance against such hazards as hurricane or tornado damage, fire or flooding and earthquakes. Health insurance companies insure people against injury or illness, while disability insurance companies insure people against loss of income for being incapacitated. Liability insurance is also used to protect a policyholder against their own negligence; it is commonly used for automobiles, but is also available for accidents that happen on the client's property or for medical malpractice for doctors.

Retirement Plans

Retirement plans are set up by employers, governments or unions to help provide financial benefits for people after they retire. Early retirement plans were known as defined benefit plans, because the plan was designed to offer the employee a specific monthly amount for the rest of their life. The amount was determined by the employee's age, salary and years of service at the time of retirement. In these plans, the employer is legally obligated to provide each retiree with the promised amount until their death. These plans became quite expensive as life expectancies climbed, and plans of this type are now only offered by governments. In 2018, the Illinois Auditor General revealed in the annual State Actuary's Report that the state will be required to contribute $9.39 billion to six pension funds in 2020 to cover underfunded pension obligations.[3]

Current retirement plans are known as defined contribution plans. In these plans, the employer promises to make a specific monthly contribution to the plan on the employee's behalf, often matching the contribution made by the employee, and it is up to the employee to determine how to invest those funds to build for their retirement. In this plan the risk is shifted from the employer to the employee, as the company is only responsible for the contributions it makes.

Summary

The financial landscape is changing all the time; new types of securities are constantly being created. The first decade of the twenty-first century saw the introduction of bitcoin and the subsequent development of new cryptocurrencies. Finance is a dynamic field with interesting work, and it can be very lucrative.

   Finance professionals need to have a thorough understanding of all the financial options available to the firm in order to put together the right mix of debt and equity to minimize the firm's cost of capital. Knowledge of the financial markets, and the institutions that make them work, is just the starting point.

End of Chapter Problems

1. What is the essential purpose for financial markets?
2. Which is more important, the primary market for stocks or the secondary market?
3. What is the biggest difference between the money market and the capital market?
4. On January 28, Krumholz Industries announced in their annual report and in their annual analyst call with Wall Street that earnings for the prior year were down 6.2% over the prior year. On January 29, Krumholz' common stock had a capital gain of 3.6%. What reason could there be for the increase in the stock price?
5. Yancy Products' common stock has a required return of 14.65% and a beta of 1.33. The risk-free rate is 2.66%, and the return to the stock market is 12.12%. Is Yancy beating the market? Prove your answer using the data.
6. Based on the efficient market hypothesis, what type of data may be used to earn excess returns if the market is:

    a. Weak form efficient.
    b. Semi-strong form efficient.
    c. Strong form efficient.

7. What are the forces that help make markets efficient?
8. What are institutional investors?
9. What do all money market securities have in common?
10. There are two big differences between common and preferred equity. What are they?
11. What are derivatives?
12. What is a mutual fund?
13. What are the two main differences between a forward contract and a futures contract?
14. What does a call option offer the purchaser?
15. Starbucks' common stock (SBUX) is currently selling for $64.24. SBUX has call options with a strike price of $62.50 and three weeks remaining until maturity that sell for $2.28. Determine the following things with regard to the SBUX call options:

    a. Their moneyness.
    b. Their intrinsic value.
    c. Their profit or loss if exercised.

16. What are the three tasks mandated to the Federal Reserve Bank?
17. What does the Federal Open Market Committee do?
18. What is the difference between a defined benefit retirement plan and a defined contribution retirement plan?

Notes

1 *Pensions & Investments*, April 25, 2017.
2 Ibid.
3 "State Must Pay $845 Million More to Pension Systems Next Year, Report Finds," by Greg Bishop. *Illinois News Network*, December 28, 2018.

Bibliography

Fundamentals of Corporate Finance, 12th edition. S. Ross, R. Westerfield and B. Jordan. McGraw-Hill Education, 2019.
Financial Management: Principles & Practice, 8th edition. T. Gallagher. Textbook Media Press, 2019.

Index